SUPER BOWL BY THE BAY

CONTENTS

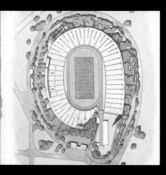

bohn & bland
Publishers, Inc.

Publishers
James C. Bohn, David C. Bland

Editorial

Editor-in-Chief
Karen E. Sweetland

Assistant Editors
Richard Keller, Sabrina E. Johnson

Design

Designer/Art Director
Henry R. Mollenauer
Talenz Associates, Ltd.

Illustrators
Jeff Ishikawa
Terry Mollenauer

Assistant to Art Director
Rick Bernard

Production

Production Coordinators
Richard Stubblefield, Arnold N. Kirschner

Typesetter
Jeannine Asturias

Graphics
Blakeley Graphics, Andrew Jones

Marketing & Advertising
Jack Little, Les Duke
Talenz Associates Ltd.

Sales Research
Cecil Patrick, Jr.

Public Relations Consultant
Myra Baillie

Director of Sales
Ronald M. Miller

Special Projects—Non-Profit
Beverly H. Case, Phyllis Martin

Sales Representatives
Barry F. Baruh, Judy K. Baruh, Frank Cygan, Neale Johnson,
Alfred Lee, David Llewellyn, Alfred Moreno, Martha Murray,
Denise Negles, Richard Novoa, Jr., Kenneth A. Packer,
Albert Whitlock, Bill Roush, Ed Baltz

Southeast Region
John F. McGinn, Jr.

Office Manager
Jennifer Roberts

Administrative Assistant
Annette O'Leary

Accountant
Dennis Venturoni

Secretary
Jackie Battaglia

he Super Bowl. Two weeks of super speculation for fans, two weeks of super pressure for the competing teams. One game, one shot at the title. The winner captures the glory, the loser waits for another chance.

The Super Bowl. That uniquely American event one Sunday each January when the nation virtually comes to a halt. More than 100 million television sets from Walla Walla, Washington to Bangor, Maine spark to life. People who may not have seen a football game all year will tune in almost out of a sense of patriotic duty.

But the Super Bowl is more than a game. It is a stylish celebration, an attention-grabbing national spectacle, building to a gameday crescendo. And after all the hype, the partying and predicting, the players finally take the field and attempt to match the excitement of pre-Super Bowl festivities.

Each Super Bowl has its own story — of heroes and goats, of brash talkers and silent leaders, of determination, exhilaration, and frustration. Already it has established its own unique history, its own tradition. And it all started in 1967 at the Los Angeles Memorial Coliseum, site of Super Bowl I.

On January 15, 1967, the Kansas City Chiefs of the seven-year-old American Football League battled the Green Bay Packers, one of the granddaddy franchises of the long-established National Football League. Back then, it was called simply the AFL-NFL World Championship Game, and experts likened it to a heavyweight-versus-unranked contender mismatch.

The teams' philosophies were as radically different as the personalities of their coaches. The Packers, winners of four NFL titles in the previous six years, were an experienced, well-drilled team. They were molded in the style of their coach, Vince Lombardi, who stressed a no-nonsense attack based on

Max McGee caught only four passes in the 1966 regular season. Playing behind Boyd Dowler, he expected to see little action in the first Super Bowl. But after Dowler was injured, McGee ignited the Packers with seven catches and two touchdowns.

18 MAGIC SUNDAYS:
A Super Bowl Retrospective
by Adam Sachs

Green Bay's Elijah Pitts slashes through the Kansas City Chiefs' line in Super Bowl I. Veteran Pitts scored two second-half touchdowns helping the Packers turn a tight game into a 35-10 romp.

photo: James Flores

Perhaps no other player had a greater impact on the early years of Super Bowl history than Joe Namath of the New York Jets. Quarterback Namath led the Jets to victory in Super Bowl III, gaining respect for himself, his team, and the upstart American Football League.

© Eastman Kodak Company, 1984

How to stop a mid-air collision.

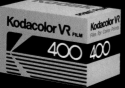

Great action shots are no accident with Kodacolor VR 400 film. So fast, it can catch the big play. So sharp, it can pick up all the fury and frustration of the players. So sensitive, it can capture all the color of the game. Kodacolor VR 400 film. For pictures that could sweep you off your feet.

Kodak

Because time goes by.

previous six years, were an experienced, well-drilled team. They were molded in the style of their coach, Vince Lombardi, who stressed a no-nonsense attack based on fundamentals and execution.

The Chiefs, coming off their first AFL championship in Kansas City, had size, speed, and raw talent, but little big-game experience. Their coach, Hank Stram, was a colorful innovator who had installed a multi-set offense.

In Lombardi's opinion, the Packers had to win. "Vince was really hooked on this thing about carrying the flag for the NFL," said Green Bay guard Fuzzy Thurston. "Before we left for Los Angeles, he called us together and told us this was going to be the biggest game we ever played."

"Vince respected the Chiefs, therefore we had to respect the Chiefs," commented fullback Jim Taylor. "He told us to forget the point spread (Packers favored by 14) and get our heads into the game. He said we had worked hard to get where we were, but we could blow it all by losing to Kansas City."

As it turned out, Lombardi had nothing to fear. His Packers saved face for the NFL in workmanlike style, 35-10.

The game produced an unlikely hero. Max McGee, a 34-year-old reserve receiver behind Boyd Dowler, had caught only four passes all year. Not expecting to play much, he reportedly stole away from the Lombardi camp during Super Bowl week to sample the Los Angeles nightlife. However, when Dowler reinjured a shoulder two plays into the game, McGee stepped in like an all pro. He caught seven passes for 138 yards, including two spectacular touchdown grabs.

As for the Chiefs, cornerback Fred Williamson became the first player to attract widespread media attention with mock-serious, Muhammad Ali-like pregame predictions. He claimed that he would put the Green Bay receivers out

photo: James Flores

The powerful Packers defense kept the Chiefs in check throughout Super Bowl I. Led by future Hall of Famers Willie Davis, Ray Nitschke, and Herb Adderley, they held the Chiefs to 72 yards rushing and kept the pressure on quarterback Len Dawson.

Matt Snell scored the Jets' only touchdown in their 16-7 victory over the Baltimore Colts in Super Bowl III. The hard-nosed Snell's 30-carry, 121-yards performance was overshadowed by the Joe Namath hoopla.

photo: Vernon Biever

Ben Wilson, normally a reserve fullback, led the Packers in rushing in Super Bowl II with 62 yards and 17 carries in Green Bay's 33-14 triumph over the Oakland Raiders.

photo: Malcolm Emmons

of commission with his patented forearm blow known as "The Hammer." Ironically, it was Williamson who was knocked out of the game in the second half.

Fifty million viewers watched the game, televised for the first and only time by both CBS and NBC. A total of 61,946 fans witnessed the game at the Coliseum — less than two-thirds of capacity — a far cry from today's guaranteed Super Bowl sellouts.

And although the game turned out as most people had expected, the idea of a world championship game was established, and it was executed in a style like no other game before it.

In 1968, the Packers bulldozed their way back to the Super Bowl and again were heavily favored to defeat the AFL champions, the Oakland Raiders. If the Packers had any trouble motivating themselves, they received an inspirational jolt two days before the Super Bowl when coach Lombardi announced it would be his farewell game. "This may be the last time we're all together," Lombardi told his team.

So the players dedicated the game to Lombardi. "We all had lumps in our throats," said quarterback Bart Starr.

Surely the Raiders had picked the wrong time to challenge the NFL's best. But if any team in the AFL could lock horns with the Packers, it was the Raiders, who had finished the season with a 13-1 record. Daryle (Mad Bomber) Lamonica directed an explosive aerial attack to a corps of talented receivers. Their defense was simply tenacious, perhaps best personified by man-mountain defensive end Ben Davidson.

But the intangible motivation factor proved too much for the Raiders. The Packers, led by Starr's second straight most valuable play-

13

Joe Namath (12) connects with tight end Pete Lammons (87) for one of 17 passes the Jets quarterback completed in Super Bowl III. Namath's favorite target was George Sauer (eight catches, 133 yards).

14

er performance (202 yards passing), and Don Chandler's four field goals, coasted to a 33-14 victory.

As the final gun sounded, guard Jerry Kramer and tackle Forrest Gregg hoisted Lombardi onto their shoulders and carried him to the Orange Bowl tunnel. "This is the best way to leave the field," the smiling coach said.

The title "AFL-NFL World Championship Game" needed a change. It was too long and failed to inspire visions of greatness. It lacked the one key ingredient necessary to attract attention. Pizzazz.

The team owners had brainstormed before the first title game. First they considered "The Big One," but dismissed it as juvenile. Next they rejected "The Final Game," reasoning that the sun would rise the next morning regardless of who won. Finally, Chiefs owner Lamar Hunt suggested "Super Bowl." It was put on the back burner.

The problem was that no one really knew if this annual clash between the young and the established leagues would turn out to be a Super Bowl or a Super Dud. Two convincing victories by the Packers hadn't helped matters.

Still, "Super Bowl" became the game's official name when the New York Jets met the Baltimore Colts in 1969. And when the Jets stunned the sports world with their upset win, the owners knew that the game could indeed be super.

Super Bowl III was Joe Namath's chance to bask in the limelight. The Colts were 17-point favorites on the strength of their 13-1 season mark and a 34-0 massacre of a strong Cleveland team in the NFL Championship Game. Nobody gave the Jets a chance. However, Broadway Joe thought otherwise.

Namath met Baltimore kicker

Unintimidated by the Jets, Colts running back Tom Matte charged for 116 yards on 11 carries in Super Bowl III. Despite Matte's efforts, the Colts had trouble mounting scoring drives against a spirited Jets defense.

He was right. Joe Namath's brash predictions became a reality in Super Bowl III, making believers of Jets coach Weeb Ewbank and the rest of the pro football world.

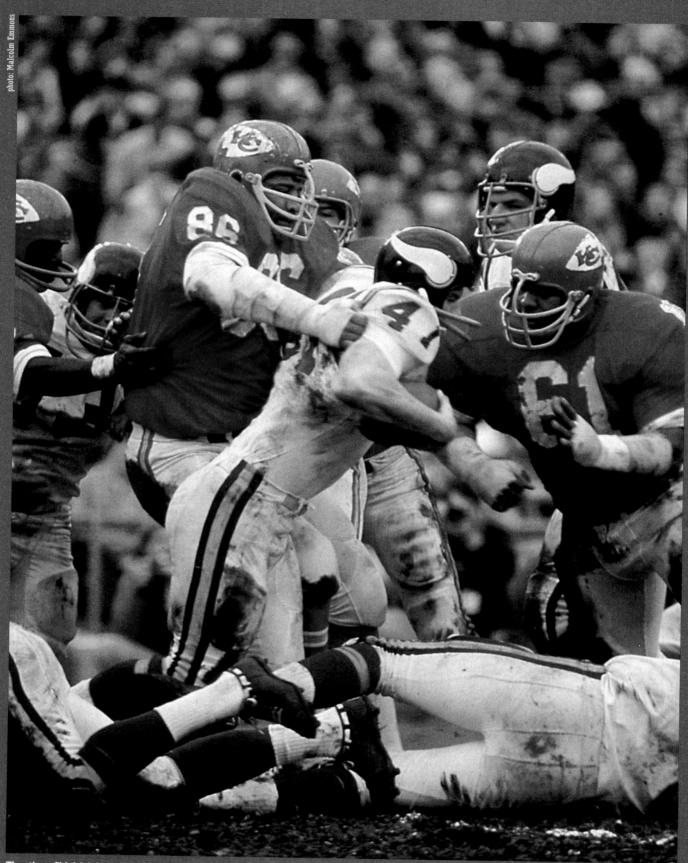

The stingy Chiefs' defense kept a firm grip on the Minnesota Vikings' running attack in Super Bowl IV. It held running back Dave Osborn to 11 of the Vikings' paltry 67 yards rushing for the game.

Lou Michaels in Ft. Lauderdale a week before the game and told him, "We're going to kick the hell out of your team." Four days later, Namath appeared before the Miami Touchdown Club and guaranteed a Jets victory. In so doing, he set himself up to be either the game's greatest prophet or its most humiliated loudmouth.

The proud Colts were appalled by such irreverence. In fact, they were so infuriated that they taped copies of Namath's quotes to their lockers and mirrors, figuring the mere sight of those words would stir them into an angry, aggressive mood.

This didn't affect Broadway Joe. On the contrary, he detected insecurity building in the Colts' quarters. "If they need newspaper clippings to get up for a game, they're in a helluva lot of trouble," he observed.

When it came time to perform, Namath lived up to his words. He deftly engineered a second-quarter drive climaxed by Matt Snell's four-yard touchdown run. Gradually the Jets' confidence grew as they sensed the Colts losing their poise.

Uncharacteristically, Baltimore turned to razzle-dazzle in an attempt to put points on the board. With 30 seconds left in the first half, they ran a flea-flicker play with quarterback Earl Morrall handing off to Tom Matte, who then lateralled back to Morrall. Receiver Jim Orr stood alone in the end zone wildly waving his arms, but Morrall never saw him. Instead, he passed to the other side of the field and was intercepted.

The Colts trudged into the locker room with a look of impending doom. "Our self-assurance was draining away, little by little, like beans out of the bottom of a torn sack," said Morrall.

The Jets took complete command in the second half, never allowing the Colts to regain their confidence. Namath, calling frequent audibles and mixing his

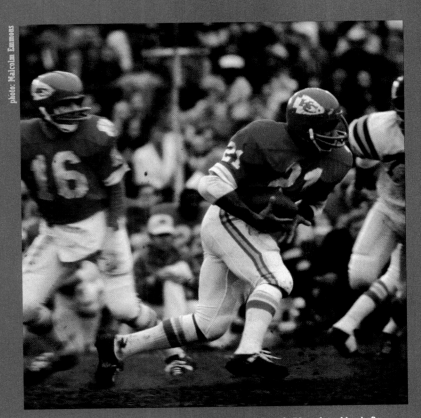

Len Dawson hands off to Mike Garrett. Although he accounted for only 39 yards rushing in Super Bowl IV, running back Garrett scored an important five-yard touchdown, paving the way to the Chiefs' 23-7 win over the Vikings.

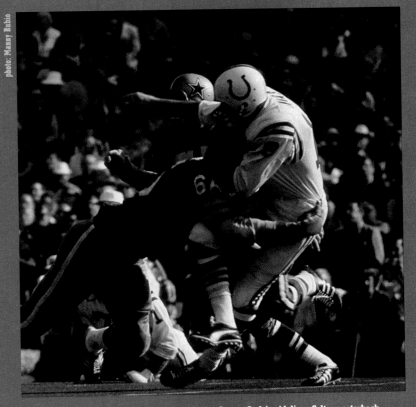

In a game of errors and mishaps, Cowboys defender George Andrie sidelines Colts quarterback Johnny Unitas with a bruising sack in Super Bowl V. Earl Morrall replaced Unitas and led the Colts to a come-from-behind 16-13 victory.

plays brilliantly, finished with 206 yards passing and was fittingly named most valuable player. Snell, the often-overlooked Jets hero, battered his way through the Colts defense for 121 yards on 30 carries. Jim Turner hit three second-half field goals to give New York a 16-0 lead in the fourth quarter before injured Johnny Unitas came off the bench to lead Baltimore to its only score.

The AFL's first Super Bowl victory made Broadway Joe Namath a hero. More importantly, it brought hard-earned and well-deserved respect to the AFL.

  SUPER BOWL IV

The story of Super Bowl IV centered around Kansas City quarterback Len Dawson. Four days before the game against the Minnesota Vikings, NBC news reported that Dawson was one of seven players under investigation by a U.S. Justice Department Task Force for alleged gambling connections with "underworld figures."

The media had a hot story and ran with it. Under pressure, Dawson isolated himself. Chiefs safety Johnny Robinson, Dawson's roommate, spoke on his behalf. "Lenny said he's never been through anything like it," Robinson stated. "I know it hit him real hard. It ate him up inside. It looked to me as if he aged five years from Tuesday to Thursday."

Chiefs coach Hank Stram even got a phone call from President Richard Nixon before the game. Nixon told him that the team should forget the rumors and play like champions.

On Super Sunday, Dawson left his personal troubles off the field and performed with precision and an icy nerve. Nicknamed "Lenny the Cool," he consistently moved the Chiefs into scoring position in the first half, setting up three field goals by Jan Stenerud and Mike Garrett's touchdown run.

The Dallas Cowboys rebounded from the loss to the Colts in Super Bowl V by subduing the Miami Dolphins 24-3 in Game VI. After years of near-misses, the Cowboys finally gave head coach Tom Landry a long-awaited victory ride.

Jim O'Brien, with Earl Morrall holding, kicks the decisive field goal in Super Bowl V. Rookie O'Brien missed an extra point earlier, but redeemed himself with the game-winner with five seconds remaining.

photo: Dick Raphael

Kansas City dealt Minnesota the crushing blow in the third quarter. Leading 16-7, Dawson continued to pick the Vikings' defense apart with short passes. He threw a safe five-yarder to Otis Taylor, who managed to elude a Minnesota tackler and sprint down the sideline to the end zone, turning a short "out" pattern into a 46-yard touchdown play.

The Chiefs' defense, spearheaded by Buck Buchanan, Bobby Bell, Curly Culp, and Robinson (who played with a cracked rib), never allowed fiery quarterback Joe Kapp and the Vikings to generate much offense.

Dawson was voted the most valuable player, and later was cleared of all gambling charges. Kansas City had evened the AFL-NFL Championship series at two wins apiece with their victory in the final game before the merger of the leagues.

 SUPER BOWL V

Super Bowl V ushered in a new era in professional football. The merger agreement between the AFL and NFL, implemented during the 1970 season, realigned the 26 pro football teams into the American and National Football Conferences and introduced interleague regular season games.

The Baltimore Colts, now representing the AFC, gained the chance to redeem themselves for their Super Bowl III loss to the Jets. Their opponents, the Dallas Cowboys, had finally reached the Super Bowl after five consecutive division titles and two championship game losses. Both squads were hungry for victory — perhaps too hungry.

It was a sloppily played game from start to finish. There were dropped passes, blocked extra points, 10 turnovers, 14 penalties. All three quarterbacks — Earl Morrall and Johnny Unitas for the Colts and Craig Morton for the Cowboys — had sub-par days.

Super Bowl VI most valuable player Roger Staubach scrambles away from Bill Stanfill of Miami. Staubach completed 12 of 19 passes and threw two touchdowns (to Lance Alworth and Mike Ditka) to lead the Cowboys to a 24-3 victory.

The Colts managed both of their scores through a combination of luck and Dallas miscues. John Mackey scored the first touchdown on a 75-yard pass that was tipped by Colts receiver Eddie Hinton and Cowboys cornerback Mel Renfro. Their second score was set up by Rick Volk's interception return to the Dallas 3-yard line.

Still, it was the only Super Bowl in history in which the outcome was decided in the final seconds of play. In keeping with the game's pattern, the Cowboys gave the Colts a golden opportunity to win. With a minute left, one of Morton's passes deflected off the hands of running back Dan Reeves into the arms of Colts linebacker Mike Curtis. Baltimore ran the clock down to nine seconds, then summoned rookie kicker Jim O'Brien to break the 13-13 tie.

The rookie felt the pressure. Dallas called a time out to make him think about it a little longer. He asked Morrall, the holder, which way the wind was blowing. "There is no wind," replied Morrall. "Just kick the ball straight." O'Brien did, then leapt into Morrall's arms, fist in the air. The Colts had gained their redemption.

In Super Bowl VI, the Cowboys were determined to win the Super Bowl trophy, newly-named after the late Green Bay head coach Vince Lombardi. They had gone to the Super Bowl the year before, and they had come away empty. They didn't intend to let that happen again.

Their opponent was the Miami Dolphins, a budding powerhouse under coach Don Shula, making his second Super Bowl appearance after coaching the Colts in Super Bowl III.

The young Dolphins proved to be no match for the Cowboys. Dallas dominated every phase of the game, posting an impressive

24-3 victory.

Their rushing attack, spearheaded by Duane Thomas (95 yards), Walt Garrison (74), and Calvin Hill (25), racked up a Super Bowl record 252 yards. Roger Staubach, who took over for Craig Morton at quarterback, fired touchdown passes to Lance Alworth and Mike Ditka, earning most valuable player honors along the way.

Dallas' Doomsday Defense, anchored by Bob Lilly, Jethro Pugh, and Lee Roy Jordan, stymied Miami's prolific rushing attack. The Dolphins' Larry Csonka and Jim Kiick were held to 80 yards combined. Quarterback Bob Griese found the Cowboys' defense no friendlier. He was sacked for losses totaling 29 yards.

"I never saw a Cowboys team so intense, so ready to play," said Lilly. "And it had nothing to do with the money. We would have paid the league to play in that game. That's how much we wanted it."

So the Cowboys had silenced their critics at last. And the Dolphins, following an established pattern, would rebound from their Super Bowl loss. They would do so in grand style.

  SUPER BOWL VII

Preparing for Super Bowl VII, Miami had everything to lose. They came into the game with a 16-0 record, and if they came out on the winning end after 60 minutes on that Sunday in January, they would become the first undefeated, untied team in NFL history.

Their obstacle was the Washington Redskins, a collection of cast-offs and overachievers crafted in the image of coach George Allen. Allen was equal parts psychologist and strategist, who used emotional speeches to coax his rejuvenated veterans, the "Over the Hill Gang," into giving their maximum effort.

Man for man, the teams matched up perfectly. The Dolphins started the crafty Bob Griese at quarter-

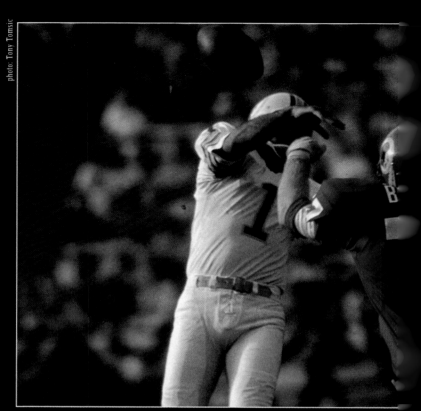

No time for a fumble. Trying to protect a 14-0 lead over the Washington Redskins in Super Bowl VII, Dolphins place kicker Garo Yepremian tried to pass after his field goal attempt was blocked late in the game. Instead he fumbled and Redskins defender Mike Bass recovered for a 49-yard touchdown. Despite the setback, the Dolphins clung to a 14-7 victory and preserved their perfect season.

Running back Larry Brown was the Redskins' workhorse in Super Bowl VII. He carried the ball 22 times for 72 yards and caught five passes. But the rest of Washington's offense could do little against Miami's "No-Name Defense."

back. The Redskins countered with Billy Kilmer, a quarterback with the uncanny knack for winning through determination, despite his reputation for throwing the NFL's most wobbly passes.

Miami had the most potent rushing attack in the history of the game, overpowering defenses all season to accumulate 2,950 yards. Both Larry Csonka and speedster Mercury Morris had 1,000-yard seasons, and Jim Kiick was a backfield receiving threat. Washington relied on workhorse Larry Brown, the NFC's top rusher.

The Dolphins boasted graceful receiver Paul Warfield and surehanded Howard Twilley. The Redskins had two great receivers of their own — Charley Taylor and Roy Jefferson.

Nevertheless, defense was the cornerstone upon which each team had built its success. For Miami it was the "No-Name Defense" led by Jake Scott and Manny Fernandez. Although individually anonymous, they were well recognized collectively, posting three shutouts and allowing less than 13 points a game in the regular season.

Washington's defense thrived on Allen's motto, "The future is now." In the twilight of their careers, defensive players such as Jack Pardee, Ron McDole and Pat Fischer all were getting their first shot at the Super Bowl well past their thirtieth birthdays.

Miami controlled the game throughout. Griese connected with Twilley on a 28-yard pass to give the Dolphins a 7-0 first-quarter lead. Miami drove onward, powered by the pounding, straight-ahead running of Csonka, who gained 112 yards. They expanded the margin to 14-0 on Kiick's touchdown plunge before halftime.

Meanwhile, the "No-Name Defense" held the Redskins in check. Tackle Fernandez plugged the middle of the line and never let Brown get loose. Safety Scott, the game's most valuable player, stopped two drives with timely interceptions, one in the end zone

Super Bowl VII most valuable player Jake Scott intercepted two key passes for the Dolphins. Linebacker Nick Buoniconti intercepted a third pass to set up the Dolphins' victory.

Running back Larry Csonka bulldozed his way to two touchdowns as the Dolphins coasted to a 24-7 win over the Vikings in Game VIII. Csonka broke Matt Snell's Super Bowl rushing records by carrying 33 times for 145 yards.

which he returned 55 yards.

The Dolphins looked like sure winners. But with two minutes left, kicker Garo Yepremian lined up for the field goal which would have given Miami an insurmountable 17-0 lead and assure the dream season. What followed was unquestionably the most comical and bizarre play in Super Bowl history.

Yepremian's line-drive kick was cleanly blocked by Bill Brundige. The ball could have bounced out of bounds or the Redskins could have fallen on it, but fate was not so kind to the Dolphins. Instead it bounced right into Yepremian's hands. Fleeing from the charging 270-pound Brundige, little Garo tried to pass the ball to no one in particular.

The ball slipped from his hand and bounced off his helmet. In the confusion, Washington cornerback Mike Bass plucked the ball out of the air and raced 49 yards for a touchdown. The perfect season was suddenly in jeopardy.

After this remarkable turn of events, the Dolphins held the ball for only six plays and had to punt with 1:14 remaining in the game. But Miami's No Names stopped Washington's last-minute desperation effort to hold on for a 14-7 win and preserve the unprecedented perfect season.

 SUPER BOWL VIII

In 1974, the Dolphins made their third straight Super Bowl appearance. Although their consecutive regular season winning streak had stopped at 18, they finished with a strong 12-2 record and a shot at the Minnesota Vikings for the championship.

The Vikings became the fourth team to earn the chance at Super Bowl revenge after suffering a previous loss. This time they had the scrambling Fran Tarkenton at quarterback and a much-improved running attack led by do-it-all

Steelers linebacker Jack Ham's crunching tackle of the Vikings' Chuck Foreman typified the relentless Pittsburgh defense in Super Bowl IX. The Steelers held Minnesota to a microscopic 17 yards rushing.

Running back Franco Harris used superior blocking and intelligent running to lead the Pittsburgh Steelers' 16-6 march over the Vikings in Super Bowl IX. Harris, the game's most valuable player, amassed 158 yards on the ground, breaking Larry Csonka's year-old rushing record.

photo: Vernon Biever

Franco Harris continued his rugged running for the Steelers in Super Bowl X. He trudged for 82 yards on 27 carries and added 26 yards on a pass reception.

Steelers quarterback Terry Bradshaw passed over the outstretched arms of Cowboys defender Ed Jones in Pittsburgh's 21-17 victory over Dallas in Super Bowl X. Bradshaw completed nine passes for 209 yards and two touchdowns.

rookie back Chuck Foreman.

As always, the Vikings relied heavily on their punishing defense, the "Purple People Eaters," spearheaded by Carl Eller, Gary Larsen, Jim Marshall, and Alan Page. It figured to be a game won in the trenches.

Miami won that battle, and the game, 24-7. Most valuable player Larry Csonka steamrolled his way to 145 yards on 33 carries, both Super Bowl records. He also scored two touchdowns. Miami moved the ball at will on the ground, scoring on its first two possessions to knock Minnesota out of the contest early. The running game, featuring misdirection blocking, was so successful that quarterback Griese only had to throw seven passes.

For Miami, there were predictions of a dynasty. For Minnesota, there was only more frustration and talk of "next year."

 SUPER BOWL IX

In their third Super Bowl championship attempt, the Vikings were determined to win against the AFC champion Pittsburgh Steelers. Their mood was apparent before the game, as Pittsburgh defensive tackle Joe Green remembered. "All ninety-four of us (Vikings and Steelers) were standing in the tunnel, waiting to be introduced. We were loose and joking around. The Vikings were standing there stone-faced. They looked like they were at attention. I saw Alan Page. I smiled and said hello. He didn't say anything."

The Vikings played the game as stiffly as they looked. The Steelers, making their first-ever NFL Championship appearance, used the running of Franco Harris and the mettle of the Steel Curtain defense to post a workmanlike 16-6 victory. Harris, the most valuable player, set Super Bowl records with 34 carries and 158 yards, and scored one touchdown.

Graceful Lynn Swann of the Steelers dazzled the crowd with four long receptions for 161 yards in Super Bowl X. His biggest catch came with 3:02 left in the game, when he took a pass from Terry Bradshaw and sprinted 64 yards for a touchdown.

But the real story was the domination of the Vikings by the Steel Curtain. The front four of Greene, L.C. Greenwood, Ernie Holmes, and Dwight White held the Vikings to a paltry 17 yards rushing. Fran Tarkenton didn't fare much better, throwing three interceptions and being sacked for a safety.

Pittsburgh was on its way to becoming the NFL's next powerhouse. The Vikings, meanwhile, were left wondering what it takes to win.

SUPER BOWL X

The tenth Super Bowl proved to be one of the most wide open and exciting to date. Pittsburgh repeated as the AFC champion. Dallas, thought to be in a rebuilding year, became the first wild card team to reach the NFL Championship Game.

Super Bowl X would also be remembered as Lynn Swann's day, not for the number of passes he caught, but for his acrobatic flair in catching them.

The underdog Cowboys sandwiched a Roger Staubach-to-Drew Pearson scoring pass and Tony Fritsch's field goal around a Pittsburgh touchdown to take a 10-7 lead at the half.

The Steelers' aggressive linebacker Jack Lambert was not happy with the way things stood. "I felt we were intimidated a little bit in the first half. The Pittsburgh Steelers aren't supposed to be intimidated. We're supposed to be the intimidators. I decided to do something about it."

He did. After Steelers' kicker Roy Gerela missed a field goal, Cowboys defender Cliff Harris gave him a taunting pat on the helmet. Lambert didn't approve, and he hurled Harris to the ground.

Lambert's display of emotion seemed to fire up the Steelers in the second half. A safety on a blocked punt and Gerela's two field goals put the Steelers ahead

Oakland Raiders running back Clarence Davis accounted for 137 of his team's 266 rushing yards in a 32-14 conquest of Minnesota in Super Bowl XI. The Raiders set a Super Bowl record for 429 yards total offense, and turned those yards into points.

30

The joy of winning. Raiders coach John Madden receives the requisite victory hoist from his troops after a convincing victory over the Vikings in Game XI.

photo: Michael Zagaris

15-10 in the fourth quarter.

Then it was Swann's turn. He already had set up one field goal with a bobbling catch of a Terry Bradshaw bomb while falling over Cowboys defender Mark Washington. Bradshaw sent him long again. Washington again matched Swann stride for stride as they headed toward the goal post. Bradshaw waited until the last possible moment, unleashing the ball just before tackle Larry Cole and Harris decked him.

The pass was perfect. Swann scaled the air and pulled it down for a 64-yard touchdown. Bradshaw, who was knocked cold on the play, didn't even realize that the Steelers had scored until 10 minutes later in the dressing room. Most valuable player Swann gained a Super Bowl record 161 yards on just four receptions.

Despite Swann's heroics, the Cowboys and their courageous leader Staubach (playing with bruised ribs) weren't about to throw in the towel. A 34-yard bomb to sparingly-used receiver Percy Howard brought the Cowboys to within four points, 21-17. Staubach, the master of miracle finishes, received a final chance to pull out a victory.

The Steelers and the 100 million viewers across the nation held their breath through a tingling series of plays until Glen Edwards intercepted Staubach's "Hail Mary" desperation pass in the end zone with no time remaining. The Steelers were champions again, but they had been through a fight.

 SUPER BOWL XI

In Super Bowl XI, the Vikings made a fourth appearance, and turned in another disappointing performance. This time they fell prey to the marauders of the AFC, the Oakland Raiders.

The Raiders were a team that mirrored the character of their coach, John Madden, an eccentric

In the mid 1970s the Pittsburgh Steelers became pro football's dominant team. Led by the powerful running of Franco Harris (above) and a solid defense, the Steelers won four Super Bowls in a six-year span.

emotional orchestrator. The defense had earned the reputation as hit-men and outcasts. Safeties Jack Tatum and George Atkinson were the most feared tandem in the league.

Minnesota's hopes crumbled even before the first half was over, falling behind 16-0 and never mounting a serious threat to win.

Oakland quarterback Ken Stabler connected frequently with the game's most valuable player, wide receiver Fred Biletnikoff (4 receptions, 79 yards), and tight end Dave Casper to set up short touchdowns. Running back Clarence Davis, following the blocks of Art Shell, Gene Upshaw, and Mark van Eeghan, had a productive day. He slashed through Minnesota's unusually porous defense for 137 yards.

The Raiders set two Super Bowl records on their way to a 32-14 victory. The offense amassed 429 total yards, and Willie Brown returned an interception 75 yards for a touchdown. With a performance like that, it was no contest.

 SUPER BOWL

Dallas carried the "Doomsday Defense" to Super Bowl XII. Denver brought the "Orange Crush." The experts felt that the team which could move the ball would win the game. Dallas did both, devastating the Broncos 27-10.

Denver had blazed to a 12-2 regular season record and playoff victories over past Super Bowl champions Pittsburgh and Oakland. Offensively, they had scored enough points to rejuvenate quarterback Craig Morton, in his third football life after lean years with the Cowboys and Giants.

Their defense, led by end Lyle Alzado and linebackers Randy Gradishar and Tom Jackson, had given up only 148 points all year. Still, they faced a tough chore in trying to stifle Roger Staubach, Tony Dorsett, Drew Pearson and company in "the money game."

Wide receiver Fred Biletnikoff, the Super Bowl XI most valuable player, made four receptions for 79 yards, each of them setting up Raiders' scores.

Cowboys receiver Butch Johnson's fingertip catch for a touchdown sealed Denver's doom in Dallas' 27-10 victory over the Broncos in Super Bowl XII. Johnson's score put the Cowboys ahead 20-3, and the "Doomsday II" defense kept the Broncos' offense under wraps thereafter.

Dallas again was led by their "Doomsday Defense" featuring Randy White, Harvey Martin, Ed (Too Tall) Jones, and Jethro Pugh. Morton would find out the hard way that "Doomsday" and Super Sunday were one and the same.

White and Martin, the co-most valuable players, terrorized Morton into a horrendous passing day — 39 yards and four interceptions. Morton fared so poorly that the "who's he?" of Super Bowl quarterbacks, Norris Weese, had to come to the rescue in the second half in an attempt to pump some life into the Denver attack. Dallas forced eight Broncos turnovers in all and allowed only 156 total yards.

On offense, the Cowboys had just enough punch to decarbonate the "Orange Crush". Butch Johnson made one of the most spectacular catches in Super Bowl history in the third quarter — a diving, fingertip grab of a Staubach bomb to give Dallas a 20-3 lead en route to their second Super Bowl victory.

In Super Bowl XIII, Dallas and Pittsburgh picked up where they left off three years before. The rematch was for high stakes. The winner would become the Super Bowl's first three-time champion. Both teams were armed with explosive offenses and bullish defenses. The result was a fast-paced, high-scoring, thoroughly entertaining game.

Many people considered the game to be the second round of a battle between two of football's all-time greatest quarterbacks, Roger Staubach and Terry Bradshaw. As usual, Staubach excelled under pressure. But he couldn't match Bradshaw, who burned the Cowboys' secondary for 318 yards and four touchdowns. The Steelers held off a late Cowboys charge for a 35-31 victory.

"Bradshaw was the difference," said Dallas safety Charlie Waters of

It was a long day for Broncos quarterbacks in Super Bowl XII. Reserve quarterback Norris Weese fumbled after replacing Broncos starter Craig Morton who left the game with four interceptions.

Steelers coach Chuck Noll ministers to quarterback Terry Bradshaw after a bone-shaking play in Super Bowl XIII. Bradshaw survived the blow to lead Pittsburgh to a 35-31 win over Dallas.

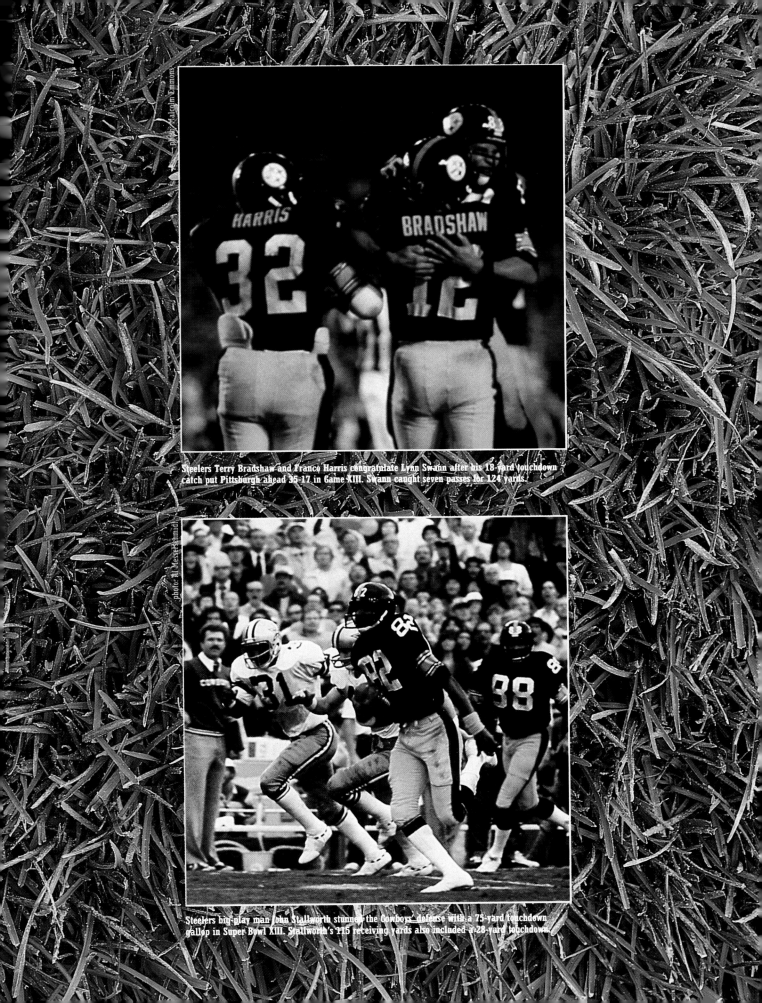

photo: Malcolm Emmons

Steelers Terry Bradshaw and Franco Harris congratulate Lynn Swann after his 18-yard touchdown catch put Pittsburgh ahead 35-17 in Game XIII. Swann caught seven passes for 124 yards.

photo: Al Messerschmidt

Steelers big-play man John Stallworth stunned the Cowboys' defense with a 75-yard touchdown gallop in Super Bowl XIII. Stallworth's 115 receiving yards also included a 28-yard touchdown.

Franco Harris storms up the middle for a 22-yard fourth-quarter touchdown giving Pittsburgh a 28-17 lead over Dallas in Super Bowl XIII. Harris led Steelers rushers with 68 yards.

the game's most valuable player.

"He can throw a ball twenty yards like I can throw a dart twenty feet," added cornerback Cliff Harris.

Bradshaw's first dart went for a 28-yard touchdown to John Stallworth. Staubach came back gamely, teaming with Tony Hill for a 39-yard score later in the first quarter.

Dallas linebacker Mike Hegman stunned Bradshaw early in the second quarter when he stripped the ball from the quarterback and raced 37 yards to give Dallas its only lead of the game, 14-7.

The margin vanished quickly. Bradshaw beat the Cowboys' zone on a 75-yard pass-and-run play to the ubiquitous Stallworth. A leaping, fingertip grab by Rocky Bleier in the Cowboys' end zone put the Steelers back on top at halftime, 21-14.

"It was a game where we could never seem to catch our breath," Pittsburgh safety Mike Wagner said. "It was back and forth, back and forth, like a basketball game. It was one of those days when you knew no lead was gonna be safe."

Dallas threatened Pittsburgh's lead in the third quarter, driving inside the Steelers' 10-yard line. Then came perhaps the most heart-wrenching play in Super Bowl history, and one that foreshadowed the Cowboys' fate.

Jackie Smith, one of the game's greatest tight ends for 15 years with the St. Louis Cardinals, finally got a shot at a Super Bowl ring with the Cowboys in his sixteenth and final season.

On this play, he curled through the Steelers' zone into an open spot in the end zone. Staubach spotted him and drilled a perfect pass. Smith dropped to his knees to be sure he made the routine catch, but the ball bounced off his hip.

Smith fell back in disbelief. Even Staubach showed rare emotion, slapping his hands and grimacing in disappointment. Dallas had to settle for a field goal.

After Pittsburgh scored twice on a run by Franco Harris and a Bradshaw-to-Lynn Swann touch-

Super Bowl XIII most valuable player Terry Bradshaw completed 17 of 30 passes for 318 yards and four touchdowns to lead the Steelers over Roger Staubach and the Cowboys.

To have and have not. Fifteen-year veteran Jackie Smith's dropped pass in the end zone may have cost the Cowboys victory in Super Bowl XIII. After Smith's miscue, Dallas settled for a field goal and ultimately lost the game by four points.

down pass, Dallas was forced to play catch-up. Touchdown passes to Billy Joe DuPree and Butch Johnson (after a recovered onside kick with 26 seconds left) put a temporary damper on the Pittsburgh victory party.

Staubach had a hot hand. There was a feeling in the Orange Bowl that if he got the ball back once more, anything could happen.

The Cowboys had to try another onside kick. Bleier recovered to end the suspense and start the champagne corks popping in Pittsburgh.

No Super Bowl is a cakewalk, but the Steelers had every reason to believe that they would register a resounding victory in Super Bowl XIV and become the game's first four-time champions.

The Los Angeles Rams had done the Steelers a favor by eliminating their arch-rival, the Cowboys, in the divisional playoffs. The Rams had stumbled into the Super Bowl after a 9-7 season and a less than convincing 9-0 NFC Championship Game victory over Tampa Bay.

The Steelers had a decided edge in experience and talent, but the Rams had plenty of heart — exemplified by defensive end Jack Youngblood, who played despite a hairline fracture to his left leg. Los Angeles also had the advantage of playing before 104,000 fans in their own backyard, Pasadena's Rose Bowl.

For three quarters it appeared that the underdogs might dethrone the champions, but the Steelers showed their mettle in a two-touchdown fourth quarter to come away with a hard-fought 31-19 triumph.

Paced by the passing of Vince Ferragamo (212 yards) and a Lawrence McCutcheon-to-Ron Smith option pass for a touchdown, the Rams took a 19-17 lead into the decisive fourth quarter.

Defensive end Joe Greene re-

Behind powerful blocking, Los Angeles Rams fullback Cullen Bryant scores his team's first touchdown in Super Bowl XIV. The spirited Rams held a 19-17 lead over the Steelers after three quarters, before losing 31-19.

called, "That was the first time I could ever remember playing against a team that was more intense than we were. They were beating us in the trenches, moving us out. We were shocked."

The Steelers overcame the shock. Terry Bradshaw, in his second consecutive most valuable player performance, again delivered one of his patented big plays. He hit another big-play man, John Stallworth, to finally silence the Rams' upset hopes.

The Steelers had claimed their fourth Lombardi Trophy, closing out the 1970s with a flourish.

 SUPER BOWL
XV

Everybody loves a rags-to-riches story. That's why the tale of Jim Plunkett's 1980 season has been recounted so often. Plunkett had been battered and often injured in his five years as New England's quarterback and was traded to San Francisco in 1976. After two disappointing seasons with the 49ers, Plunkett was placed on waivers. Many people believed he was through.

However, the Oakland Raiders decided to give him one more chance. Plunkett rusted on the bench for two years before finally getting his chance when starter Dan Pastorini broke his leg four weeks into the 1980 season.

"All Jim needed was someone to believe in him," said Raiders coach Tom Flores. Plunkett sparkled for the rest of the season and led the wild-card Raiders to three playoff victories.

In Super Bowl XV, the Raiders took advantage of Plunkett's accurate passing and their strong, opportunistic defensive play to assume an early command over the Philadelphia Eagles, a team of veterans and free agents in their first Super Bowl.

Linebacker Rod Martin set up Oakland's first touchdown with the first of his Super Bowl record

photo: Ross Lewi

A yellow ribbon around Louisiana Superdome at Super Bowl XV welcomed back the hostages Iran had held captive.

Raiders linebacker Rod Martin intercepted three Ron Jaworski passes en route to a 27-10 victory over the Philadelphia Eagles in Super Bowl XV. Martin's three interceptions set a Super Bowl record.

Raiders running back Kenny King takes a pass and runs 80 yards for the longest touchdown reception in Super Bowl history. King's score gave the Raiders a commanding 14-0 lead over the Eagles in the first quarter.

three interceptions. Plunkett capped the drive with a scoring pass to Cliff Branch.

Late in the first quarter, Plunkett scrambled out of the pocket, and patiently waited until he spotted Kenny King near the sidelines in front of the Raiders' bench. The catch-and-run covered 80 yards, a Super Bowl record, and the Raiders were on their way to a 27-10 win.

Plunkett, shielded by an inspired offensive line, finished the day with 261 yards passing and three touchdowns. "I'm not a real emotional person," said Game XV's most valuable player. "I don't jump up and down, but I'm as happy as I can be right now."

Having gone from benchwarmer to Super Bowl hero in less than a season, Plunkett had every right to be happy.

Super Bowl XVI matched two teams of similar character. The San Francisco 49ers and the Cincinnati Bengals both had finished 6-10 in 1980 and figured to be at least a few years away from Super Bowl contention. Both teams also lacked the common prerequisite of most Super Bowl teams of the past. Playoff experience.

Nevertheless, both teams had passed stiff challenges in their conference championship games. San Francisco beat Dallas with a dramatic last-minute drive and Cincinnati froze out San Diego in a 10 degree-below-zero survival test.

The 49ers and the Bengals also had abundant young talent and two of the league's best quarterbacks in Joe Montana and Ken Anderson, respectively. Coaches Bill Walsh of San Francisco and Forrest Gregg of Cincinnati each emphasized the passing game, throwing as often as 50 times per game.

On Super Sunday, Montana outshined Anderson in the first half,

San Francisco quarterback Joe Montana completed 14 of 22 passes for 157 yards as the 49ers outlasted the Cincinnati Bengals 26-21 in Super Bowl XVI. Montana's performance included an 11-yard scoring pass to Earl Cooper and a one-yard touchdown run.

directing touchdown drives of 68 and 92 yards. The 49ers held a commanding 20-0 halftime lead. To make a game of it, the Bengals knew they had to score quickly.

Anderson, who finished with 300 yards passing, began to find holes in San Francisco's secondary, manned by standout rookies Ronnie Lott, Eric Wright, and Carlton Williamson. He drove the Bengals 83 yards to a score to start the third quarter.

But when he brought them to the verge of another touchdown, the 49ers defense became a brick wall, executing the greatest goal line stand in Super Bowl history. Cincinnati had three opportunities to punch the ball over from the 1-yard line (including two attempts by 260-pound fullback Pete Johnson), but they failed to find a crack in the 49ers' armor.

The Bengals' momentum had been stalled just enough to allow the 49ers to weather the comeback and hold on for a 26-21 victory.

The streets of Georgetown , the posh nightlife section of Washington, D.C., overflowed with jubilant citizens. College students and young professionals romped on car hoods, champagne bottles bubbling in one hand, index fingers pointing to the sky. Normally reserved lawyers and businessmen slapped each other with high fives and blasted the horns on their Mercedes. Everywhere drinks were on the house.

What brought about this festive commotion? The Washington Redskins had just beaten the Miami Dolphins 27-17 in Super Bowl XVII.

It was a 10-year reunion of the Super Bowl VII matchup, but the nicknames had changed. The Redskins had the Hogs (the mammoth offensive line), the Smurfs (the diminutive receivers), and the Fun Bunch (the end zone cele-

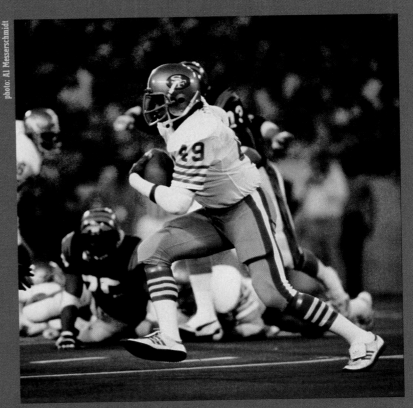

photo: Al Messerschmidt

Earl Cooper ran for 34 yards and caught two passes to help the 49ers build a 20-0 halftime lead over the Bengals. Cooper's output contributed to the 127 yards the 49ers' rushers gained that day.

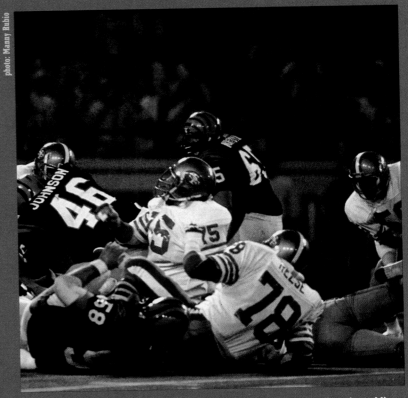

photo: Manny Rubio

The moment of truth in Super Bowl XVI. San Francisco's defense held the Bengals at the goal line on four consecutive plays in the third quarter. Their dogged determination was the difference in the 49ers' thrilling victory.

Miami's Fulton Walker raced through the Redskins' defense for a Super Bowl record 98-yard kickoff return for a touchdown in Game XVII. Walker's effort gave the Dolphins a 17-10 advantage which disappeared in the Redskins' 27-17 triumph.

Alvin Garrett of the Redskins accounted for his team's first score in Super Bowl XVII with a four-yard touchdown completion from Joe Theismann. Charlie Brown added a touchdown reception in the second half to seal Washington's victory.

bration crew). The Dolphins boasted the stinging Killer Bees defense (Bob Baumhower, Doug Betters, the Blackwood brothers, etc.).

Washington coach Joe Gibbs made no attempt to conceal his game plan — John Riggins right, John Riggins left, John Riggins up the middle, with an occasional Joe Theismann precision pass mixed in to keep the defense off balance. Riggins, who enhanced his flaky image by wearing top hat and tails to a pregame press conference, had amassed over 400 yards in three playoff games. The Hogs had specialized in wearing down opponents in the second half. Miami would be this game's victim.

Washington had tied the game at 10-10 in the second quarter when lightning struck. Miami's Fulton Walker took the kickoff and bolted untouched up the middle for a record 98-yard score. Washington cut the lead to 17-13 in the third quarter and gradually began to dismantle the Dolphins' defense.

With 10 minutes left in the game, the Redskins faced fourth-and-one on the Dolphins' 43. The scene was set for Riggins. With the Dolphins' defense bunched up on the line to stop him, Riggins broke outside where only cornerback Don McNeal remained in his path. He took McNeal's shot and bounced off. McNeal desperately grabbed Riggins' jersey, but Riggins ripped away and sprinted to the end zone.

The Redskins added an insurance touchdown on Theismann's pass to Charlie Brown to spark the victory celebration. Washington's defense, though overshadowed by Riggins and the Hogs, had held Miami without a pass completion in the second half.

Riggins had gained a record 166 yards on 38 carries and was named the most valuable player. "At least for tonight," he said, "Ron (Reagan) may be the President, but I'm the King."

Although the Dolphins lost Super Bowl XVII to the Redskins, they had their high points in the game. Besides Fulton Walker's record 98-yard kickoff return to a touchdown, Jimmy Cefalo (81) raced 76 yards to score on a pass from David Woodley. The Dolphins generated 176 yards rushing, 96 yards passing.

"At Audi the future of the automobile is being decided."

—Car and Driver, December 1983

Have you noticed where the great developments in automotive engineering have been coming from?

Many of them have come from one place: From Audi.

They have come from a group of hand-picked engineers working under a man they respect: Ferdinand Piëch, Audi's Chief of Research & Development in Ingolstadt, Germany.

Consider these Audi engineering achievements:

The five-cylinder gasoline engine. A six would have been too big and heavy; a four would not have been smooth enough for the kind of luxury car Audi had in mind.

It was the innovative five that made the Audi 5000 feel just right.

The quattro permanent all-wheel-drive system for sports coupes and sedans: A major breakthrough in performance and driving safety that increases mobility about 100% on wet or snowy roads. This all-weather system enabled the Audi racing quattro to win the World Rally Championship. It was recently introduced on the Audi 4000S quattro at $16,830.*

Audi 5000S & 5000S Turbo: The technology that makes these the most aerodynamic luxury sedans sold in America also makes them two of the quietest.

We solve problems. Audi's engineers proved the world's fastest luxury sedan need not be the most powerful, and started an aerodynamic revolution that sent the industry back to its computers and wind tunnels.

Many people believe Audis are beautiful. We believe they are buying them in record numbers for more important reasons. For your nearest dealer, call toll-free 1-(800) FOR-AUDI within the continental U.S. *Mfr's sugg. retail price. Title, taxes, transp., registration, dealer delivery charges add'l. **PORSCHE+AUDI**

Audi: the art of engineering.

Super Bowl XVII most valuable player John Riggins shed Miami cornerback Don McNeal and ran 43 yards for the Redskins' decisive touchdown. Rigins, the central figure in Washington's offense all season, set Super Bowl records with 38 carries for 166 yards.

hey billed it as a dream game — Super Bowl XVIII, a fantasy meeting between two of the NFL's most dominant identities. In one corner stood the Washington Redskins, defending world champions, winners of their last 11 straight, confident that they would retain their title. Staring back across the field were the Los Angeles Raiders, self-proclaimed Darth Vaders of professional football, a surly conglomerate of misfits and vagabonds with two Super Bowl victories already to their credit.

The stage had been set in week five of the regular season when Redskins quarterback Joe Theismann engineered a thrilling 37-35 victory over the Raiders at RFK Stadium. As the 72,920 fans crowded into Tampa Stadium for the rematch and millions of others fine-tuned their television sets, they had every reason to expect another spine-tingling battle to the finish.

The cast of players was universally renowned. The Redskins, guided by third-year coach Joe Gibbs, boasted seven All-NFL players, including Theismann and running back John Riggins, who had helped Washington set the NFL record for most points scored in a season. Theismann, the league's most valuable player, had connected with the likes of Art Monk, Charlie Brown and running back Joe Washington for 29 touchdown passes in 1983. Riggins, a legend in post-season play, entered Super Sunday with an NFL record six consecutive 100-yard games.

The Raiders, coached by Tom Flores, countered with a diversified attack featuring quarterback Jim Plunkett, MVP of Super Bowl XV, and amazing Marcus Allen, who had darted his way to 1,014 yards on 266 carries during the regular season.

Defensively, both teams were noted for stinginess. The Redskins were number one in the NFL

photo: Dave Bush

against the run, fifth in least points allowed, and sixth in sacks. The Raiders had improved their defense dramatically since their earlier confrontation with Washington by acquiring six-time Pro Bowl cornerback Mike Haynes from New England. Haynes joined Pro Bowl standouts Howie Long, Ted Hendricks, Rod Martin, Lester Hayes and Vann McElroy to uphold the renegade image of the Raiders' defensive unit.

All week long, the two teams had been brashly self-assured. Raiders' defensive end Lyle Alzado claimed he would tear Riggins' head off. Hayes proclaimed himself the only true Jedi in the NFL. Gibbs said simply, "We'll enjoy everything going on, then we'll play our hearts out on Sunday."

But from the early moments of the game, there were indications that the close encounter would never materialize. On the Redskins' first punt, Raiders' special teams captain Derrick Jensen found an opening up the middle, stormed through to smother Jeff Hayes' kick, and recovered the rolling ball in the end zone. This sudden blow seemed to ignite the Raiders and deflate the Redskins' confidence. It set the tone for the remainder of the game.

The pace continued into the second quarter when Plunkett isolated big-play receiver Cliff Branch on cornerback Anthony Washington. The combination clicked twice, on a 50-yard bomb and a 12-yard touchdown strike to give Los Angeles a 14-0 lead.

Forced to settle for a field goal after a first-and-goal on the Raiders' 7, the Redskins appeared to be headed to the locker room down 14-3, but still in the game. Then came the play that Theismann and Gibbs might have wished they hadn't run.

With 12 seconds showing on the clock, Gibbs called for a screen pass from the Redskins' 12. "We wanted to get ourselves a little breathing room and get out of there," said Theismann. Instead,

51

substitute linebacker Jack Squirek emerged from a crowd to pick off Theismann's floater intended for Washington. A few steps later, he was in the end zone.

It was a devastating play for the Redskins. An 11-point deficit at halftime had seemed manageable. Eighteen points would prove insurmountable.

The Redskins came to life briefly in the second half, driving 70 yards after the kickoff to cut the Raiders' lead to 21-9. Riggins capped the drive with a 1-yard run.

But Los Angeles quickly extinguished any thoughts of a Washington comeback with a score of their own. Aided by a key 38-yard pass interference penalty, the Raiders rambled 70 yards to stretch their lead to 28-9 on Allen's first touchdown dash.

In the next series of plays the Raiders applied the knockout punch in the Redskins' day of agony. Riggins, virtually unstoppable in short-yardage situations all year, needed one yard on fourth down on the Raiders' 26.

As Raiders' linebacker coach Charlie Sumner explained, "A lot of linebackers play so deep that they (the Redskins' line) can double down on the nose man to give Riggins a lane. We put our inside linebackers (Matt Millen and Bob Nelson) right up on the line and forced them to take us man-to-man."

The strategy worked. With the middle of the line jammed, Riggins broke outside where linebacker Rod Martin was waiting. Martin, UPI's AFC Defensive Player of the Year, absorbed the impact and dropped Riggins to the turf for no gain. Riggins managed only 64 yards on 26 carries against the stubborn Raiders' defense.

The game then became "The Marcus Allen Show." On the Raiders' first play after stopping Riggins, Allen took a handoff and started a sweep to the left where Redskins' defensive back Ken Coffey stood waiting to drop him for an eight-yard loss.

A crowd of 72,920 fans filled Tampa Stadium to witness what most people thought would be a classic confrontation between two pro football superpowers. Only the Raiders' fans would come away happy.

photo: R. Mackson

photo: Dave Bush

Instead, Allen abruptly reversed his field, accelerated through a huge opening up the middle, and outsprinted the entire Redskins' defense 74 yards to the end zone. With that run Allen wrapped up both the game for the Raiders and the MVP award for himself.

But the day belonged as much to the Raiders' defense as to Allen. The line and linebackers won the battle with the Hogs and dominated the scrimmage line. They sacked Theismann six times and pressed him into numerous hurried passes.

In the aftermath of their victory, the Raiders were rightfully jubilant. In their 38-9 thrashing of the Redskins, they had virtually rewritten the Super Bowl record book. Allen set records for most yards gained rushing, most combined yards rushing and receiving, and longest run from scrimmage. The Raiders set new team marks for average gain rushing and most points in a game.

Perhaps Raiders' managing general partner Al Davis was justified in telling his team, as he received the Lombardi Trophy, "Not only, in my opinion, are you the greatest Raiders team of all time — I think you rank with the great teams of all time who ever played any professional sport."

His appraisal may have been somewhat exaggerated. But one thing is certain — the Raiders had just played the best all-around game in Super Bowl history, thoroughly dominating the Redskins in every category.

Nose tackle Dave Stalls summed up the feelings of his teammates, "We were not awed by the Redskins or playing in the Super Bowl. We knew all along that we could win and confidence really helps you be successful."

Successful they were, by the largest victory margin in Super Bowl history. In the loser's locker room, Redskins middle linebacker Neal Olkewicz expressed his team's dejection, saying quietly, "In my wildest dreams, I never believed this could happen to us."

Preparing for battle is a personal business. For Raiders tackle Bruce Davis, stretching exercises loosened muscles and soothed pregame tensions.

Derrick Jensen (31) gave Raiders a 7-0 lead with a blocked punt for the TD.

Cliff Branch's two key catches led to a 14-0 Raiders' advantage.

Mark Moseley's FG brought the Redskins within striking distance, 14-3.

Rugged Raiders' defense applied pressure on Theismann.

Ray Guy held Washington at bay with seven long punts.

Mike Davis (36) matched Clint Didier (86) step for step.

Stalled Redskins' drives kept punter Jeff Hayes on the field.

Raiders' Squirek, right man in right place at right time.

The beginning of the end for the Redskins. With just 12 seconds left in the first half, reserve linebacker Jack Squirek's interception for a touchdown gave the Raiders a commanding 21-3 lead.

Marcus Allen became the center of attention in the second half.

Raiders' Greg Townsend dropped Theismann to the turf.

Don Hasselbeck (87) celebrates blocked Moseley PAT.

A long day for Redskins' quarterback Theismann.

Finishing off the Redskins. In the longest run from scrimmage in Super Bowl history, Marcus Allen races 74 yards to cap the Raiders' dominating victory over Washington, 38-9.

photo: Peter Read Miller

Chris Bahr contributed a field goal and five PATs to Raiders' cause.

photo: John E. Biever

Raiders' defenders sense victory after shutting down the Redskins.

photo: John E. Biever

Jubilant Reggie Kinlaw knows who's number one.

photo: Dave Bush

MVP Marcus Allen delivers the victory kiss.

photo: Michael Zagaris

59

o the average sports fan, the third week in January bestows the crown jewel of professional football. The Super Bowl. Indeed it is a game filled with mighty men, magic moments and considerable media hype. But to a first-time Super Bowl attendee, it is more, much more. The name of the game is party, a day-in, day-out, week-long festival that could easily be labeled "America's Annual Company Picnic."

Many of the 60,000-80,000 seats available each year are occupied by executives, their clients and employees, arriving in corporate jets, private aircraft, chartered planes, trains and yachts. Football fan and executive may not always be one and the same, but chances are they will rub elbows with one another at a party—one of dozens held during Super Bowl week.

This marathon of merriment finds Guccis with hootchie cootchies, Brooks Brothers jackets flung carelessly over barstools, bejeweled matrons aflush with anticipation as they vie for the attention of this week's hero, and young ladies (lots of them) giggling and strutting their stuff. And the beat goes on....

Despite the apparent spontaneity of the moment, the buildup to Super Bowl XVIII began long before. To be selected as Super Host, the City of Tampa had to guarantee adequate hotel space for the NFL contingent, the teams and the fans, as well as the facilities for meetings, parties, dinners and the like. They had to organize a Task Force to handle traffic, transportation (900 buses, 350 limousines), civic events, housing and problem solving. For over two years, some 200 volunteers, broken into committees, addressed these and dozens of other issues.

The end result? A civic spirit that endured despite poor weather and lower visitor-spending than local merchants had anticipated. Resi-

SUPERFANITIS ATTACKS TAMPA

dents thought that Super Visitors would spend Super Bucks for all kinds of consumer goods. In fact, the hottest items (besides official Super Bowl souvenirs) were gloves, scarves, and rain gear needed to ward off the elements. It is unlikely that many microwaves, television sets or automobiles were grabbed up in the eagerness to spend money.

True, it was reported that local revenue swelled by more than $87 million. But to an emerging city like Tampa, the Super Bowl was not seen as a short-term money generator. It was considered a priceless public relations vehicle designed to gain national exposure and emphasize that not all the action here was football-related. The real Tampa action involved booming growth projections for the business community. What better way to attract the movers and shakers of industry, even if their attention was on more urgent matters than company relocation? In Redskinland, they call it "lobbying." And still the beat goes on....

In a dizzying effort to prepare Tampa for its "coming out party," welcome signs adorned highways, hotels and motels, bars, stores and more. For weeks prior to Super Sunday, hordes of workmen spruced up the more visible areas, planting flowers, shrubs and trees into soft warm soil. Whammo! The area was hit by one of its worst freezes in years, and flora and fauna shriveled up like old parchment. Undaunted, the crews rushed to replace what nature had torn asunder, working from sunup to sundown right up to game day.

Certainly one of the more impressive elements of the organized hoopla was the list of daily activities open to the public. Although the events were staged mainly for residents, they drew visitors and media members as well. Four days of festivities included special movies and exhibits, parades and fireworks, luncheons and banquets, the racing of dogs, horses and cars (separately, of course), sporting events and concerts. On hand to entertain the troops were such luminaries as Frank Sinatra, John Denver, Lou Rawls, Tony Bennett, Merle Haggard, and the Royal Winnipeg Ballet.

Many activities planned for outdoors were hurriedly moved inside to cramped quarters or cancelled by rain. Those visitors who came expecting heat, humidity and the chance for a running start on this year's tan were in for a grey awakening. Except for one muggy day, they shivered in their spring frocks and short-sleeved shirts, before the assault on rain apparel began. Mother Nature and the natives had the last laugh, though. On Super Sunday the Superfans would lug umbrellas and warm clothes to the game, only to be met by a sudden and most welcome sunsplash.

In preparation for the big day, the NFL and the media arrived early to set up shop. One side of the stadium became the CBS command post, barricaded and heavily guarded. From the massive mobile units parked in rows, thousands of feet of cable were run into the stadium to handle the audio/visual hookup which would beam Super Extravaganza around the world.

Meanwhile, the NFL staff attended to logistical details. Media registration and on-going liaison was a hefty project since, according to NFL Special Events Director Jim Steeg, over 2,100 press credentials had been issued.

Thursday before the game the majority of the press legion poured into town from the far corners of the globe. Hyatt, the headquarters hotel, bustled with hundreds of mediamen, good ol' boys who had been through it all many times before. Every turn brought a fresh whiff of cigar smoke and a hearty "Howya doin', Buddy? Haven't seen ya since Detroit."

The good ol' gang was handsomely cared for by the NFL. Little could have been wished for that was not provided: private lounge, complimentary beverages, courtesy

Thousands of balloons mark the game's commencement.

cars, and a never-ending array of leisure activities and parties.

As the media prepared stories, attended press conferences, swapped tales and otherwise enjoyed themselves, the fans were busy playing.

SUPERFANITIS: A mental and physical condition lasting from one week to five months; primarily attacking adults (sex is unimportant — although not to be mistaken for a symptom); causing an itching, twitching desire (nay, need) to drink, laugh, wear ridiculous get-ups, be loud and silly, and forget who you are. Treatment: Super Bowl. Cure: At this writing, absolutely none!

All week long, restaurants bulged and bars overflowed, literally and figuratively. Although most establishments expected a booming trade and planned accordingly, some spots actually ran out of booze and had to send out to neighborhood liquor stores for reinforcements. It would be interesting to know if the sale of headache remedies also surpassed previous local records. One can only imagine.

For the captains of industry, the party scene was chic, pricey and private. Behind closed doors and away from the gawkers, the rich sipped imported champagne, nibbled exotic hors d'oeuvres, and supped on sumptuous meals hosted by executives, franchise owners and local civic leaders.

The hottest tickets in town, for which even the moguls wrestled, were invitations to the commissioner's party, historically the *number one* social event of the week. This year, 4,000 people traveled by motor coach to the fairgrounds for an elegant circus featuring animal and aerial acts from the Ringling Bros., Barnum and Bailey Circus.

A host of clowns, mimes and jugglers ushered guests into the tent. Before them, bars and tables brimmed with delicacies. As the throng sipped and munched, the animals entertained.

If you're a friend of Jack Daniel's, we hope you'll visit us sometime soon.

WE CAN'T BLAME THE BOYS for having a water fight now and then. If you worked in Jack Daniel's rickyard, you'd start one too.

Looking after a burning hard maple rick is a hot job. But it's one we can't do without. You see, we take the charcoal that results and use it to help smooth out our whiskey.

That's done by seeping it down through huge vats packed tight with this charcoal. Just a taste of Jack Daniel's, we think, and you'll agree it's worth a water fight or two.

CHARCOAL
MELLOWED

◊

DROP

◊

BY DROP

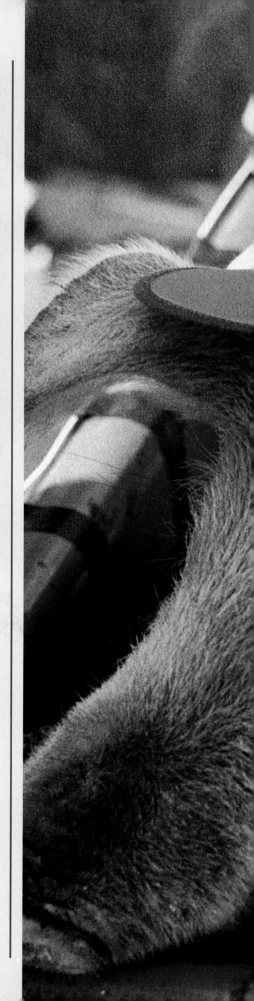

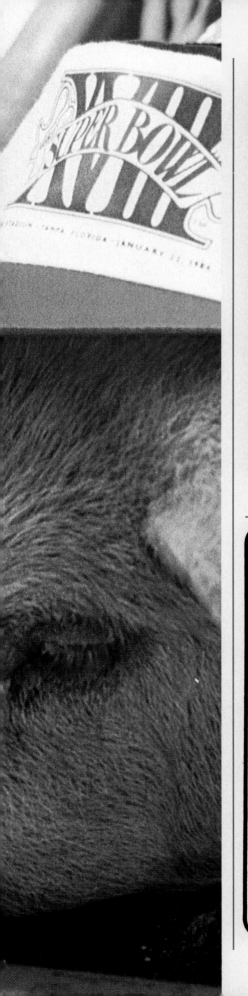

Later, the ringmaster invited everyone into the main arena—a maze of tables, soft lights and dozens of food stations. Amid the subdued din of tableside chatter, a driver zoomed a motorcycle up a cable and the "really big show" ensued, followed by dancing, socializing and a miniature carnival.

The beat continued into game day. A profusion of brightly colored tents sprang up in the fields near Tampa Stadium. Inside, businessmen held luxurious versions of tailgate parties. Barron Hilton hosted a gathering for 1,000 guests on the grounds adjacent to his hotel. The party was in keeping with the NFL "circus" theme, with a heavy emphasis on food. Each table—and there were dozens— resembled a groaningboard from an Elizabethan banquet. According to a Hilton representative, eight chefs were flown in from around the world to prepare the feast. Selections included crepes, blintzes and waffles with various toppings; fresh, succulent seafood; a carving station with ham, beef, and corned beef; a table of Texas and Mexican specialties; fruits, juices, pastries piled high; and a table brimming with every conceivable type of cheese.

Meanwhile, the stadium grounds swarmed with ticket holders hours before gametime. They came in all shapes, sizes, ages, and colors of dress, with a predominance of red and gold. Though outnumbered, the black-clad Raiders' patrons stood out among the multitude.

Others came looking for tickets. Scalping was outlawed, but the market demands precipitated remarkable forms of invention. Two enterprising, law-abiding young men offered tickets at the face price, with a loophole requiring the purchaser to buy their *hats*, at $250 apiece!

As kickoff approached, the stands swelled with eager, noisy fans. Tampa Stadium was designed for college games, and though the seating capacity had been in-

A sandcastle replica of the old Tampa Bay Hotel located on the University of Tampa campus. Dating back to 1890, this landmark, with its Moorish architecture and 13 minarets, has become the city's trademark.

creased considerably for the Super Bowl, walking space was reduced to narrow pathways. The field was littered with people, making sideline movement risky to impossible. CBS cameras, photographers, cheerleaders, the teams and staffs, and NFL security combined to create a traffic jam akin to a Los Angeles freeway at rush hour.

Then the game began. That's right, after a week's worth of non-stop social functioning, of late hours and drink after drink and plate after plate of food, they actually got down to playing football. The fact that the action became one-sided early on did not dampen the spirits of the exuberant crowd. Fueled by 80-proof varieties and/or excited determination in support of their chosen teams, the fans reached high levels of frenzy by halftime. Each crushing tackle, dazzling run, completed pass or quarterback sack met with boisterous approval or disapproval, depending on the point of view.

But aside from bystanders leaping over cables and bodies, most of the field action occurred during the spectacular halftime show presented by Disneyworld.

After months of drawing, designing, organizing and coordinating, the field grew ablaze with color as 2,100 local students ran through demanding dance and marching routines. Billed as a "Sparkling Salute to the Silver Screen," the show featured production numbers spanning the entire field, accompanied by a musical score of show tunes recorded in Los Angeles and aired over Disney's sophisticated sound system.

To pull it off, the Disney staff put in thousands of man-hours over the course of a year. Their involvement had begun with a special request from NFL Commissioner Pete Rozelle to Ron Miller, President and Chief Operating Officer of Disney Productions. Although Disneyworld had previously produced Orange Bowl halftime

Pro Football's Brightest Stars Shine On These Unique Solid Brass Engravings

Limited Editions, Each Personally Autographed and Beautifully Framed, Ready to Hang in Your Office or Home

History-making moments in history-making careers—Joe Montana's, Dwight Clark's, Joe Theismann's—are captured dramatically for fans and collectors in this remarkable and original graphic art form!

These exciting game-action scenes are meticulously engraved on heavy sheets of solid brass. Each is individually engraved (not stamped), protected by a coating of clear acrylic, and double matted under glass in a handsome 20" x 16" Nielsen Gallery Frame.

Each is personally autographed—the star's big, bold signature is centered on the mat—and comes with a Certificate of Authenticity mounted on the back.

"Air Montana"

San Francisco 49ers' QB Joe Montana is shown in Super Bowl XVI action, snapped by 49er photographer Michael Zagaris. This edition is limited to 2,621 to commemorate the 49er 26-21 victory over the Cincinnati Bengals, and Joe himself owns engraving #1/2621.

"Dwight's Flight"

49er Wide Receiver Dwight Clark is pictured leaping for his famous game-winning TD catch in the 1981 NFC Championship game, from an original pen and

ink drawing by artist Donn Knepp. "Something got me up there," said Dwight. "It must have been God or something." The 28-27 49ers/Cowboys score got our Limited Edition up to 2,827—minus Dwight's #1/2827.

"Super Joe/MVP"

The NFL's 1983 Most Valuable Player, Washington Redskins Quarterback Joe Theismann is depicted in a series of action shots by 'Skins photographer Nate Fine. Our Limited Edition of 2,717 honors the Redskins 27-17 triumph over the Miami Dolphins in Super Bowl XVII. Joe, of course, has #1/2717.

Order Now!

For each Limited Edition engraving, autographed and framed, send only $125 plus $10 to cover sales tax, insurance, postage. Enclose your personal check or money order or your VISA or MasterCard number and expiration date. Or order by phone:
1-800-453-7404

Team Effort Sports, Inc.

P.O. Box 770, Drawer 84
Burlingame, California 94010

49ers fans exhibit their disappointment.

Kids are Superfans, too.

Pint-sized Redskins fan upset over loss

The evil Darth Raider emerges victorious.

An apple a day keeps Darth Raider away.

Riggins' Raiders storm the stadium.

Clowning around at Hilton's circus bash

Mickey and Minnie salute Hollywood.

Barry Manilow serenades fans with "The Star Spangled Banner."

Military brass band trumpets the opening of NFL-Alumni Awards Banquet.

'Skins fans display anticipated souvenirs.

Hopeful fans "sign" for tickets.

Performers strut their stuff during halftime.

Watch the game with a wide receiver.

A pair of Bushnell precision binoculars lets you get more of what you pay for when you buy football tickets: more excitement, more color, more action. Bushnell wide angle models have the power to put you on the field from any seat in the stadium, and the wide angle view lets you keep all the action in focus. Bushnell makes the largest selection of wide-angle binoculars and other high-quality sports optics. See them at your Bushnell dealer.

BUSHNELL
DIVISION OF **BAUSCH & LOMB**
2828 E. Foothill Blvd., Pasadena, CA 91107

photo: Dave Bush

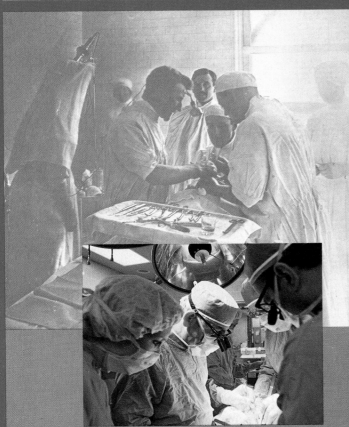

Raiders fan surveys the competition.

Outlandish garb, the norm at Super Bowl

Hilton's circus-theme brunch with all
the trappings

The Hugh O'Brians arrive for Barron
Hilton's extravaganza.

Superfan sports Super moustache.

A pause for the cause

Commissioner's circus party—SRO

Bear less than grisly during cocktails

Multiple cameras were positioned to cover every aspect of the game.

Jubilation rose to a frenzied pitch by halftime.

shows and complex productions on their own grounds, this would be their first Super Bowl.

Logistically, it was a super challenge, requiring Disney personnel to move to Tampa six weeks prior to Super Sunday. A major hurdle was the recruitment of student performers through individual auditions. Working with eleven local high schools, dance studios, private schools and colleges, Disney staff and local contacts surveyed the talents of more than 3,500 young people. In October, final auditions were held, and the 1,800 successful candidates were individually fitted for costumes.

In December, five choreographers traveled from school to school and led 280 separate rehearsals. The entire company was assembled only twice and never had the luxury of a complete run-through from opening to finale. The scheduled final rehearsal had been canceled by rain.

The promise of the Disney spectacular kept most people glued to their seats while thousands of balloons soared above and staging units were rushed onto the field. As the show unfolded in the manner of a Busby Berkeley extravaganza, 200 support staff and 300 staging technicians scurried about behind the scenes preparing performers and arranging the 3,000 props to be used.

Divided into 14 groups ranging from "Bathing Beauties" and "Body Builders" to "Lounge Lizzies" and "Tap Dancers," the young entertainers handled the 12-minute program like seasoned professionals. The show was broken into six distinct segments centering around famous Hollywood tunes: "Let's Go to the Movies," "You Oughta Be in Pictures," "Puttin' on the Ritz," "Tico Tico," "Singin' in the Rain," and the grand finale, "When You Wish Upon a Star."

To showcase the songs, a 47-foot hexagonal stage with five staircases and a revolving lift was positioned at midfield. Other props

photo: Ray DeAragon

Radiant Raiderette cheers the fans and inspires shouts of admiration.

Marcus Allen and Matt Millen congratulate each other on a job well done.

To the victor go the spoils—the Lombardi Trophy.

included 14 baby grand pianos, two 60-foot swimming pools, 80 chaise lounges, 60 giant lighted stars, 180 helium-filled beach balls, 80 dance discs, 200 balloon head-dresses, five swing units and 1,000 yellow umbrellas.

And if all of that wasn't enough, the spectacle ended with an elaborate fireworks display, on the field and into the heavens. Through it all, the fans offered "oohs" and "aahs" and thunderous applause. "BRAVO." "The best show ever!"

In the aftermath of the Disney show, the second half of the game seemed anticlimatic, a lackluster competition with the Raiders rolling over the Redskins play after play. Most observers felt the 'Skins would storm the field in the second half and give the Darth Raiders a run for the money. But it was not to be.

As the game progressed, the tone in the stands began to change. Redskins supporters were bombarded with pig calls. "Oink Oink." "Souiee." "Let's have a pig roast." And then, but for the shouting, it was over.

The press poured into the Raiders locker room and the term "pressing of flesh" took on new dimensions of meaning as they jockeyed for position to photograph and interview the season's champions. Meanwhile, the mass exodus from the stadium to neighboring bars and post-parties proceeded smoothly. It was difficult to distinguish the victors from the vanquished. Each group happily toasted its team.

The next morning, the corporate jets and commercial airliners headed skyward for the trip home. A common bond had grown among the 70,000 Superfans. They had shared the excitement and the experience, and they came away with a secret:

To those who have yet to become a Super Bowl Rookie and to feel the magic of the third week in January firsthand, remember this paraphrase, "Yes, Virginia, there is a Super Bowl. And it is a blast!"

"Autograph my ball, Mister?"

INTRODUCING THE WINNING TEAM IN REAL ESTATE.

Good football takes teamwork and attitude and strategy and solid basic skills. Put them all together and you've got a winner.

The same can be said about McGuire Real Estate. The winning team in real estate. You see we know about teamwork and attitude and strategy and all of the solid basic skills it takes to get you into the property you're looking for.

So if it's time to buy or time to sell, we'd like you to meet the winning team in Real Estate. McGuire Real Estate. We've been selling prime property in San Francisco since 1919.

McGUIRE REAL ESTATE

Prime Property/Properly Represented
(415) 929-1500

Super Bowl, the movable feast of American sport, makes its Northern California debut in a most uncharacteristic setting. Not since Super Bowl IX at Tulane Stadium, New Orleans, has this blend of pro football and show business been held amid the tranquil atmosphere of a college campus. Stanford University, long noted for its low profile and high academic ideals, finds itself in the spotlight, the site of Super Bowl XIX.

Situated in Palo Alto, 40 miles south of San Francisco, Stanford University has long been considered the "Harvard of the West." Leland Stanford, the western pioneer, set out to establish a university which would break tradition with the eastern schools and forge new academic pathways.

When the school opened in 1891, there were approximately 500 students, 17 professors, an Inner Quadrangle of 12 classroom buildings and more than 8,000 acres of land, donated by the Stanfords. A noteworthy graduate of the first class was Herbert Hoover (the football team's first water boy), for whom Stanford's Hoover Institution is named.

Since 1891, the private university has grown and prospered in all respects, with a 1983 enrollment of more than 13,000, an endowment of nearly $1 billion and leading graduate programs in business, education, psychology, computer science and chemical engineering. Its medical center is world-renowned, a pathfinder in medical research and development.

Surely, Leland Stanford would not have been the least surprised at the great progress that Stanford has made. But he might possibly have been a bit overwhelmed at the prospect of a football game of this magnitude taking place on Stanford soil. Still and all, the pleasure of the day will belong to the fans who will gain a rare glimpse of this magnificent campus.

SUPER BOWL GOES TO COLLEGE
Stanford 1985

The stadium nestles in a bucolic setting, obscured by rather than dominating the eucalyptus trees that cover the Stanford University campus. The look is early Ivy League; not exactly what you might expect from a school whose football team is a regular contender in the conference that almost yearly sends more players into the NFL than any other.

Despite its rustic charm, Stanford Stadium was a logical choice as the site of that most modern and urban of championship games, the Super Bowl. Although Super Bowl XIX will be the first NFL game ever played there, it is just another link in a long and rewarding relationship between the NFL and Stanford. From that association have come innovations and players who have profoundly influenced NFL history and strategy.

The NFL's "Stanford Connection" dates back to Ernie Nevers, who played only five years of professional football (1926-27 with the Duluth Eskimos and 1929-31 with the Chicago Cardinals), but still was selected as a charter member of the Pro Football Hall of Fame.

"I coached Jim Thorpe at Carlisle, and I saw virtually every great football player for over half a century," coaching great Glenn S. (Pop) Warner once said. "But Ernie Nevers was the greatest player in the history of the game."

Nevers was an All-America at Stanford and the star of the 1925 Rose Bowl game against Notre Dame's "Four Horsemen," coached by Knute Rockne. But he was even better in the NFL. His signing in 1926 made almost as much of an impact on NFL attendance as Red Grange's enlistment with the Chicago Bears had the year before. As a rookie, he missed only 26 minutes during the entire season. Then, in 1929, he set an NFL record that still exists by scoring 40 points in a game against the Bears.

NOT JUST A PASSING FANCY
The Stanford-NFL Connection: A Remarkable History

By Beau Riffenburgh

photo: Stanford Alumni Association

While Nevers was with the Cardinals, a man across town was helping develop the future for both Stanford and all of football. Clark Shaughnessy, head football coach at the University of Chicago, was the epitome of the absent-minded professor. But on the football field, he was perhaps the most imaginative coach of all time. He was obsessed with football strategy and nothing else, and had the distracting habit of diagramming plays on sheets of paper while carrying on a conversation.

It was from his creative, eccentric mind that the modern T-formation sprang. In the early 1930's, Shaughnessy was introduced to Bears owner and head coach George Halas. Shaughnessy began visiting Bears' practices, watching their use of the T-formation, and returning to his own team to experiment.

After studying the strengths and weaknesses of the T, Shaughnessy converted it from a dying formation used by only one NFL team into a bold new scheme based on quickness, motion and deception. His major innovation was the counter play. He split one end wide, motioned away from him, then ran back to the side of the spread end.

Having developed new theories for the T, Shaughnessy only needed a forum in which to try them out. He found it at Stanford. The Indians (as the Stanford team was known at the time) had a 1-9 record in 1939, but Shaughnessy thought his new T could help turn that record around. He had his doubters. Pop Warner said scornfully, "If Stanford ever wins a single game with that crazy formation, you can throw all the football I ever knew into the Pacific Ocean."

But Shaughnessy proved to be right. With Frankie Albert running the offense, Stanford's "Wow Boys" used Shaughnessy's tactics and reversed their season of the year before, sweeping to nine consecutive victories and into the Rose Bowl.

But Shaughnessy had one more

stop to make before January 1. In the weeks prior to the Rose Bowl, he returned to Chicago to help Halas and the Bears in their NFL Championship Game against Washington.

With Shaughnessy calling plays from the press box, Chicago was unstoppable, winning 73-0, the widest margin of victory in NFL history.

Three weeks later, Stanford beat Nebraska 21-13 in the Rose Bowl to complete the perfect season. Football would never look the same again. In one season, with two different teams, Shaughnessy had set the offensive course of the game. Team after team began converting to the T.

Shaughnessy was not finished with either the NFL or college football, however. He remained at Stanford one more year before moving on to Maryland and then Pittsburgh. In 1948, he became the head coach of the Los Angeles Rams and took them to the NFL Championship Game against Philadelphia in 1949.

He joined the Bears in 1951 as a technical advisor specializing in offense. Four years later he transferred to defense, where he had as many theories as he had on the other side of the ball.

Shaughnessy retired in 1962, but he left pro football one last legacy. "I learned a great deal from him," said former Rams and Redskins coach George Allen, who was a defensive assistant with the Bears under Shaughnessy. "He was a great man with a very fertile mind. He worked ungodly hours and was always making notes on things to do in the future. He passed a lot of his habits and beliefs on to me."

Shaughnessy also passed his teachings along to the four members of his initial Stanford backfield. They, in turn, became successful NFL players.

Norm Standlee and Hugh Gallarneau, who both were seniors in 1940, joined the Bears the next year. In the 1941 NFL Champion-

Football has been played at Stanford since 1891. In that time, Stanford teams have produced coaches and players who have profoundly influenced the evolution of the pro game.

In the leather helmet days, Stanford teams were as gutsy as they were innovative. As the game advanced, Stanford has continued to be a forerunner in football strategy and player development.

ship Game against the New York Giants, Standlee broke open a tie game with two third-quarter touchdowns, as the Bears won another championship. After missing the next four years because of World War II, he returned to pro football in 1946 as a fullback for the San Francisco 49ers, remaining with them for seven years.

Gallarneau was one of the Bears' leading rushers and receivers in 1941 and 1942, before joining the service. He returned to the Bears in 1945 and led the team in rushing in 1946, when the Bears won yet another NFL title.

Albert, a two-time All-America and the first draft choice of the Bears in 1942, and halfback Pete Kmetovic both entered the service after their senior years in 1941. After the war, Kmetovic played with the Eagles and Lions, while Albert went on to a distinguished seven years with the 49ers. By the end of his career, he had passed for the fifth most yards in pro football history.

Albert was named San Francisco's head coach in 1956. He constructed a team that included quarterback Y.A. Tittle and running backs John Henry Johnson, Joe Perry and Hugh McElhenny. In his second year, Albert led the 49ers to their first-ever title, as they tied for the Western Conference championship. But after a bitter loss to Detroit in the 1957 playoff and a disappointing season in 1958, Albert retired with a three-year record of 19-16-1.

He never played in the NFL, but Chuck Taylor, a little-known sophomore offensive lineman on the 1940 Stanford team, went on to make more significant contributions to Stanford and the NFL than any of his better-known teammates.

Taylor served as the Indians' freshman coach for several years, then served on Buck Shaw's 49ers staff before returning to Stanford as head coach in 1951. Like Shaughnessy, he led the Indians to nine consecutive victories and into the Rose Bowl in his first year.

"I learned fast that Stanford wasn't going to run over anybody," Taylor said, recalling his first year at the helm. "But passing could keep us in almost every game, and could allow us to upset a team that was physically stronger than we were."

So Taylor devised a passing strategy that was unique at the time. Instead of using the run to establish the pass, he worked it the other way around. His shift of emphasis laid the foundation for the style of attack that has become synonymous with Stanford football. In the larger picture, he started football down the path toward being the pass-oriented game it is today.

The traditional passing approach had the receiver run down ten yards and turn around, with little deviation from the pattern. "But we changed that," Taylor said. "We divided the field into nine zones and called zone patterns instead of specific routes. That way, it was up to the receivers to get open, and it was the quarterback's responsibility to read both the defense and his own receiver."

Taylor's use of the passing game also started Stanford on its continuing string of outstanding passers and receivers. His first great passing duo—Gary Kerkorian and Bill McColl—finished their Stanford careers in the 1952 Rose Bowl. But neither player was finished with football. Kerkorian played four years in the NFL with the Steelers and Colts. He started for the Colts in 1954, but his career came to a halt with the emergence in 1956 of rookie Johnny Unitas.

McColl, an All-America in both 1950 and 1951, played for the Bears from 1952-59, becoming the team's number three career receiver before retiring to pursue a medical career. However, his influence at both Stanford and in the NFL continued well beyond his own playing days. His son Duncan was an All-America defensive end at Stanford in 1976 and the first draft choice of the

The 84,804-seat Stanford Stadium will be the site of Super Bowl XIX. However, its connection with professional football is long-standing. From Frankie Albert to John Elway, Bill McColl to Chris Dressel, Stanford has given pro football great passers, receivers—and more.

photo: Gerald French

Washington Redskins the next year. Another son, Milt, a Stanford linebacker, joined the 49ers and played on the club's Super Bowl XVI championship team.

In 1953, another passing combination, consisting of two players who were sophomores in Taylor's first season, continued Stanford's passing trend. Bobby Garrett became the first of six Stanford quarterbacks to lead the nation in passing, and end Sam Morley was named All-America. Garrett was the first draft pick of the Cleveland Browns and went on to play for the Green Bay Packers. Morley played for the Washington Redskins.

The following year, Taylor started another sophomore quarterback, predicting that if he continued to develop, there was no telling how far he could go. Indeed, despite not having a football scholarship, John Brodie was about as successful as a quarterback can be.

Brodie led the nation in passing and became the All-America quarterback as a senior, winning the honor over Heisman Trophy winner Paul Hornung of Notre Dame, Sonny Jurgensen of Duke, Milt Plum of Penn State and Len Dawson of Purdue. He then took his talents to the 49ers, where, in 17 years, he threw for more than 31,000 yards and guided his team to three NFC West titles.

Taylor retired as head coach in 1958 to become the assistant athletic director. His successor, Jack Curtice, didn't win as many games as Taylor, but he continued to put the ball in the air.

In 1958, Stanford became the only college team ever to have two quarterbacks — Dick Norman and Bob Nicolet — finish among the nation's top 10 passers. The next year, Norman led the nation in passing and total offense, and his favorite end, Chris Burford, led the college ranks in receiving.

Norman later played with the Bears, while Burford went on to an eight-year career with the Dallas Texans and Kansas City Chiefs. He

Jeff Siemon is the only consensus All-America linebacker in Stanford history. Minnesota's first-round draft choice in 1972, Siemon led the Vikings in tackles 5 times, made 11 interceptions, and didn't miss a game for 10 consecutive seasons.

Although he led Stanford in rushing as a junior and senior, Scott Laidlaw was a relative unknown. Drafted by the Cowboys, he played five years in Dallas.

finished among the top five AFL receivers three times and started for the Chiefs in Super Bowl I.

When Curtis stepped down after the 1962 season, Stanford's passing tradition received a serious threat. The new coach was John Ralston, who had built strong teams at Utah State concentrating on a bruising ground attack and a tough defense, led by such players as All-America Merlin Olsen.

For his first several years at Stanford, Ralston had moderate success. His teams were led by a series of quarterbacks who would play in the NFL at other positions. Steve Thurlow would go on to the Washington Redskins as a halfback. David Lewis would twice lead the NFL in punting with the Cincinnati Bengals. And Gene Washington would be an all-pro wide receiver with the 49ers. Ralston also coached guards Blaine Nye, later an all-pro with Dallas, and John Wilbur, who played with several NFL teams.

It wasn't until 1968 that the urging of Taylor (who had become the athletic director), and the development of a quarterback whom the Stanford coaches had once considered playing at defensive end, finally convinced Ralston to go back to Stanford's basic approach. The Pass.

"The key to our change in strategy was Jim Plunkett," Ralston said. "He came in as a sophomore and in the initial game completed ten of thirteen passes for 277 yards and four touchdowns. Jim continued from that point, never satisfied, always with a vision of what he wanted Jim Plunkett to accomplish."

In his senior season (1970), Plunkett accomplished almost everything he wanted. It started with his team goals, which he had always placed above personal advancement. That year, the Indians defeated USC for the first time in 13 years and went to their first Rose Bowl in two decades, defeating unbeaten Ohio State 27-17.

Plunkett also earned personal

honors aplenty. He won the Heisman Trophy, was named Player of the Game in the Rose Bowl, was a consensus All-America, and finished as the leading yardage producer in the history of college football.

Plunkett was the first player chosen in the 1971 NFL draft, and followed that by becoming the NFL's rookie of the year. Injuries cut short his career with the New England Patriots (1971-75) and kept him from blooming again with the 49ers (1976-77). Down but never out, he was signed as a free agent by the Raiders in 1978 and led the team to victories in Super Bowls XV and XVIII.

During his years at Stanford, Plunkett shared the college spotlight with three fine receivers. As a sophomore, he threw to Gene Washington, who set conference records for receiving after being moved from quarterback. Washington then spent nine years with the 49ers, setting the team record for most career yards receiving. He also teamed with Bob Moore (who later played with the Raiders, Tampa Bay and Denver) and with flanker Randy Vataha, who joined Plunkett for several years in New England.

He even shared his own position. The year after Plunkett graduated, his former backup, Don Bunce, encored for Plunkett by taking the Indians to the Rose Bowl. There Bunce was named Player of the Game, leading a come-from-behind 13-12 victory over undefeated Michigan.

Although Bunce played only one year in Canada and went to medical school instead of playing in the NFL, others from his team had successful NFL careers. Benny Barnes played for 11 years with the Dallas Cowboys. Jeff Siemon became a Pro Bowl linebacker at Minnesota. And Greg Sampson made a successful switch from defensive line at Stanford to offensive line with the Houston Oilers.

Even the coaches from those

Mike Boryla's NFL career didn't match his two brilliant years as Stanford's starting quarterback but he did have his moments of glory. Representing the Philadelphia Eagles in the 1976 Pro Bowl, Boryla's two fourth-quarter touchdown passes turned a 20-9 deficit into a 23-20 NFC win over the AFC.

John Brodie came out of Stanford to become one of the NFL's most productive passers. In 17 seasons with San Francisco, Brodie completed 2,469 passes for 31,548 yards and 214 touchdowns, leading the 49ers to three conference championships.

two Rose Bowl teams made significant contributions to the NFL. Ralston became the head coach of the Broncos and led the team to its first winning season ever. Quarterback coach Dick Vermeil became the NFL's first special teams coach with George Allen in Los Angeles, served as head coach at UCLA, then took the Eagles to Super Bowl XV. Assistant Roger Theder is now on Frank Kush's staff in Indianapolis.

After Ralston's Rose Bowl triumphs, the passing game at Stanford became a national model, and the Cardinals (as they officially became known in 1972) were able to recruit a nonstop succession of outstanding passers.

In 1972 Ralston was succeeded as head coach by Jack Christiansen, a member of the Pro Football Hall of Fame as a Detroit Lions defensive back, and a former head coach with the 49ers. Five seasons under Christiansen yielded only mediocrity in the win-loss columns, but they did produce several outstanding players who moved into the NFL ranks.

Quarterback Mike Boryla succeeded as the starter in 1972-73. Boryla then played for the Philadelphia Eagles, and in the 1976 AFC-NFC Pro Bowl, threw two fourth-quarter touchdown passes to bring the NFC from behind to a 23-20 victory.

Christiansen also turned out wide receiver Tony Hill, who later made all-pro with the Cowboys; running back Scott Laidlaw, who also played with Dallas; defensive back Randy Poltl, who played with Denver; and three All-America defensive ends—Pat Donovan (now a Pro Bowl offensive tackle with Dallas), Roger Stillwell and Duncan McColl.

Stanford's passing game perhaps reached its most innovative stage under Christiansen's successor, Bill Walsh. A veteran NFL assistant coach and mentor to Ken Anderson and Dan Fouts, Walsh brought new diversity to the Stanford attack, while refining the passing game

Frequently injured with the New England Patriots and San Francisco 49ers, Jim Plunkett led the Raiders to two Super Bowl titles. He was Game XV's most valuable player when Oakland defeated Philadelphia, 27-10. In Super Bowl XVIII in 1984, he directed the Raiders over Washington, 38-9.

Gene Washington was the 49ers' first-round draft pick in 1969 after setting season and career receiving records at Stanford. In nine pro seasons, Washington caught 371 passes and scored 59 touchdowns.

even further.

"Only a limited number of college teams are able to play conservatively and overwhelm their opponents physically," Walsh said, repeating the message of Chuck Taylor a quarter of a century earlier. "So we decided to utilize a high-percentage passing offense with selective, but effective, use of the run."

Walsh's strategy was successful. In only two years at Stanford, he twice led his teams to bowl victories and twice coached the nation's leading passer—Guy Benjamin in 1977 and Steve Dils in 1978. He became head coach of the 49ers in 1979 and two years later led them to the Super Bowl XVI Championship.

But Walsh contributed more than just his offensive theory to the NFL. In his two years at Stanford, he helped develop a bundle of current NFL players, including Benjamin, who is now with the 49ers; Dils, who started in 1983 for the Vikings; Turk Schonert, who led the nation in passing in 1979 and is now with the Bengals; all-pro wide receiver James Lofton of the Green Bay Packers; and tackle Gordon King of the New York Giants. He also coached Darrin Nelson who, as a freshman in 1977, became the first player in NCAA history to rush for 1,000 yards and catch 50 passes in the same year. Nelson did it twice more before moving on to the Minnesota Vikings in 1982.

In the past five years, Stanford has continued to be among the nation's leaders in passing. Rod Dowhower coached the Cardinals in 1979 before moving on to the NFL, where he is now offensive coordinator for the improving St. Louis Cardinals. And although Paul Wiggin (who became Stanford's head coach in 1980) didn't contribute to the NFL the theory and innovation of Walsh, he did send the league perhaps the ultimate passer, John Elway.

The latest and potentially the best of the Stanford quarterbacks,

Southwest Airlines & Hertz:
The Winning Combination for Business and Pleasure.

Whether you're going to work or play, you'll enjoy Southwest Airlines' style of keeping spirits high and fares low.

FLY SOUTHWEST
"Love that Spirit!"

Plus at each of the 22 Southwest destination cities, Hertz is there to serve you with great daily, weekly and weekend rates. And all the service and quality that Hertz is famous for. So choose the winning combination. Call your travel agent, Southwest Airlines or Hertz today for reservations.

Hertz

The #1 way to rent a car.™

Hertz rents Fords and other fine cars.

SOUTHWEST AIRLINES DESTINATION CITIES:

Amarillo, Austin, Corpus Christi, Dallas, El Paso, Houston, Lubbock, Midland/Odessa, Rio Grande Valley, San Antonio • New Orleans • Kansas City, • Little Rock • Oklahoma City, Tulsa • Albuquerque • Denver • Las Vegas • Phoenix • Los Angeles, San Diego, San Francisco.

Starting Sept. 2nd from Southwest Airlines & Hertz

SUPER BOWL BONANZA!

You could win a trip for two to Super Bowl XIX in San Francisco or many other exciting prizes. Pick up your game cards from Hertz or Southwest Airlines today.

No purchase necessary. Void where prohibited.

Randy Vataha was one of Jim Plunkett's favorite receivers during their days at Stanford. Vataha accounted for 1,234 yards on 83 catches before going on to join Plunkett with the New England Patriots.

Elway set a number of NCAA records before becoming the first pick of the 1983 NFL draft. He entered pro football with the most glowing press clippings and the highest praise of any quarterback in over a decade. Despite a rocky start as a rookie, he helped lead the Broncos to the playoffs.

Unlike Walsh and Dowhower, Wiggin was not primarily an offensive coach. In fact, he had earned a reputation as a defensive wizard. But, like Walsh, Wiggin did have a strong NFL connection before becoming head coach of the Cardinals. He had been an All-America tackle and the co-captain of Stanford's 1956 team with John Brodie. He then was an all-pro with the Cleveland Browns, and head coach of the Kansas City Chiefs from 1975-77, before returning to his alma mater.

Also like Walsh, Wiggin sent a number of players into the NFL. Besides Elway, he coached such current NFL players as running back Nelson, wide receivers Ken Margerum of Chicago and Andre Tyler of Tampa Bay, Pro Bowl tackle Brian Holloway of New England, tight end Chris Dressel of Houston, and the 49ers' Milt McColl and Rick Gervais.

Wiggin resigned at the end of the 1983 season, but that shouldn't signal an end to the NFL's "Stanford Connection." After all, Stanford's new coach is Jack Elway, John's father, and one of the nation's most innovative advocates of the passing game.

With an Elway again on the Palo Alto campus, the NFL will be seeing more of Stanford than its stadium at Super Bowl XIX. Whether it be with new offensive strategies, or better and better passers and receivers, Stanford will continue to influence and contribute to the NFL — through the air, of course.

photo: Alan Kaye

Tony Hill broke Gene Washington's career receiving records at Stanford. In eight years with Dallas, he has led the team in receiving four times and caught 298 passes, third-best in club history.

photo: John H. Schaff

Turk Schonert spent most of his Stanford career on the bench before leading the nation in passing in 1979. As a pro, he is backup for Cincinnati's all-pro quarterback Ken Anderson.

One of Stanford's all-time great defensive players, Pat Donovan moved to offensive tackle with the Dallas Cowboys. Before retiring at the end of the 1983 season, he played ten years and appeared in four Pro Bowls.

John Elway virtually rewrote the Stanford record book for passers during his years there. Upon graduation in 1983, he joined the Denver Broncos. Although his performance was less than spectacular, he helped Denver reach the playoffs.

For Great Steaks, The Old West Can't Beat The Far East.

Going out for steak today is about like it was out on the Chisholm Trail. Basically, it's still take it off the fire and put it on the plate.

At Benihana, we do steak like you've never tasted or seen before. Tender, choice filets of beef. Fresh mushrooms, onions, zucchini, and bean sprouts. All prepared hibachi style, right at your table. By a chef who makes sure you not only have a great steak, but a great time.

And what we've done for steak, we've also done for seafood and chicken. So don't head for the Old West. Come to the Far East.

BENIHANA
THE JAPANESE STEAKHOUSE

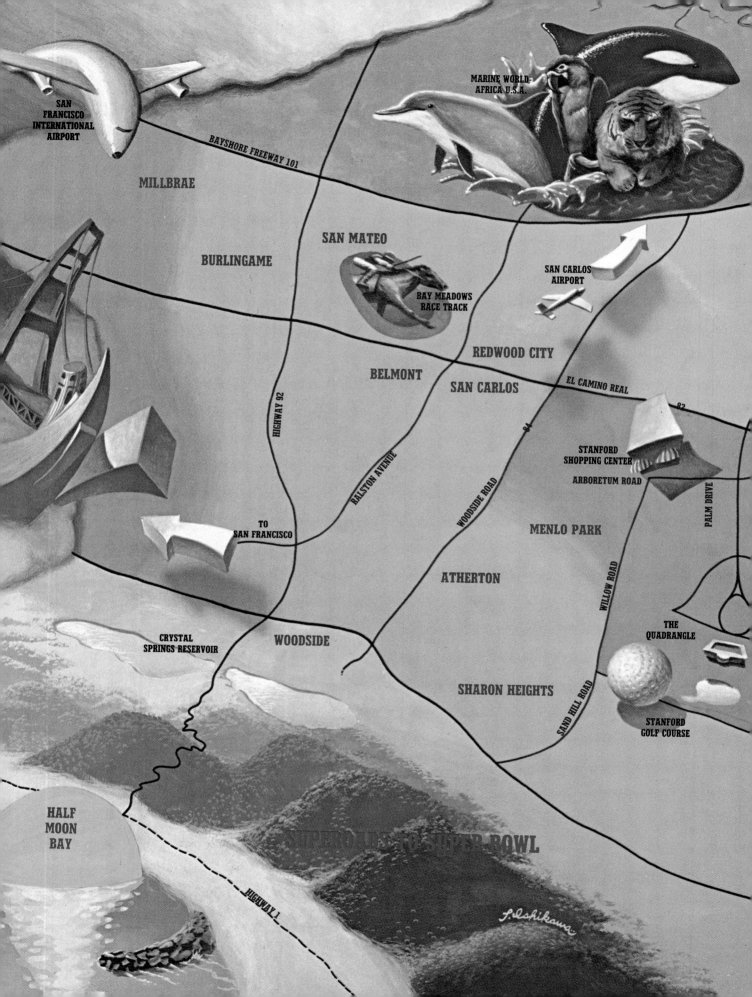

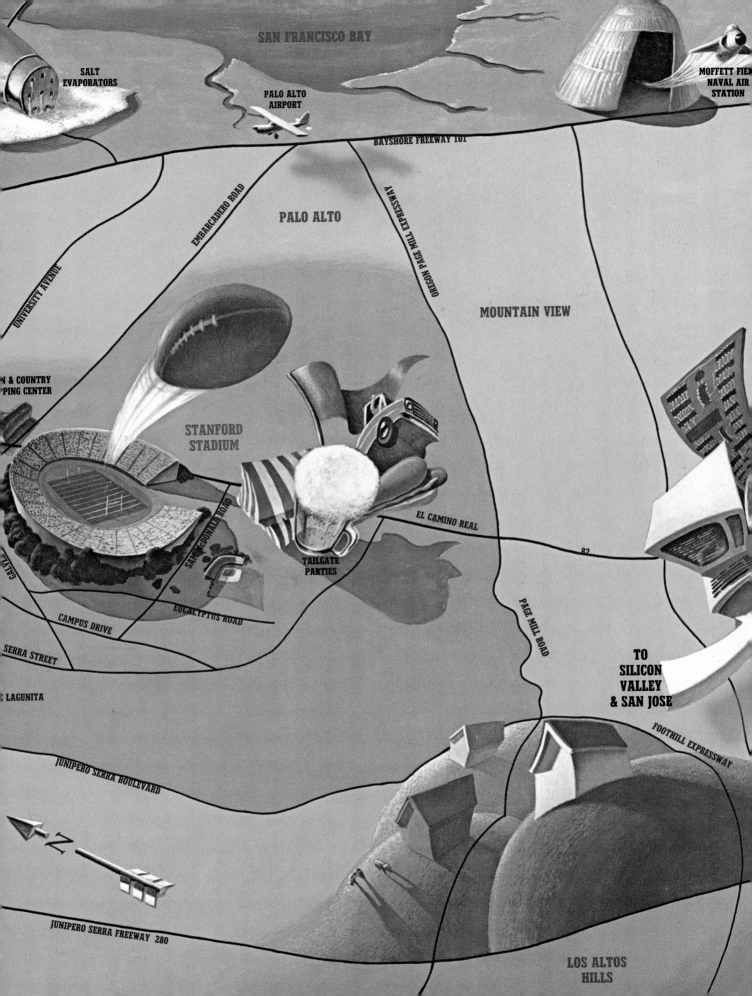

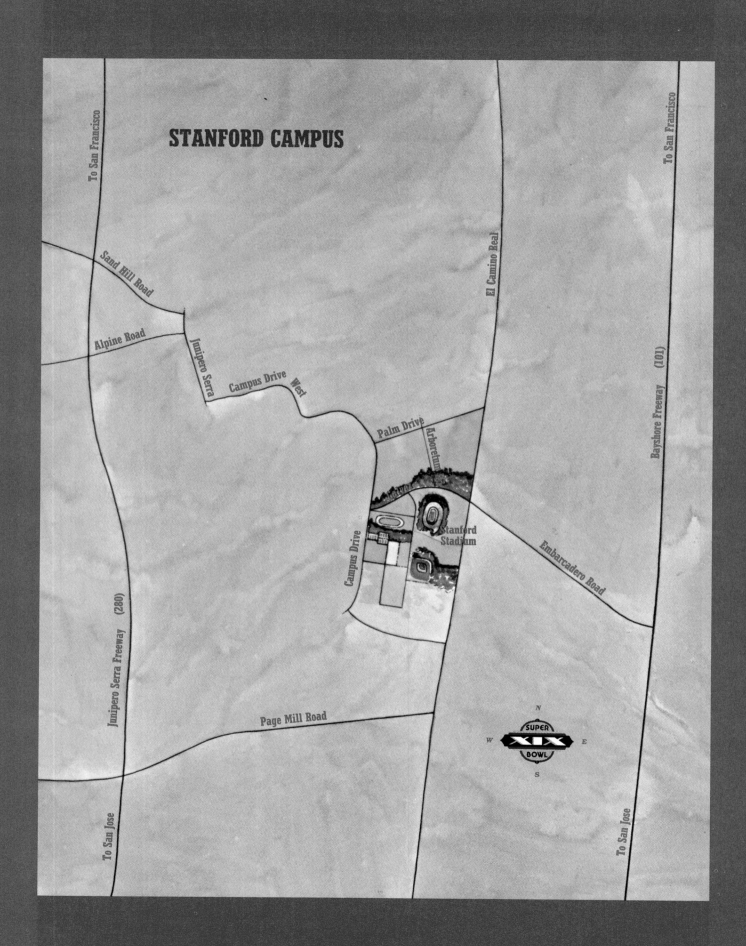

STANFORD CAMPUS

STANFORD STADIUM

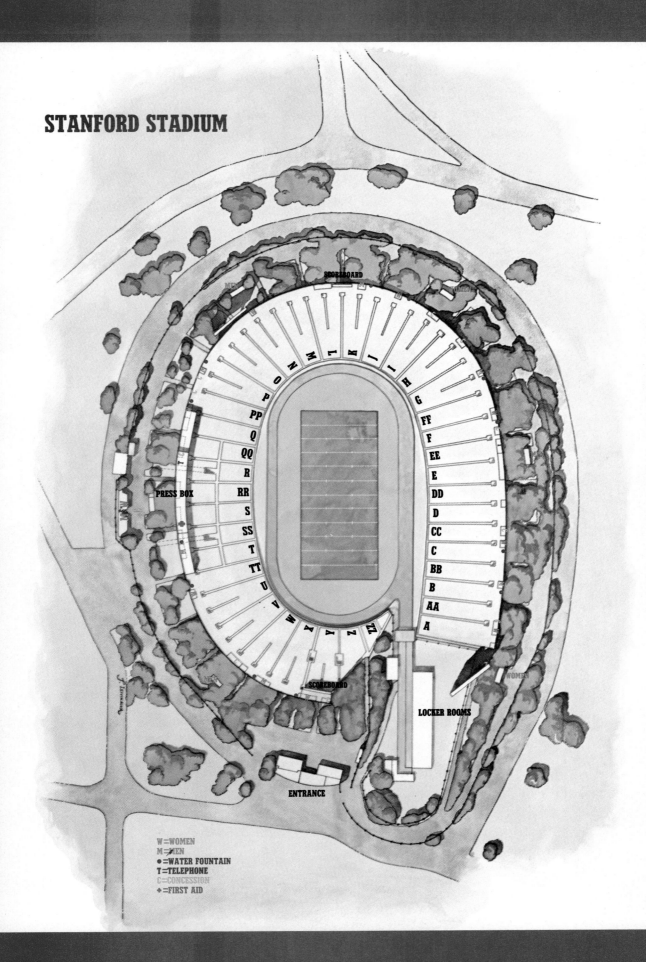

The San Francisco experience starts in The Center.

It is most definitely San Franciscan.
Free validated parking. Evenings after 5:00 P.M. and all day Saturday. Free parking Sunday.

Once the Long Wharf of the Barbary Coast, Embarcadero Center is now a landmark of shops, restaurants and fountains. Nestled within four spectacular office towers and the Hyatt Regency Hotel, it's an essential part of the city, like a visit to Fisherman's Wharf and Union Square, or a Cable Car ride.

Feel the pulse of San Francisco's nightlife.
From funky in-spots to a laid back wine bar, Embarcadero Center sets the pace for San Francisco's nightlife. The music ranges from jazz to new wave. There's even big band dancing. When the sun goes down, The Center lights up with a vengeance.

The city's famed district for shopping and dining.
There are 175 distinctive shops and tantalizing restaurants to explore. You'll find the latest fashions and sportswear for men and women. Plus dozens of specialty shops. Even an optometrist, a dentist, repair shops and a chapel.

And we have dozens of restaurants to enjoy. From a world of expertly prepared cuisine — Mexican, Japanese, Indian, Italian and Continental — to classic American, and of course, famous San Francisco Seafood. Even your favorite burgers, pizza and ice cream.

It's in the center of town.
Embarcadero Center is right in the heart of the city. Where Market Street meets the Embarcadero, from Battery and Sacramento Streets to the Hyatt Regency Hotel. BART and Muni Metro run through the city to Embarcadero Station. The Cable Cars come right down California Street to the Hyatt Regency.

Wake up in the center of everything.
The Hyatt Regency is Five Embarcadero Center. Enjoy the luxury and

service, plus the convenience of being downtown in the morning. There's also Big Band dancing on Friday evenings, a sumptuous Sunday brunch, and the city's only revolving rooftop restaurant.

Come visit. The atmosphere is refreshing. Civilized. One visit to this famed district will convince you.

Open Monday through Saturday. Sundays during the Summer.

From Battery and Sacramento to the Hyatt Regency Hotel.

embarcadero center
Refreshing. Civilized. Most definitely San Franciscan.

NORTHERN CALIFORNIA:
A Panorama of Scenic Beauty and Lifestyle

nique. Spirited. Spicy. Diverse. Urbane. The list of adjectives appropriate to San Francisco could fill page after page. And yet, all the superlatives in the world fail to capture the essence of this uncommon community known to its inhabitants simply as "The City."

Over the decades, nature has conspired with the populace to create an environment that stirs the senses, a living canvas emitting nonstop stimuli. Hear the clanging bells of man's merriest mode of transport, the cable car, climbing the majestic hills. Listen for the deep-throated horns announcing the fog billowing through the Golden Gate. Tune in to the symphony of music and foreign tongues at every turn. Touch the rough shell of a crab, the weathered wood of a pier, the crunchy crust of sourdough bread and the cool marble of a museum. Breathe deep the crisp sea air. Sniff the pungent aromas wafting from mysterious restaurants, the odor of expensive perfume, the fresh scent of the flowers and trees.

San Francisco — a dazzling dame whose bawdy past lingers in her campy, sophisticated present. Everything anyone could possibly want can be discovered here, amidst a lifestyle that has become its own art form.

Its 47 square miles contain a never-ending smorgasbord of attractions. In San Francisco, you don't eat. You dine — in your choice of almost 2,700 restaurants. A full calendar of festivals celebrates holidays, ethnic causes, neighborhoods and themes. Shopping areas feature innovative clothing and gift items conceived by world famous designers as well as California's own. Museums and galleries house impressive collections. Performing arts and nightlife venues appeal to every taste and budget. And one of the most beautifully functional urban parks in the United States cuts straight through the center of town.

Baghdad-By-The-Bay, City of Love, The City...
SAN FRANCISCO

photo: Rick Cummings

photo: Rick Cummings

San Francisco! A great place to visit and you'll probably want to live there. Its allure can be so sweet, its charm so captivating, you may never want to leave. And if you do leave, chances are you will come back one day.

Yes, indeed, the magic of "Baghdad-by-the-Bay" derives from a heritage of odd foods, sounds and smells; grimy Argonauts and the mind-boggling wealth they generated; million-dollar mansions adorned with gingerbread from apparently-crazed wood carvers; an emporium of vendors and shops; "nymphes du pave" lurking in doorways and dimly lit alleys.

Throughout its history, the city gave birth to terms like "hoodlums" (roving youth gangs), "shanghai" (drugging unwary citizens for the purpose of selling them into white slavery), "beatnik" (coined by our own Herb Caen, referring to the forerunners of the hippies), and "malarkey" (produced by local boasters). We had it all then, and we still do.

"San Francisco has a lovely sense of the absurd, preserved in the artful foolishness of old Victorian houses and the ding-dong cable cars, sure cures for depression." (from *The Pacific States of America*.)

Rest thy weary bones if you must, but linger no longer than necessary for there is much to do and see. Your spirits will soar and a feeling of giddiness will come over you, making each day a long-cherished memory.

In planning your visit here, consider some of the unique means of travel that will make your trip a high adventure—even before you arrive. Of special note is a new dimension in zany—a sleuthing expedition aboard a specially-chartered train from Los Angeles to San Francisco where unsuspecting passengers take part in a creative whodunit, playing out roles from a script prepared by "Pickwick Productions," the creators of this heavenly madness. Call (714) 494-4116 for information.

Above: After nightfall, Grant Avenue in Chinatown becomes a maze of pulsating colors.
Below: "San Francisco—the city that got too big for its bridges."

Columnist Herb Caen

"Well, it hasn't taken long to fall in love with San Francisco."

T.H. White

110

Modeled after the Palm House at Kew Gardens in London, the Conservatory of Flowers is the oldest existing building in Golden Gate Park. The conservatory sponsors seasonal flower shows, and tours are given by prior arrangement.

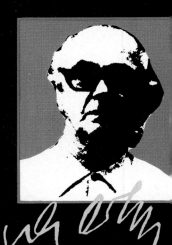

San Francisco's rich cultural life can be vividly seen through its performing arts. Its highly respected companies include the symphony, the ballet, and the opera, pictured above in *Die Meistersinger von Nurnberg,* 1981.

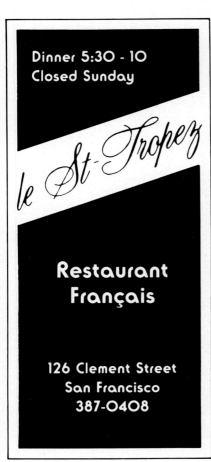

photo: Rick Cummings

The 20-story atrium lobby of the Hyatt Regency rises above the famous *Eclipse* sculpture. Conveniently located downtown for business and pleasure, the Hyatt boasts quality dining in the Marketplace Restaurant and Friday evening tea dances.

For nearly one hundred years, small commercial fishing boats have docked at Fisherman's Wharf. Established by Italians at the end of the 19th century, the Wharf today is both a marketplace for crab, shrimp, and fish and a tourist center crowded with restaurants and souvenir shops.

Photo: Rick Bernard

Regent Air, a lavish new airline with daily service between New York and Los Angeles, will wing you westward in a fashion rarely experienced in even the most elaborate corporate jets. Gourmet cuisine, fine wines, a luxurious lounge, private compartments, hairdresser, and manicurist are but some of the amenities available, for little more than a first-class ticket on most airlines. Call (800) 538-7587 for the flight of your life.

Upon arriving in San Francisco, there are transportation choices for any budget: sleek limousines offering custom tours of the city and outlying areas (try Opera Plaza Limousine, Ltd., Vista, and Carey Nob Hill—the latter providing outstanding drivers and service); helicopters for touring or delivery to the stadium on Super Sunday (Commodore Helicopters is the official helicopter service for the Super Bowl); and luxury yachts for small groups or parties (Hornblower Yachts is unequaled in this regard). Horse-drawn carriages or buggies are available through Buggies in the Park (761-8272) and Carriage Charter (398-0857).

Among the hundreds of tours available to visitors, there are several that could be termed "out-of-the-ordinary." For the physically fit, the Sierra Club conducts weekend cycling, hiking, skiing, horseback riding, and sports outings. Marine Life Tours (921-3676) offers tidepooling, whale watching, hiking, scuba diving and more. National Park Service (556-0560) leads dozens of explorations of coastal areas, parks, archeological sites, sailing ships and old forts, with the added benefit of rangers who combine history with amusing anecdotes.

Walking tours are especially popular, albeit challenging, with itineraries to keep feet a-movin' for days. Fred Baumeister, a native San Franciscan (673-2894), can arrange all manner of strolls around the city. Walks geared to local architectural history are conducted by Heritage Foundation (441-

3000). Historical tidbits, lore, and neighborhood browsing are the highlights of Judith Kahn's Cafe Walks (751-4286), which include stops at interesting cafes along the route.

For a one-of-a-kind experience, explore the old haunts of famed author Dashiell Hammet with merry chases up alleys and down back streets where heroes and villians once lived and worked, led by Don Herron (564-7021). Mystery buffs and Sam Spade fans will likely never find a more fun-filled stroll.

Secrets of Chinese cooking and culture unfold on various tours offered by the Chinese Culture Foundation (986-1822). The itinerary includes tea shops, markets, a fortune-cookie factory, and a stop for mouth-watering dim sum (a unique Cantonese dining experience). The aromas and spicy flavors of Chinatown might best be soothed by a cold glass of brew, perhaps while on a private tour of the Anchor Brewing Company (863-8350).

An insider's look at San Francisco can be arranged by On Target Tours (346-6808), such as a cook's tour of North Beach (our Italian neighborhood) led by a noted food writer. For a docent-led tour of the Performing Arts Center, contact 552-8338. Guest of the Chef will arrange banquets, wine tastings or cooking demonstrations for groups (421-0220, Annette Clark).

The whole family will want to take the Alcatraz tour, conducted by highly informed and amusing park rangers, with stories of murderous thugs and evil dudes who inhabited "the rock" over many decades. Tickets should be purchased at Red & White Fleet, Pier 41, *well in advance* (546-2805).

If children are less than enthusiastic about the planned events of the day, Katy Schatz of Youth Tours (for ages 5 to 18) will delight your darlings and keep them happily occupied for the better part of the day (457-9218).

"East is East, and West is San Francisco, according to Californians. Californians are a race of people; they are not merely inhabitants of a state."

O. Henry

Cliff House, circa 1900

Golden Gate Bridge construction began in 1933. It opened to foot traffic in 1937.

By 1890, the cable car system operated 600 cars over 100 miles of track.

Built in 1875, the Palace Hotel catered to the world's rich and famous.

The 1906 earthquake and fire made street refugees of the city's populace.

For those traveling in groups, Tour Service Unltd. (885-2510) offers distinctive custom-designed tours to match a variety of interests.

San Francisco's tradition of unparalleled lodging was born in the late 1800s when William C. Ralston built the world-famous Palace Hotel. Since that time, world-class hotels have flourished here. One of the most magnificent, the Fairmont Hotel, featured in the television series "Hotel", offers every amenity and one of the last elegant supper clubs in the country where major headliners perform. The Westin St. Francis has been at the center of life in San Francisco for over 75 years. One curious evolution in its service was the "coin laundry," created in the 1930s to keep ladies' white gloves from soiling. Few guests now sport white gloves, but you can bet your last dime that the shiniest coins in town were "laundered" at the St. Francis.

Many alternatives to the grand hotels exist that are less costly, charming, and first-rate. In the downtown area, five small, lovely hotels restored to stately elegance beckon visitors: Nob Hill Inn, Inn at Union Square, Campton Place, Vintage Court and Galleria Park Hotel. Each boasts unusual comforts and distinctive furnishings (a glass cage elevator, footed tubs, antique or oppulently modern furnishings, and truly fine restaurants in the latter three).

You'll feel like a guest in a millionaire's retreat when staying at the Spreckels Mansion. Built in 1887, this small hotel is spacious, comfortable, filled with treasures and convenient to all areas of the city. The Mansion, owned by consummate adman Robert Pritikin, is a joy—of whimsey, creativity, eclectic yet tasteful decor, and good service. Its Music Room is the setting for classical concerts and magic shows. The gardens display many Beniamino Bufano sculptures. The lobby restroom is especially dazzling and the dining room, with its stained glass

In 75 years, San Francisco's "Bay to Breakers" has grown from a field of 186 men to an estimated present-day registration of 100,000 men, women and children.

49ers' fans turn tailgating into an art form.

Opening day at the 'Stick mixes baseball with civic pride.

Innovative stylist Yosh is frequently noted in national fashion magazines.

Delights of Japanese bathing and massage can be found at Kabuki Hot Spring.

Ambassador Health Club, a haven for business-weary travelers and executives.

Cowboys participate in the world-class Grand National Rodeo, Horse Show and Livestock Exposition, held annually at the Cow Palace. Built by the WPA during the depression, the Cow Palace's use as an arena for livestock shows prompted a local official to exclaim, "three million dollars for a palace for cows!" It has been the scene of sports, conventions, concerts, trade shows and circuses.

Sakura Matsuri, Japantown's annual Cherry Blossom Festival is an eighteen-year-old tradition celebrated over two consecutive weekends in April. The festival has gained a reputation as the foremost showcase of Japanese culture and customs in the United States. Events include dance performances, a food bazaar, drum concerts, martial arts demonstrations, and a 2½-hour parade.

windows and soft lighting, offers excellent cuisine.

The Union Street Inn is a soothing hideaway in the middle of a bustling area known as Cow Hollow, once dairy and farmland, now teeming with stylish shops and cafes. The Inn blends the old with the new and style with rich textures and maintains a charming garden.

San Francisco has an abundance of museums, acting companies, dance troups and musical offerings. Our casual lifeltyle carries over into the perfoming and cultural arts scene without sacrificing quality.

A case in point is the American Conservatory Theatre, one of America's finest acting companies with an award-winning, 18-year history. This fine group of performers presents new and classical productions each season. The San Francisco Ballet is one of this country's most venerable dance companies, newly housed in its own facility (the first of its kind in the history of American dance). Opera in San Francisco dates back to the late 1850s, with such performers as Tetrazzini, Emma Nevada, and Enrico Caruso. Its tradition of lavish grand opera continues today with the excitement of world-famous performers. In 1911, the city established its own symphony and it has since thrived under the direction of several noted maestros. Regular concerts are held in the beautiful, though controversial, Davies Symphony Hall.

On the lighter side, a zany show called Beach Blanket Babylon (at Club Fugazi) draws crowds and rave reviews year after year. Songs blend, one into another, for 90 minutes of camp, outrageous costumes (hats that tower several feet in all directions), dance routines and take-offs on fairy tales and movie plots. It's a combination of Busby Berkeley, Disney, Alice Cooper and tongue-in-cheek humor. It's pure, sheer FUN!

During the 1960s, San Francisco

was a training ground for stand-up comics and musical groups. The Hungry I spawned dozens of success stories. Today, new clubs like the Punch Line keep the tradition alive. Musical entertainers appear everywhere, from the swank Venetian Room at the Fairmont Hotel to the funky Plush Room at Hotel York to wild Wolfgang's for rock, new wave, and comedy. A local favorite is the Great American Music Hall, a beautifully restored building from bygone days. Literally all musical forms have been featured at one time or another—classical, chamber, jazz (some of the "greats" appear here), country, 60's rock'n'roll, blues, instrumental, and ethnic.

Many museums present history and the arts in dynamic settings and provide visitors with hours of aesthetic appreciation and greater understanding of foreign cultures and varying art forms.

M.H. de Young Memorial Museum houses an impressive and extensive permanent collection of paintings, sculpture and decorative art objects depicting artistic development in America, Europe and Africa. Each year, temporary exhibitions from around the world supplement this valuable collection.

The California Palace of the Legion of Honor's permanent collection of French art spans the 16th to the 20th century and features a magnificent grouping of Rodin sculptures. Here, too, is a beautiful display of porcelain objects.

At the California Academy of Sciences, rooms are filled with graphic displays of the evolution of our civilization. In addition, the building houses an aquarium and a planetarium.

Each of these museums has an excellent docent program, whose members are thoroughly trained in conducting informative, enlightening tours. Be sure to call for docent schedules and museum hours.

In 1915 San Francisco hosted the Panama Pacific International

Located in Golden Gate Park, the Japanese Tea Garden is one of the few structures remaining from the 1894 Mid-Winter Exposition. The fortune cookie was invented here by Makato Hagiwara. Until World War II his family tended the gardens, which contain bridges, foot paths, pools, and statuary such as the Bronze Buddha which was cast in Japan in 1790 and donated by the Gump brothers.

The Galaxy at Sutter and Van Ness is the first new theater to be built in downtown San Francisco in approximately thirty-five years.

Photo: Rick Bernard

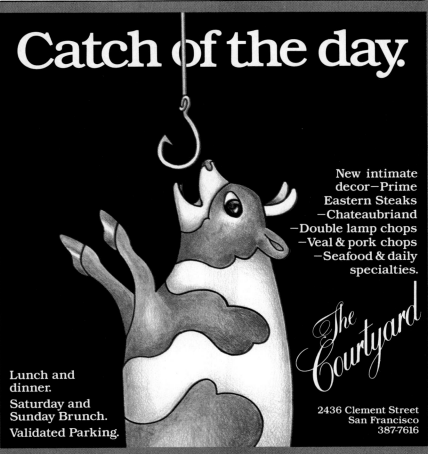

Exposition in an area adjacent to the U.S. Army Presidio, now known as the Marina District. The only remaining restored building, The Palace of Fine Arts, is home to the Exploratorium, a hands-on museum where children and adults alike are fascinated by the dizzying, dazzling experiments and working exhibits. This is probably the *best* science museum in the world, serving both as an educational institution and as a tribute to creative scientific enterprise and achievement. It richly deserves the international recognition and support it receives and is worth a visit by all travelers to the Bay Area.

Mark Twain once said, "The coldest winter I ever spent was a summer in San Francisco." But when the weather calls for outdoor activity, Golden Gate Park is the place to be.

In 1866, the Board of Supervisors met with Frederick Olmstead, the designer of Central Park in New York. The result—1,000 acres of "outside lands" reserved for park development. Years later, a young Scottish gardener, John McLaren, put existing plans into action and lovingly transformed wind-swept sand dunes into what is now one of the most magnificent urban parks in America. Developed along the lines of an English garden, it encompasses meadows, playfields, gardens, lakes, waterfalls and pathways for walking and bicycling.

There is much to see and do within the park, aside from enjoying the beauty of thousands of varieties of flora and fauna. There's the Japanese Tea Garden with an authentic tea house, Oriental trees and shrubs, pools and streams; the de Young Museum, Asian Art Museum, and Academy of Sciences that line the band concourse; the graceful Victorian conservatory surrounded by lavish gardens; the Murphy Windmill built in 1905 to pump fresh water into the gardens; and Stow Lake for boating. Here you can rent horses, roller skate, view a herd of buffalo, visit the

For almost 30 years, Williams-Sonoma has provided San Franciscans with the best of the best in kitchen utensils, gadgets, and cookware. Now operating 21 stores across the United States, it also has a thriving mail-order business. Williams began his career as a gourmet and hardware store owner in Sonoma.

The Four Seasons Clift Hotel offers grace, every modern convenience, and the little European touches that make all the difference—high tea service, for instance. Located within walking distance of Union Square, it affords the weary shopper an elegant resting spot.

In business for 139 years, Louis Vuitton began his career as a "packer" for royalty. Known for quality trunk-making craftsmanship and specializing in custom designs for any and every need, his shops are located in major cities throughout the world. His trademark—canvas bags with leather and brass trim.

The atrium forms the visual centerpiece of the Galleria at Crocker Center, a recently opened specialty shopping center in the Financial District. There are 60 shops for men, women and children offering international as well as domestic items. One restaurant, The Old Poodle Dog, is named after a restaurant dating back to the Earthquake, when it served as a refugee soup kitchen.

"model boat" basin at Spreckels Lake, have a picnic and play various sports. The park is a multifaceted, priceless gem that brings continued pleasure to residents and visitors alike.

South from the park is the San Francisco Zoo, covering approximately 70 acres. Newest of the exhibits is the Primate Discovery Center which includes open atriums, meadows, pools, and a unique hands-on learning center. The zoo has undergone extensive refurbishing and expansion since 1977 and is now among the finest in the nation.

To the Bay side of the city is the ever-popular Fisherman's Wharf. The adjoining area offers browsing in Ghirardelli Square (a former chocolate factory converted to stylish shops and restaurants), Aquatic Park and nearby Maritime Museum, and Hyde Street Pier where old ships are docked (some open for viewing). While in the area, stop at Buena Vista Cafe, the birthplace of Irish Coffee. Nearer to the Wharf is the Cannery, once a Del Monte canning plant (1909) and now another complex of shops and restaurants. If wine and the history of viticulture interest you, be sure to visit the Wine Museum on Beach Street, just a few blocks from the Wharf.

It is from Piers 41 to 39 that Bay Cruises on the Red and White Fleet, Gold Coast Cruises, and the Blue and Gold Fleet depart. Each offers a cruise around the Bay, from bridge to bridge.

Just east of Fisherman's Wharf is the vast complex, Pier 39. Once a cargo pier, it has been transformed into a boardwalk, with quaint shops reminiscent of a turn-of-the-century village. Street musicians, a carousel and games palace, and "The San Francisco Experience" video show make for pleasant breaks between shopping and dining. From the pier, you can also rent a bareboat or a skippered boat (Sailtours, 986-2590).

The city has many buildings designated as historic landmarks, but only one "district" so proclaimed. Jackson Square dates back to the 1850s and is the only downtown area to survive the 1906 earthquake and fire. These buildings have been carefully restored and serve as a major decorator and furniture showroom center. On Osgood Place, a shop called William Stout Architectural Books, is identifiable only by a window heaped with books. On the inside, an international assortment of books devoted to architecture, design and art is piled atop tables, crammed into nooks, and otherwise carelessly mounts toward the ceiling. First-timers are agog at the sight!

One of the most colorful areas of the city is North Beach, perched partially atop landfill where the Bay's waters once lapped at the cliffs of Telegraph and Russian Hills. In those days it was both a settlement of Italians and a center of the lusty, lurid section called the Barbary Coast. During the 1950s, the area gave birth to the "beat" movement. City Lights bookstore, owned by '50s poet Lawrence Ferlinghetti, is one of the few remaining symbols of this era and, of course, it has an excellent poetry section.

Finally, although many ethnic groups are represented in San Francisco, the Chinese community, said to be the largest such settlement outside the Orient, now brims with exotic markets, architecture, shops and restaurants. Streets bustle with activity from sunup to late night. Although parking is next to impossible to find, Chinatown is compact and within walking distance of downtown.

Over the years, designer boutiques and imposing department stores have burst upon the scene. Long-standing traditions like I. Magnin, Saks and Macys have been joined by Neiman Marcus, and the streets surrounding Union Square are lined with exclusive shops. International names like Gucci, Bally, Alfred Dunhill, Jaeger, Courreges, and Vuitton adorn

Celebrating its 80th anniversary, the Westin St. Francis today remains a center of social, theatrical and business life. The St. Francis has hosted guests of international prominence from Emperor Hirohito to Ethel Barrymore. Topping the 32-story Tower which opened in 1972 is Oz (above), an elegant dance club which offers a spectacular view of the city and the Bay. Be sure to ride one of the outside elevators to the top.

Opulence abounds at the Fairmont—grand dame of local hotels.

One of the San Francisco Ballet's performances, "Stars and Stripes Ballet"

The American Conservatory Theater company in final curtain call

San Francisco Opera performance, Act I from Rigoletto

Irish coffee was born at the Buena Vista Cafe.

photo: Rick Bernard

storefronts. But San Francisco has produced her share of noted designers and shops. Jeanne Marc, Jessica McClintock and Helga Howie are regularly featured in leading fashion magazines.

Beautifully designed, lacy lingerie of Victoria's Secret first appeared as mail-order items in magazines and later in shops bearing the name. Every conceivable kitchen gadget and appliance can be found at Williams-Sonoma, which also boasts a successful catalog business. And fabulous little luxuries featured in the Sharper Image catalog now can be found in the company's own retail outlet.

If quality is a criterion and price no object, there are stores like Wilkes-Bashford where terms like "chic" and "pricey" are inadequate to describe its clothing for men and women. Elizabeth Arden's is where women can be coiffed, groomed and outfitted from head to toe. Smartly dressed sports enthusiasts find clothing and equipment at Eddie Bauer. Gumps is the place for traditional gift items, jade in every form and lovely clothes for women, while Alfred Dunhill's has a dramatic assortment of gifts and clothing, primarily for men. Few jewelry stores can compare with the quality, reputation and selection of Tom Wing & Sons. Messrs. Tom are experts in fine jade, pearls, and gems—all displayed in a lovely setting of Oriental collectors' pieces.

It is advisable to select an area of the city devoted to shopping and to travel on foot, so as not to miss the hundreds of stores that make San Francisco a shopper's mecca. Must-see areas include Union Square, Sacramento Street (above Union Square as well as the section between Divisadero and Arguello), Embarcadero Center (four high-rise buildings creating a unique shopping center), Pier 39, The Cannery, Ghirardelli Square, quaint Union Street with its restored Victorians, and

Both the recently restored Murphy Windmill and its soon-to-be-restored sister date back to the early 1900s. Built to take advantage of westerly winds to pump much-needed water from sunken wells into Golden Gate Park, they are primarily responsible for maintaining the park as one of the world's horticultural masterpieces.

Chinatown is noted for having the best and most reasonably priced produce and fish markets in town. The delights of Chinese cuisine and markets are no longer a mystery to occidentals.

Above: The California Palace of the Legion of Honor, replica of its namesake in Paris, and completed in 1924. *Below:* Bay view of Aquatic Park, Maritime Museum, and Ghirardelli Square, which served as a chocolate-manufacturing plant from 1856 to the mid 1960s.

Ghirardelli

Passenger ships and cargo and military vessels enter and depart San Francisco Bay from all parts of the world.

TAKE ADVANTAGE
OF YOUR OPPORTUNITIES

You've earned the right to enjoy the best, so add *The Robb Report* to your list of the finest. Each month you'll find the best the world has to offer among its pages. Whether it's news on investments, stories on art and collectibles, interviews with famous personalities or looks at advances in sports technology, *The Robb Report* has it all. Don't let this opportunitity pass you by. Subscribe now.

ᵀʰᵉ Robb Report

One Acton Place
Acton, MA 01720
(617) 263-7749

Filmore Street above California Street.

Dining is an important part of every holiday and in San Francisco people "live to eat." Historically known as a home to cabbages and kings, the city's order of the day is gourmet—pate, quiche, and innovative sauces.

The hottest of the hot spots is Masa's in the Vintage Court Hotel. Mastaka, the former chef of Le Plaisir (New York) and Auberge du Soleil (Wine Country), is again creating extraordinary meals amid a softly lit, tranquil setting. One must be totally dedicated to dining at Masa's and commence phoning (415/989-7154) *exactly* three weeks prior to the desired reservation. The phone rings from 10 o'clock each morning, and only the most persistent callers are rewarded with voluptuous soups, tantilizing entrees and delicate desserts. Another "in" spot is the dining room at Campton Place (hotel), serving delectable, creative food.

Many wonderful Italian restaurants dot the city, but a few stand out: Donatello's (Pacific Plaza Hotel) is elaborately decorated with imported marble, glass, and muted earth tones. The food is, quite simply, elegant. The rudest waiters in town can't succeed in thinning the crowds at Caffe Sport (North Beach), where accomplished chefs turn out mouthwatering food. It is always packed, noisy and great fun, but expect a long wait. A more artistic atmosphere, in which the owner's extensive art collection adorns the walls, is found at Modesto Lanzone's (Opera Plaza). Pasta here is delicate and divine.

In America many people have yet to discover the subtle complexities and dramatic flavors found in the regional cooking of China. The gastronomic pleasures of Mandarin cuisine were introduced to the United States many years ago by Cecilia Chiang. It is impossible to describe the nuance of flavors to be experienced at her beautiful

"Above all, I have always loved the restaurants."

Spencer Tracy

photo: Rick Bernard

135

"The Saroyan-Sam Spade city—perhaps that was the last of it as far as the storybooks are concerned, but there is no way to give up on San Francisco once you have fallen under its spell. You keep looking for the magic, and now and then, when the wind and the light are right, and the air smells ocean-clean, and a white ship is merging from the Golden Gate mist into the Bay, and the Towers are reflecting the sun's last rays—at moments like that you turn to the ghosts and ask, 'Was this the way it was?' and there is never an answer..."

Herb Caen
One Man's San Francisco, 1976

restaurant, The Mandarin (Ghirardelli Square). Sleekly modern Yank Sing (Battery Street) has perhaps the best example of dim sum—an adventure of bite-sized delicacies served from rolling carts, creating an ideal brunch or lunch. Local critics and aficionados continually give high marks for skillful execution to Tsing Tao, a plain little neighborhood cafe serving Szechwan dishes (mild to hot).

At this writing the long-awaited opening of Barbara Tropp's new restaurant, China Moon, has been delayed until fall of '84. It is anticipated that Ms. Tropp's reputation and skill will draw crowds and acclaim.

Classic French culinary preparation is found in many local commercial kitchens, though nouvelle influences often are evident in many of the newer restaurants. Of these, Le Club and The French Room (Clift Hotel) combine outstanding food and service with utterly romantic settings. The Blue Fox and La Bourgogne remain notable "institutions," serving French and continental cuisine.

Dining at the California Culinary Academy affords patrons the opportunity to observe "chefs in the making," under skillful tutelege by noted chefs. The dining room is separated from classrooms and kitchens, with large viewing windows, where students prepare an amazing profusion of delights.

Le Castel, a lovely converted home on Sacramento, is a tribute to French and nouvelle cooking. Greens (Ft. Mason) is an airy oasis devoted to the most creative, appetizing vegetarian dishes found anywhere. Brunch is elevated above the norm at Doidges (Union Street), and the Zuni Cafe (off Market Street) combines classic Mexican with Western influences for what is called New Mexican—delicious!

Even though, according to Herb Caen, "We get baseball weather in football season and football weather in July and August," on sunny days a picnic is ideal to while away

The Cadillac Bar, one of San Francisco' s "in" spots and authentic Mexican restaurants

the midday. Select goodies from Oakville Grocery or Vivande.

When you've seen the sights and supped divinely, pause briefly to pamper yourself before journeying to other wonderous locales in the Bay Area. Ladies will find complete grooming services at Julie Moran and superb haircuts from David Windsor (788-8829), both on Maiden Lane. Ambassador Health Club is perfect for men to unwind, while the Kabuki Hot Spring (Japantown) is a relaxing, restorative oasis for men and women.

That done, you are ready to venture forth, to explore and enjoy!

art by Terry Mollenauer

139

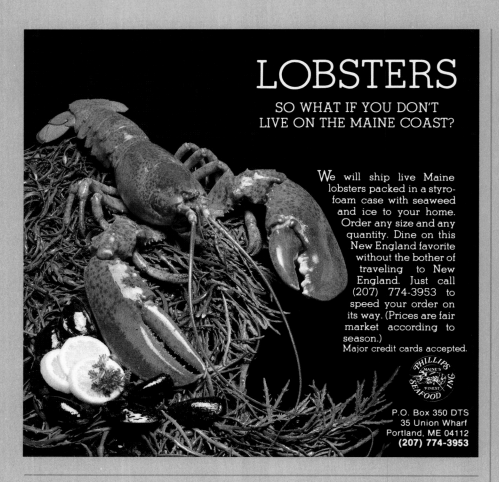

*Tea dancing at the Hyatt Regency San Francisco
—a favorite Friday evening pastime*

photo: Rick Cummings

141

Beniamino Bufano statue guards
entrance to the Mansion Hotel.

The zoo's a favorite spot for young and
old alike.

Treasures await beneath the colorful
lanterns in Japantown.

Park ranger regales Alcatraz visitors
with folklore and anecdotes.

Coit Tower, the city's monument to
volunteer firemen.

The Mansion Hotel offers distinctive dining as well as lodging.

Seoul Garden features the finest Korean cuisine.

San Francisco cartoonist Albert Tolf displays his work.

Hundreds of flower stands adorn downtown San Francisco.

Saks Fifth Avenue fashions on display

"San Francisco—with her hills she is Rome—with her Bay she is Naples—with her sometimes blue sky she is Switzerland—with her fog she is London—with her cafes and restaurants she's Paris—with the hotels and theaters she is New York—But with her people, well, with her people, bless her, she is just San Francisco."—Anonymous

QANTEL® HAS PEOPLE TALKING...

Coyne Edmison, V.P./Gen. Mgr.
Skirvin Plaza Hotel
Oklahoma City, OK.

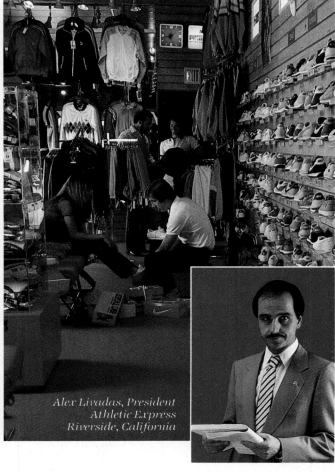

Alex Livadas, President
Athletic Express
Riverside, California

about our Hotel Management System

"I discovered the QANTEL Hotel & Leisure system while attending a trade show last year. I was very impressed. It was evident that HAL™ was written by hotel people for hotel people.

HAL clearly offered the operational control that's essential for a profitable hospitality business, as well as the flexibility to adapt to situations we might encounter years in the future. We bought the system and were operational in March with Front Office and Back Office modules, which include Reservations and Accounting. Thanks to HAL, we've never been more on top of things."

about our Retail Management System

"I used to spend a lot of my time commuting from store to store. Now I can efficiently operate most of my business from the QANTEL computer that sits on my desk.

With the QANTEL FRAME™ software, I can follow each of our six stores, category by category, with Monthly Profit Profiles. I can also condense my stock of over 2,000 plus items into 50 key items, and determine, with a Hot and Cold Report, which ones to keep or drop. I can even get print-outs of sizes in a format that conforms to the footwear industry. FRAME has given me the vision to see future possibilities."

For Hoteliers, Retailers, Manufacturers, Sports and Transit Management, MDS Qantel offers industry-specific solutions that work.

MDS QANTEL
BUSINESS
COMPUTERS

a Mohawk Data Sciences Company

©1984 MDS Qantel, Inc.

4142 Point Eden Way, Hayward, CA 94545 • Toll Free: (800) 227-1894 TWX: 910-383-0249 • Calif. Call (415) 887-7777

Among San Francisco's many districts, Chinatown is perhaps the most dazzling. Into a space of only a few blocks, it packs a multitude of restaurants, night spots and stores.

A tradition of elegant hospitality is still evident in the palatial Garden Court at the Sheraton-Palace Hotel in San Francisco. Balconied galleries extend from the marble pavement of the court to a lofty roof of opaque glass.

In the early, opulent days of San Francisco, when founding fathers and nouveau riche socialized side-by-side, the most affluent of them often made a day-long journey to the Peninsula. There they would spend weekends, holidays, and summers in their country homes, equally as grand as and frequently more elegant than their city dwellings.

As access to the "country" became more a matter of minutes than hours, many people chose to live there year-round. Today San Mateo County's population has grown to nearly 600,000. Its residents enjoy the second highest median income in California, and live in homes with the highest average price tag in the U.S.

Still, the country setting endures, the weather remains ideal, and the quality of life and convenient location to the delights of the Bay Area only add to its attractiveness.

Heading south from the City, drive down Coast Highway 1 through Devil's Slide and Montara and on to Half Moon Bay. Or fly into the Half Moon Bay Airport, a small terminal accommodating primarily privately owned planes. If boating is your real love, what better entrance to the Half Moon Bay region than through Pillar Point Harbor at the south end of the airport in Princeton-by-the-Sea. Here you will find a beautiful marina, a public pier for fishing, whale-watching tours conducted by the Oceanic Society (415/441-1106), fresh seafood shops, sportfishing charters like Huck Finn Sportfishing, and a cluster of good local restaurants. Ketch Joanne at the pier serves fresh fish, as does Paul and Barbara's Fish Trap on Capistrano Road, both with seaside ambiance, casual atmosphere and good cooking. Up Capistrano Road is the historic Princeton Inn, once a resort hotel, later a bordello and haven for rumrunners, and now a lovely restaurant.

THE PENINSULA:
A Legacy of Affluence

Nine sandy white public beaches rim the coast with numerous horseback riding stables bordering the highway. Try Friendly Acres for invigorating rides along the cliffs. Visitors to this area can't help but notice the prevalence of agriculture with roadside stands selling noted seasonal crops such as artichokes, Brussels sprouts, flowers and pumpkins. Half Moon Bay's annual Pumpkin Festival in October is a major Bay Area event.

For an authentic English meal, stop at the Village Green in El Granada, where hospitality and graciousness are the order of the day. British immigrant and owner Susan Hayward runs both the restaurant and a dance studio she opened upon arriving in America. She and her friendly staff of family and dance students try, as she puts it, "to discount the American idea that English food is bland." This restaurant, which evolved because "dance teachers are notoriously poor," certainly disproves the theory!

In Moss Beach, north of the harbor, is the beautiful Fitzgerald Marine Reserve, teeming with tide-pools, seals, and other sea life. The Moss Beach Distillery, another local haven, boasts a cliff-side ocean view and regular Sunday afternoon jazz. Speaking of jazz, a local tradition known as the Bach Dancing and Dynamite Society has delighted area residents for almost 20 years. The title springs from a Fourth of July celebration witnessed by founder Peter Douglas in which people were dancing to Bach music and setting off dynamite. However, the idea for this non-profit organization, which hosts local musicians, grew more out of Douglas' love of jazz. Be sure not to miss this one-of-a-kind experience in Douglas' home at Miramar Beach. Call (415)726-4143.

There is a variety of coastside lodging deserving special mention. Two hostels—the Point Montara Lighthouse and the Pidgeon Point Lighthouse—offer charm, natural

San Francisco's new international airport terminal will introduce millions of travelers from throughout the world to the City by the Golden Gate. Completed in 1983, this new terminal is an inventive redesign of the airport's 25-year-old Central Terminal.

Testing recipes for an upcoming issue of *Sunset* Magazine

Bangers, lemon curd and scones are the bill-o-fare at the Village Green.

Menus at the quaint San Benito House change daily.

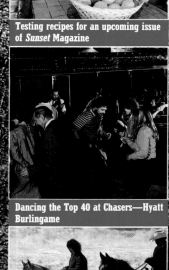

Dancing the Top 40 at Chasers—Hyatt Burlingame

Pidgeon Point Lighthouse guards coastal shipping lanes.

Galloping in the surf—a special coastside pastime

Filoli, a gracious estate featured in TV's "Dynasty" series

Concerts and jam sessions are Sunday afternoon rituals in Half Moon Bay.

Romantic location with bay view at The Castaway

Woodside Store (built 1854), first store between San Jose and San Francisco

Relaxation is in the air at the Half Moon Bay Lodge.

PGA ranks Half Moon Bay Golf Links fourth best in Northern California.

Rod McLellan's Acres of Orchids is a leading world supplier.

Elegant dining at Calcutta Cricket Club, Amfac Hotel

The Peninsula leads the country in commercial flower production.

Attractive entrance bespeaks quality lodging at San Benito House.

Filoli Gardens and Estate are open for private tours.

beauty, and something different in exchange for shared chores and less privacy than standard lodging affords. It's well worth the effort. For finer lodging, the Half Moon Bay Lodge provides every amenity and close proximity to the Half Moon Bay Golf Links, whose 18th fairway many believe rivals the 18th at Pebble Beach for beauty and challenge. Finally, in the center of Half Moon Bay proper lies the San Benito House, an acclaimed bed-and-breakfast inn with a folksy atmosphere, an excellent restaurant manned by owner/operator Carol Mickelsen, and a *croquet lawn.*

San Francisco International, the country's seventh-busiest airport, provides visitors with convenient access to the Peninsula *bayside.* A recently completed $100 million renovation project has created an exciting new terminal with warm colors, natural light and lush landscaping, linked with the boarding area by a beautiful shopping compound containing fine restaurants, shops, exhibitions and a permanant art exhibit. If you arrive in time for breakfast or lunch, try JoAnn's in South San Francisco, a tucked away, three-star restaurant with the ambience of a sparkling diner and home-made muffins to die for.

Many fine restaurants are sprinkled along the Peninsula. In the Burlingame/San Mateo area, you'll find continental cuisine at Nathan's, the Calcutta Cricket Club, and The Castaway. Classic French is on La Reserve's menu in San Mateo, and for German fare, visit the lovely Pine Brook Inn in Belmont. South Peninsula holds even more of a dining selection. Excellent French cuisine is presented by Pear Williams in Menlo Park, Alouette in Palo Alto, and Au Chambertin in Los Altos. Gourmet food for all occasions is Victoria Emmon's specialty in Palo Alto, and Avanti Pasta Cafe in Los Altos flaunts neon and pizza that will knock your socks off.

The heart of the Peninsula holds

A California Historic Civil Engineering Landmark, Crystal Springs Reservoir, with five other reservoirs, serves over 1.8 million Bay Area residents. The Pulgas Water Temple here is open to the public with horseback riding and hiking trails (no picnicking).

Dolphins delight the crowds at Marine World.

Students from Notre Dame College recreate the romance and gentility of a bygone era at the Ralston Mansion. The summer home of an 1800's San Francisco financier, the mansion is now the focal point of the Notre Dame campus.

photo: Steve Castillo

Marine World/Africa USA in Redwood City, a unique 65-acre wildlife and entertainment park full of exotic animals and exciting shows, including an impressive new stunt show. North in San Carlos is the Circle Star Theater, an every-seat-is-a-good-seat theatre-in-the-round which opened in October 1964 with "My Fair Lady" and now attracts top name performers from Richard Pryor to Wayne Newton.

There is no lack of interesting, out-of-the-ordinary tours on the Peninsula. Visit the beautifully sculptured Japanese Garden in San Mateo (415/377-4640). Ten miles south of the San Francisco Airport lies the Coyote Point Museum for Environmental Education, a hands-on exhibition hall especially attractive to children. Tour the Stanford Linear Accelerator (415/854-3300) or *Sunset* Magazine (415/321-3600) or enjoy a four-hour trip aboard the Marine Ecological Institute's 85-foot research vessel (415/364-2760). Bay Windsurfing can really give you some exercise (415/595-2285).

Take a load off and refresh yourself at the British Bankers Club, an old bank converted into a restaurant/saloon. Also investigate three great meeting and drinking establishments: 42nd Street Bar and Restaurant, Scotty Campbell's and Talbots.

Rest and relaxation from a long, eventful day can be had at the Hyatt hotels in either Burlingame or Palo Alto. The best shopping on the Peninsula is found in Menlo Park at the Allied Arts Guild, a handsome Spanish-styled complex of distinctive artisan shops; at the Stanford Shopping Center in Palo Alto, a beautifully landscaped, lively environ; and on University Avenue in downtown Palo Alto.

No trip to the Bay Area is complete without visiting the Peninsula and its grand selection of activities conveniently linked to the rest of Northern California. Further south over the Santa Cruz Mountains rest the lovely seaside communities of Carmel and Monterey.

157

Dress rehearsal for one of the many exotic animals preparing to entertain Super Bowl XIX visitors at Redwood City's Marine World/Africa U.S.A.

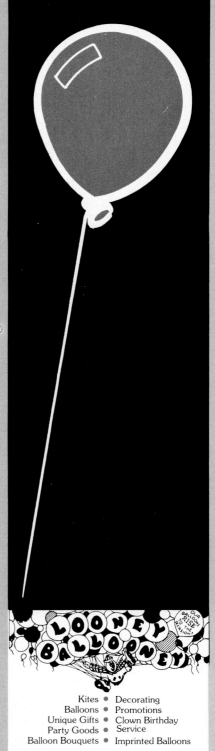

VERCELLI'S

MORI QUAM POTIUS FOEDARI

Northern Italian Dining

Reservations Recommended
(408) 374-3400
331 Hacienda Avenue, Campbell

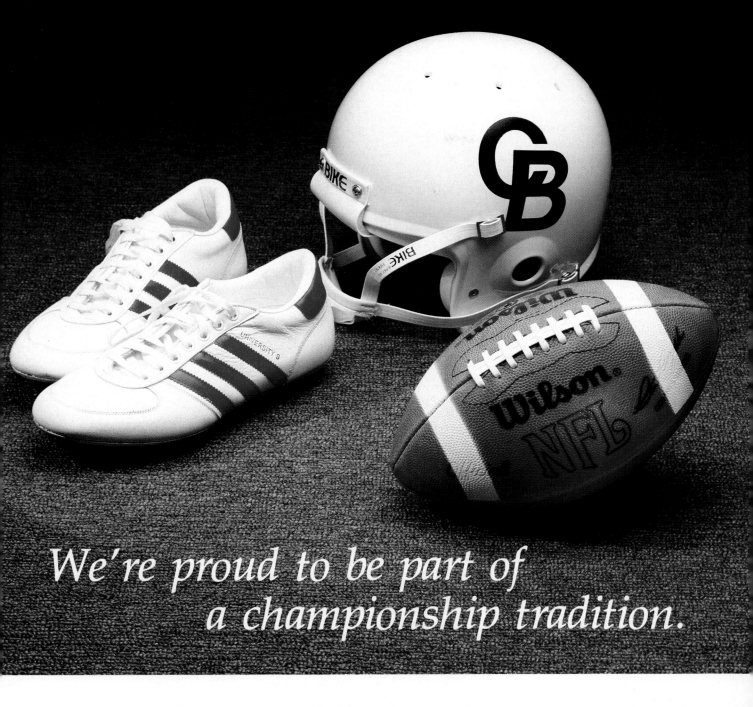

We're proud to be part of a championship tradition.

Over the past 100 years we have carried the ball and provided the best in carpeting and floorcoverings. From locker room to living room to all around the house, Conklin Bros. "your carpet store" has scored above all, in every game, commercial and residential.

ALLIED CORP. NYLON
Anso IV® HP
with HaloFresh™

(The Stanford Super Bowl Locker Rooms, Press Box and related areas are carpeted with Cambray Carpet made of Allied Anso IV® HP and installed by Conklin Bros. Anso IV® HP (High-Performance) with HaloFresh® is soil, stain, static and odor resistant with a 10-year Wear Warranty.)

OVER
100
YEARS
SINCE 1880

"You can count on us...
people have since 1880"

Conklin Bros.™
FLOORCOVERINGS

Ethereal beauty and a symphony of sights and sounds stirs the senses when visiting the Monterey Peninsula. Henry Miller described this area as "a place of grandeur and eloquent silence", but it is much more.

Jagged cliffs rise vertically from the foaming sea. Cypress trees bend in the winds. Deer lurk in forests. Meadows are filled with wild flowers. Sand dunes gently mound at ocean's edge. Happy animals of the sea sunbathe on rocks and frolic in the water. And the sunsets, well, the sunsets are a glorious profusion of vibrant reds and oranges or softly muted tones of pink and purple.

This noble area has for decades been a retreat for artists and writers, for the rich and famous, and for the vacationer in search of tranquility.

The Peninsula comprises Pacific Grove, Monterey, Pebble Beach, Carmel, and Big Sur. Its historical roots date back to the 1700s when Fathers Serra and Crespi' established missions there. In the 1800s fishing provided a solid economic base that encouraged business development and social change. To accommodate this burgeoning fishing industry, Monterey spawned a district of canneries that attracted what one writer termed "a delightful assortment of misfits," characters who came to life on the pages of John Steinbeck's novel, *Cannery Row.*

During the early 1900s the Hotel Del Monte attracted a wealthy clientele who flocked to the area for fun, relaxation and to partake of the challenges of that strange British sport, GOLF.

As word of the romantic appeal of the Peninsula spread far and wide, grand estates and cottages were built to house part-time and permanent residents. A lifestyle of European grace and charm ensued, and stringent regulations against dramatic change kept things pretty

CARMEL/MONTEREY:
Land And Sea In Aesthetic Harmony

From dizzying cliffs that snake the ocean's edge, one looks to sea and feels exposed to the eyes of God. This is a startling place, Big Sur, that remains idelibly etched on the mind, at once lonely, wild, haunting. The cacophony of crashing surf, whispering winds, and chirping birds underscores the undisturbed peacefulness of this primitive coastal area.

well intact until more recent times.

Once the fishing industry faded to a trickle, local action waned and life for all but the rich fell on hard times. It was not until the post-World War II years that the area experienced a rebirth and entrepreneurs turned rotting buildings into attractive restaurants and shops which to this day attract a happy procession of international pilgrims.

Today Pacific Grove is quietly charming, Monterey is action-filled, Pebble Beach is buzzing with golf enthusiasts, Carmel jealously guards its quaintness, and the unharnessed giant Big Sur just is.

Lodging choices in the area are excellent and diverse. In Pacific Grove, Gosby House and the Centrella Hotel place a premium on service and atmosphere, with the emphasis on nostalgia evident in the antique-decorated rooms and the myriad extra touches that make a stay very special.

At Pebble Beach, Green Gables Inn is equally charming, and of course the Lodge is serenely elegant. In Monterey try the Old Monterey Inn for charm or the Del Monte Hyatt for luxury and amenities.

Carmel is rife with inns, cottages, and hotels. Of special note are Stonehouse Inn and the modern Lobos Lodge. The venerable Pine Inn has been welcoming guests for many years and is a cozy, convenient hotel in the heart of the village. Recently refurbished, the Highlands Inn has replaced its dated atmosphere with an elegant, luxurious decor and garden setting.

Quail Lodge in Carmel Valley offers golf, tennis, swimming, hot tubs and a romantic setting away from it all, yet convenient to everything.

But what does one do here, besides laze in the sun and await mealtime, or play golf and await mealtime? Fact is, if you laze about too much you will miss a magnitude of unforgettable experiences.

California Heritage Guides (408/373-6454) and USA Holidays

The beach beckons visitors who come to surf, sunbathe, and enjoy the invigorating aspect of the sea. At Asilomar State Beach, bonfires, cookouts and beach picnics are daily rituals.

What better place to romp and enjoy an exhilarating game of touch football than at surfside.

Back in 1937, Bing Crosby decided to throw a little "clambake" for his golfing cronies. Today, the Bing Crosby Pro-Am Golf Tournament draws huge crowds to the Pebble Beach Golf Links to watch the likes of Jack Nicklaus, Tom Watson, Jack Lemmon and George C. Scott. Over the years, the Crosby has raised millions for local charities.

(408/649-5115) have a full range of tours and services to make touring a frustration-free activity. They can arrange a walking tour to trace the steps of literary giants who wrote of life in these parts, as well as cruises, shopping excursions, scenic coach rides, and more. But for the ultimate in personalized service and luxurious arrangements, Created Illusions in the San Francisco Bay Area (415/435-1753) will arrange every minute detail with care and good taste, not only for the Monterey Peninsula, but for other for parts of Northern California as well. From transportation and lodging to where you will dine and how you will occupy your time, this firm will create a trip with panache.

Whether on your own or by tour, be sure to take the renowned 17-Mile Drive. Starting in Monterey, you'll see Pacific Grove, the famed Carmel Mission Basilica, Asilomar State Beach, Point Joe (an offshore graveyard of ships wrecked in the rocks), the Dunes Golf Course, Fanshell Beach and Spyglass Hill Golf Course (one site of the Crosby "Clambake"), Cypress Point Club (ranked among the nation's top 20 courses and *very* exclusive), and Clint Eastwood's secluded home. Continuing along the drive you will encounter Gem Cove and the famous Lone Cypress (internationally recognized symbol of the Monterey Peninsula). Past other asymmetrical cypress clinging to rocky cliffs you'll come upon Pebble Beach and the Lodge (a reserved, elegant resort attracting an international clientele), and a plethora of magnificent homes. Famous local residents have included the Crockers, the Firestones, Bing Crosby and many other movie stars. You will exit at the Carmel Gate after completing the last curvy leg of the drive.

While in this area be sure to visit Point Lobos (ideal for a picnic) and Carmel Mission. A convenient side trip and a scenic "must" is a drive south on Route 1 to absorb the breathtaking majesty of Big

Monterey Bay offers a full range of nautical pleasures including yacht rentals for exploring the coastline.

For the fit and hardy, few experiences surpass the bracing sport of windsurfing, where the lone board sailor masters the sea.

Horseback riding is a perfect way to commune with nature.

photo: Courtesy of Pebble Beach Co.

Sur. Here you'll discover verdant canyons, waterfalls, redwood forests, and surf crashing beneath jutting cliffs, all making for an awe-inspiring experience. If time permits, plan to stay the night at Ventana Inn, a remarkable, luxuriously rustic retreat with an outstanding dining room, peaceful surroundings and beautiful vistas.

Those preferring more physical action and less sightseeing are in for a treat, since almost every sports discipline is available in the region. Backpacking and hiking can rarely be experienced in a more stimulating environment. Call Sierra Club (408/624-8032) for guided outings. If you'd like to camp out beneath the stars but left your gear at home, call Bugaboo Mountaineering (408/373-6433) for tents, bags, and other equipment rentals. There is roller and ice skating, raquetball, and a parcourse in Del Monte Forest for jogging. For water sports the Monterey Peninsula is an aquatic haven. Harbors and coves beckon boating and sailing enthusiasts. For yacht charter, contact Monterey Bay Yacht Charter (408/ 375-2002). The Pacific Ocean is rich with marine life and the cool, clear waters afford the perfect opportunity for scuba diving. Try Aquarius Dive (408/375-3225) for equipment rentals and instruction. A wide variety of fishing is available—freshwater, rock, surf, and deepsea—and sportfishing boats depart Monterey's Fisherman's Wharf daily. Licenses as well as equipment and bait can be obtained at the Wharf.

The crown jewel of local sporting activity is, of course, golf. In fact, the area is known as the "Golf Capital of the World." Challenge and scenic beauty abound on each of the sixteen local courses. Choose from Pebble Beach ("The Beast") that winds along the ocean; Spyglass, designed by Robert Trent Jones and maintained by the only woman greenskeeper in the country; or the less arduous but equally striking Carmel Valley Golf and

The luxurious Hotel Del Monte in Monterey in its early-century splendor, where people gathered to enjoy the good life

photo: Courtesy of Pebble Beach Co.

Country Club. Most prestigous and private of area clubs is Cypress, called the Sistine Chapel of golf by "Sandy" Tatum of the U.S. Golf Association. To play this no-nonsense course you must be "well connected." There are only 175 members, and non-members are NEVER permitted in the clubhouse.

Non-golfers and veterate shoppers have numerous locations from which to choose a bauble, bangle, or beads. Each community boasts picturesque streets lined with specialty shops, cafes, galleries and gardens. Scattered throughout the region is an impressive selection of shopping complexes, each bubbling over with distinctive boutiques for the most discerning shoppers. Pebble Beach Shops, located by the Lodge, offers more than 20 shops amid the quietly elegant setting of Pebble Beach.

In Carmel there is The Crossroads (50 shops and boutiques), Carmel Plaza (60 shops and restaurants in a vibrant garden setting), and the Barnyard in Carmel Valley. The Barnyard's distinction is derived from a rustic setting of barns, flowers, trees, and hills, with delightful shops and restaurants, and special events to make this a unique excursion. You'll feel comfortable there—be it for an hour or a day—browsing, enjoying premium wine and a good book at the Thunderbird Bookstore, or dining in one of eleven unusual establishments.

Also in Carmel you'll find a full array of merchandise at stores like Saks, I. Magnin, Macys and Ralph Lauren.

Here, too, artistic and cultural discoveries abound everywhere. Regular showings by artists (local and from afar), photgraphic exhibits, concert series, dance presentations, and the world-famous Bach Festival and Monterey Jazz Festival lend a sophisticated multicultural atmosphere to the Peninsula.

After a full day of activity you will be eager to sample some of the area's 300 restaurants. Dining

For a lively, festive evening of good music, good wine and superb dining, try Fandango's in Monterey. Native dishes and mesquite-grilled meat and fish are specialties of the house.

Old-world opulence is available for special parties in the Wine Cellar at the Sardine Factory. Chandeliers, tapestries, and woods buffed to a high patina create a mellow setting.

here is as important to the way of life as it is in San Francisco. The region's plethoric selection of restaurants is impressive—cafes, Victorian houses, converted warehouses, casual cantinas and chic bistros—and the culinary offerings are a cornucopia of scintillating sights and tantalizing tastes. Seafood is the local specialty, with calamari (squid) to be found on many a menu and in many different preparations.

Perhaps the most consistently superior fare, served in an assortment of uniquely decorated rooms reminiscent of the turn of the century, is at the Sardine Factory on Cannery Row. You're bound to have a good time!

Two magnificent culinary gems in Monterey are Fresh Cream and Their food is sublime, the atmosphere Triples. warm and intimate. Gregory's Stonehouse is a perfect spot for weekend brunch (try the Ramos Fizz), as well as creative dining (wild boar with papaya). Nearby Pacific Grove boasts many superior restaurants. Fandangos features mesquite grilling and lively atmosphere. The Old Bath House, with rich wood paneling, etched glass and romantic views of Monterey Bay, offers continental (French and Italian) dishes and specializes in mouth-watering veal preparations.

Carmel responded to the influx of tourism with a generous sprinkling of excellent restaurants, particularly French. Be sure to try San Souci, L'Escargot, and the superb Marquis, with Louis XIV decor and celebrity clientele (however, prices are moderate and each patron is given genuine VIP treatment). Casanova is a Mexican delight, and the Tuck Box serves proper English tea and teatime goodies.

If you are staying in nearby Carmel Valley, you will find some extraordinary dining establishments. Within the Barnyard, Andre's is exquisite, with attentive service and superior cuisine. The warmth and cozy charm of the classic French Chez Serge is a wonderful respite from browsing in the complex. And finally, the Covey at Quail Lodge leaves diners sated with fine continental cuisine and stylish, rustic charm.

Many visitors to the area are surprised when they are served a locally produced wine with their meal. In fact, Monterey County is California's newest, most promising wine region, receiving critical acclaim and numerous awards. Vineyards date back only twenty years (just whipper-snappers compared with their cousins to the north) and are responsible for the largest table wine production of all coastal counties. The rich alluvial soil, long a factor in making this region the country's "salad bowl," is now nurturing a vital grape-growing industry. The end result is a "grape rush" that benefits wine lovers everywhere.

Highly praised wineries such as J. Lohr, Ventana, Chalone and Jekel should be sampled. But don't overlook the newer "boutique" wineries such as Monterey Peninsula, Durney, and Chateau Julien. As with Napa and Sonoma, you can easily plan a visit to the Monterey Peninsula arranged around wine tasting.

If time permits, a trip south to the incomparable Hearst Castle is well worth consideration. This legendary estate was the home of the late William Randolph Hearst and the scene of social "extravaganzas" amid opulence no doubt unequaled in the West. Contact California Heritage Guides (408/373-6454) or Surftreks (408/649-1131) for tour information.

By now you have supped, dined, and made many new discoveries. Your eyes have feasted on the glory that is Monterey County, and chances are you will return, for you have found a home—a place to retreat to when all around you people are losing their cool!

Triples in Monterey promises sophisticated cuisine and fashionable intimate interior. Plan on lingering and savoring both the fine wines and the impeccably prepared French cuisine.

Monterey's Sardine Factory is one of the most colorful and popular restaurants in the area. Each dining room has its own menu and distinctive decor, ranging from casual to stylishly elegant.

The Old Bath House is one of many superior dining spots in the area.

Zantman's Gallery (Carmel) is a must for those seeking artistic treasures.

photo: Monterey Bay Aquarium

The new Monterey Bay Aquarium promises to be a major attraction.

A perfect way to start the day—a delightful continental breakfast at Centrella.

Clint Eastwood's Hog's Breath is a great place to go for cocktails.

Vintage autos attract ardent admirers to Pebble Beach's Concours d'Elegance.

Strolling up Ocean Avenue is a favorite pastime.

Classic cars adorn the interior of Sly McFly's bar in Monterey.

Galleries like Zantman's showcase a thriving local artists colony.

Delicious aromas draw passers-by to the Mediterranean Market.

1984 marks the 34th Annual Pebble Beach Concours d'Elegance. The event attracts vintage auto fanciers and serious buyers from around the country and is one of the largest and most prestigous such shows in the United States. Magnificent machines spanning automobile history such as Talbot-Lago, Hispano-Suiza, Cord, Bugatti, and Isotta-Fraschini are rakishly displayed for coveted awards and appreciative applause.

an Jose. The name conjures up a multitude of contrasting images. Two hundred years ago the Spanish Conquistadores established it as California's first civil settlement to produce food for military detachments in San Francisco and Monterey. Generations later, its sprawling fruit orchards earned it the title of "Garden City in the Valley of Heart's Delight." More recently, songwriter Burt Bacharach asked the popular question, "Do you know the way to San Jose?"

In fact, the predominant image of modern-day San Jose is none of the above. Her concentration of electronics and high technology is unequaled anywhere else in the country and fostered her latest nickname, "Silicon Valley." Microcircuitry, computer software, venture capital, robotics — these are among the terms properly applied to the San Jose of today.

Neatly bracketed by two mountain ranges, San Jose enjoys picture-perfect weather. The Santa Cruz Mountains screen out the Pacific fog and the Diablo Range funnels in the Central California heat resulting in warm, sunny days and cool, comfortable evenings throughout the South Bay. Combine this ideal climate with a high per-capita income and easy access to every corner of the Bay Area and it's no small wonder that so many people want to live here.

However, would-be residents are not the only ones making their way to San Jose these days. Local officials estimate that over a half-million people come to the Santa Clara Valley for business or pleasure each year, and the South Bay communities have responded with a wide range of transportation, lodging, dining, shopping, and entertainment options.

San Jose is conveniently situated within an hour's drive of San Francisco and the East Bay to the north and Carmel/Monterey to the south. Long-distance travelers or those in

SOUTH BAY:
Birthplace Of The Technological Revolution

The Hakone Gardens in Saratoga offer a tea house and other visual delights.

Gilroy's Garlic Festival features exotica like garlic wine and ice cream.

Annual multicultural festivals are a big draw in the San Jose area.

Every conceivable entertainment is offered at area festivals.

South Bay's rich cultural heritage provides a wide range of menu choices. Pictured above is Fung Lum in Campbell, an internationally acclaimed restaurant featuring

photo: Alan Negrini

Old Town in Los Gatos is notable for its crafts shops and live theater.

Vercelli's in Campbell is dedicated to preparing Northern Italian cuisine.

The Rosicrucian Egyptian Museum draws

The Decathlon Club where captains of

The famous San Jose Rose Garden

photo: Alan Negrini

a hurry will find the San Jose Municipal Airport, with its simple layout and central location, a welcome relief from the congested air terminals normal for cities of this size. For more personalized needs, over three dozen charter services can wing you in and out of town in anything from a small single-engine craft to a Learjet.

Despite the reality of urban sprawl, getting around Silicon Valley need not be the hassle it first appears. An upgraded bus system helps ease traffic snarls in the valley adequately for the present. Looking towards the future, the Santa Clara County Transportation Agency has embarked on a massive project to connect the highly populated south sector with the high tech concentration in the north. The cornerstone of the project is the Guadalupe Corridor, a three-pronged network of expressways, bicycle routes, and a 20-mile light-rail transit line. Construction is slated for completion in 1988.

Meantime, however, the automobile remains the preferred mode of travel throughout the valley. Even so, there's no need to sacrifice style and comfort en route. Dozens of limousine services stand ready with Lincolns, Rolls Royces, and the new stretch limos so popular with today's business traveler. Rental car companies abound, including T & S Motors/Repairs, which specializes in such fine autos as an '83 Ferrari Mondial, an '84 Corvette, even a '77 Gadspy Sypter, a modified replica of a 1930s touring car.

Don't worry about finding a place to stay in the South Bay. Hotel and motel rooms are plentiful, and often cost less than comparable lodging in other California cities. Downtown San Jose boasts a number of one-of-a-kind hotels. The gem of the lot might well be the refurbished Sainte Claire Hilton across from the San Jose Convention Center. A historic landmark, the Sainte Claire has long been noted for its beauty and elegance. Other recommendations

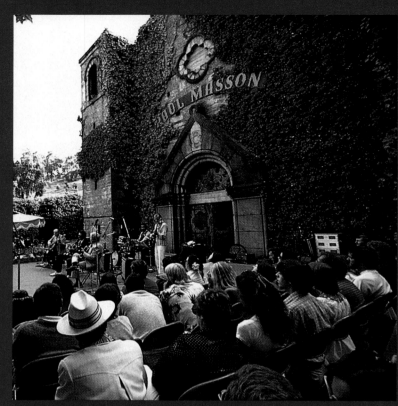

The famous Paul Masson Chateau is the setting each summer for a series of concerts, both jazz and classical, with wine intermissions at the Mountain Winery, overlooking the valley below.

photo: Rick Bernard

The Villa Montalvo Center for the Arts and Arboretum is nestled in the foothills of Saratoga, 15 miles from downtown San Jose. It's a 19-room Mediterranean-style villa and was once the summer home of former San Francisco Mayor James Duval Phelan.

The Winchester Mystery House is the result of Sarah Winchester's never-ceasing building project, apparently to ward off the vengeful spirits who wanted her to "pay" for the victims of "the gun that won the West."

San Jose's largest tourist attraction, the Rosicrucian Egyptian Museum offers a fascinating walk-in rock tomb and exhibits the only authentic reproduction of the sarcophagus of King Tutankhamen.

include the plush Le Baron downtown and the Beverly Heritage in Milpitas. For a different kind of lodging experience, a membership organization called Home Suite Homes (408/733-7215) provides accommodations in townhouses, condominiums, and restored Victorians.

Perhaps no other Bay Area locale offers a wider variety of leisure activities than South Bay. Amid a landscape of concrete and steel, the Municipal Rose Garden and the Japanese Friendship Garden pay tribute to San Jose's past dependence on the soil. The tastefully ornate Rosicrucian Egyptian Museum houses the most extensive collection of Egyptian, Assyrian, and Babylonian antiquities in the Western United States. The gigantic Winchester Mystery House with its 160 rooms, 10,000 windows, and stairways leading nowhere attests to the bizarre preoccupations of Sarah Winchester, the eccentric widow of the famed rifle manufacturer's son. For more lively entertainment, visit the Great America amusement park in Santa Clara. Covering 100 acres, its five theme parks contain live stage shows, attractions and games, restaurants, shops, and hair-raising rides.

Wine enthusiasts will find pleasant surprises in and around San Jose. More than 50 wineries flourish in the valley, a number of which have produced fine wines for over 125 years. The majority conduct regular tours, and many maintain picnic facilities. Some of the most popular names in winemaking, such as Almaden and Paul Masson, are headquartered here. Among the lesser-known but highly distinctive vintners, David Bruce, perched high in the Santa Cruz Mountains, makes premium varietals like Chardonnay and Pinot Noir; Mirassou Vineyards continues a family tradition into the fifth generation; and the Novitiate Winery, one of only two Jesuit wineries in the world, has expanded from strictly sacramental winemaking to aperitifs, table wines, and a highly regarded Black Muscat. From the Spring Cask Opening and Barbeque in April to the South Valley Wine Harvest Festival in October, a season-long calendar of wine festivals serves to educate and please the growing community of wine lovers.

Speaking of festivals, San Jose could rightfully adopt yet another nickname: "The City of Festivals." Seldom does a week pass without some form of civic celebration. The Irish Fels, Cinco de Mayo, the Greek Festival, Aki Matsuri, and the Italian American Cultural Festival bespeak the city's mulitcultural heritage. Sports fans gravitate to the Bruce Jenner Classic (track and field), the Coors International Waterski Jumping Championship, and the National Mile Motorcycle Races. The biggest blowout each year is the Great America Arts Festival on Fourth of July weekend. Spread over a 16-block area downtown, the festival has multiple stages of free entertainment, over 400 indoor and outdoor displays, and dozens of booths offering foods from many lands.

Dedicated shoppers shouldn't miss a visit to the huge shopping centers scattered throughout the South Bay. Choose from The Prune Yard, a formal Spanish plaza of cobblestone walkways encircling an elaborate hand-tiled fountain; Eastridge, with over 160 fine stores, services, and eating establishments; and perhaps the grandest of them all, the Vallco Fashion Park, two immense complexes of stores, museums, and gardens.

If your schedule permits a side trip or two, you need not venture far from the city to find plenty of excitement. Plan a day at historic Saratoga, a community dating back to 1847 which has never lost its country village charm. Here you will find the Paul Masson Winery; the Hakone Gardens, formerly a private estate with an authentic Japanese garden; and the Villa Montalvo Arboretum and Center for the Arts with its year-

Throughout the Bay Area, Victorian houses are coming alive again for businesses as well as families. This charming example is the San Jose headquarters of Talenz Associates Ltd., creators of the design, marketing and advertising for "Super Bowl by the Bay" and a wide range of other consumer and industrial products.

The history of San Jose continues to be represented in architecture, festivals, parks and museums. Another of San Jose's links to the past is the rich agricultural backdrop which remains today, punctuated by her other side—Silicon Valley.

San Jose's new Center for the Performing Arts houses the city's symphony and Civic Light Opera. Performing arts lovers also fill the 2,700 seat center for Broadway road shows, the ballet and big name entertainers.

Almost 80 years old, the Santa Cruz Beach Boardwalk has outlived all of the other West Coast Coney Island-style seaside amusement parks. Innovation, combined with a blending of vintage and modern attractions, has helped the Boardwalk maintain its popularity.

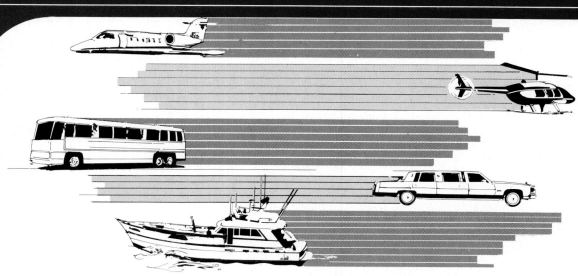

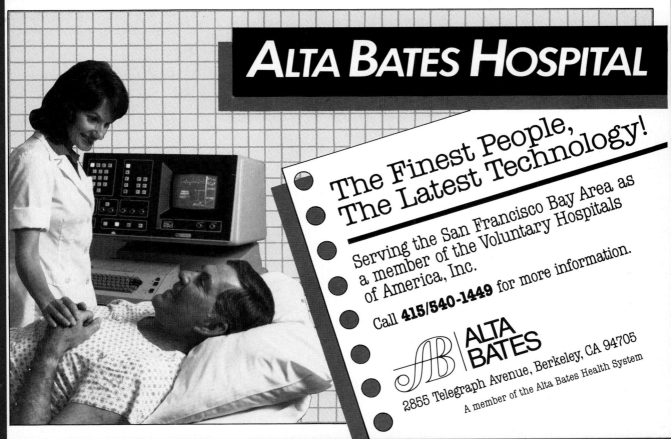

long list of cultural programs.

Scale majestic Mount Hamilton and glimpse the universe beyond at Lick Observatory. Pack a picnic and board the Roaring Camp and Big Trees Narrow-Gauge Railroad for a steam-powered ride into giant redwood forests. Venture to Old Town in Los Gatos, full of quaint shops and cafe/bars—a perfect spot for Sunday brunch. Travel south to the Santa Cruz Beach Boardwalk, California's only remaining surfside amusement park. Ride the Giant Dipper roller coaster, the classic 1911 Looff Merry-Go-Round, play indoor miniature golf, or stretch out and soak up the rays on the mile-long beach.

A day of activity will likely leave you with an insatiable hunger and an unquenchable thirst. Don't despair. There's a distinctive restaurant or lounge on virtually every corner. For drinks, check out Houlihan's in Cupertino and T.G.I. Friday's at Vallco Fashion Park, then sample South Bay's multitudinous dining choices. For Northern Italian specialties, head to Vercelli's in Campbell. Excellent French cuisine can be found at Dartanians and The Plumed Horse in Saratoga, and Emile's Swiss Alpine in downtown San Jose. For a well-rounded evening, The Garden City offers fine dining, spirits, gaming, and some of the best jazz in the valley.

After dinner, sample from the array of cultural opportunities presented in the South Bay. The 2,700-seat Center for the Performing Arts hosts San Jose's 100-year-old Symphony and Civic Light Opera, as well as Broadway road shows, the ballet, and topflight entertainers. The San Jose Repertory Company and the acclaimed Gilbert and Sullivan Society perform in the intimacy of the Montgomery Theater.

After completing your tour of the South Bay, you might wonder what is that colorful body of water to the east and what is contained in the land beyond. Continue on. The answers will unfold.

Thrilling rides at Great America include The Demon (above), a very scary roller coaster, and the world's tallest carousel.

Great America's carousel, (the world's tallest) is 100 feet high and bears 106 lacquered animals including 88 ponies and an assortment of ostriches, pigs, cats, rabbits and deer, each a fiberglass replica of a famous original.

Although less flamboyant than San Francisco, Oakland and the East Bay region boast an equally spirited history, with dramatic changes marking their evolution.

Nineteenth-century settlers who survived the treacherous journey across the plains and over the life-threatening Sierras found peaceful reward in the rolling hills of the East Bay. The tranquility was soon disrupted by Gold Rush speculators who charged into the area like a herd of wild bulls. Oakland became a bustling boomtown full of bawdy belles, gamblers, immigrants and miners, with little in common except the lust for personal gain.

As the boomtowns crumbled to dust after the mines were picked clean, eastern railroad magnates forged west, laying tracks to expand their empires and open up the country. Oakland, a prime port city, was a major stop "at the end of the line." Business, industry, commerce and manufacturing blossomed there, across the bay from the sophisticated financial empire of San Francisco.

Despite its importance, however, the East Bay languished in anonymity in comparison to its dazzling neighbor. Only in the past 15 years has energetic civic promotion brought attention to its many virtues. Oakland remains a key seaport for commercial and naval vessels, a major terminus for railroads and a thriving industrial center. Tree-lined streets and promenades, stylish shopping complexes, luxury hotels and high-rise office buildings combine to create the image of a city of the times—sleek, modern and polished.

Connected to San Francisco by the majestic, two-tiered Bay Bridge, Oakland stands as an attractive entity in itself and a gateway to the beauties contained in the land around it. Air travelers who look down from descending aircraft

photo: Stephen Frisch

EAST BAY:
An Emerging Identity

down from descending aircraft will notice a stretch of San Francisco Bay squared off in plots of still, colored water. As you move, the colors change hue—from brick red to magenta, pickle green to blue. These are the concentrating ponds of the Leslie Salt Company, engaged in the precise business of taking the Bay's early-summer water and turning out salt of near-perfect purity.

East Bay transportation officials proudly point out that Oakland International Airport is closer to downtown San Francisco than is SFO. At the recently opened Executive Terminal at the north end of the field, general and corporate aircraft use a separate tower and taxi up to a complex complete with passenger waiting area, fully equipped conference room, lounge, and private phones.

From Oakland International, you're only 20 minutes from San Francisco's business district and within easy reach of all major East Bay locales through the four long tentacles of the Bay Area Rapid Transit system. In nine years, BART's sleek, silver trains have carried more than 275-million passengers. Its most exciting stretch is the 3.6-mile transbay tunnel, one of the world's longest, deepest underwater transit tunnels, rushed through at speeds of up to 80 mph.

Where to stay in East Bay? Choices range from economical lodging units with kitchenettes to deluxe hotel suites. The grandest of the grand would be the Claremont Resort Hotel and Tennis Club spread over 22 lush, landscaped acres in the Berkeley Hills. Once the home away from home for the likes of Cornelius Vanderbilt and Eleanor Roosevelt, the Claremont is experiencing a renaissance as an urban oasis, corporate meeting site, and tennis resort. A splendid blend of luxury and centralized location can be had at the Hyatt Regency, adjacent to the new $43 million Convention Center downtown. For comparable quality away

photo: James E. Stoots,

The Lawrence Livermore National Laboratory's NOVA Laser is the biggest and most powerful in the world. Within billionths of a second, it can compress heat fuel pellets to the fusion point. The University of California operates the laboratory for the U.S. Department of Energy.

Consistent with its heritage as a transportation hub, Oakland is the headquarters of the 71-mile Bay Area Rapid Transit system. In 1983 alone, BART trains carried nearly 47,000,000 passengers.

The homes along Skyline Drive bespeak Oakland's affluence. For generations, some of the Bay Area's wealthiest citizens have resided here.

from the city, make your reservation at the Hilton Hotel in Concord. Its 340 luxurious guest rooms and suites overlook gardens and fine restaurants.

If old-fashioned accommodation is your cup of tea, try the Burlington Hotel in Port Costa, 20 miles north of Oakland. Built in the 1870s when Port Costa was a bustling seaport, the Burlington survived five major fires that ultimately leveled the rest of the town. The guest rooms are decorated with wrought iron bedframes and feature sunny sitting alcoves. For antique furnishings, private decks and an English country garden are complemented by a pampering staff.

If Oakland is your base for Bay Area exploring, you will find many surprises close at hand. For and overview of the city, take one of six guided tours sponsored by the Volunteers of Oakland (415/273-3234). More ambitious sightseers might prefer joining the docents of the Oakland Museum for a leisurely, six-mile bicycle tour examining the growth of Oakland from Spanish rancho to modern urban center. Call (415) 273-3514.

On your own, the best place to start is at Lake Merritt, 155-acres of salt water smack in the middle of town. The city's pearl, Lake Merritt is a haven for watersports (sailing, canoeing, rowing). The surrounding Lakeside Park is a recreation paradise with picnic grounds, lawn bowling greens, show gardens, a science center, Children's Fairyland and baby animal zoo, and Sunday band concerts.

At the southwestern edge of the park, behold the three-story magnificence of the Oakland Museum. Styled like Babylonian hanging gardens, it is at once a public park, cultural showcase, and an architectural marvel. Its exhibits trace the scientific, social, and artistic histories of California in a peaceful atmosphere.

Heinold's First and Last Chance Saloon, Jack London's old haunt

UC-Berkeley's shaded walkways provide moments of contemplation.

NAS Alameda is home port to carriers and support vessels.

The East Bay Regional Parks are a haven for horseback riders.

Lunchtime concerts pack in the crowds at Berkeley campus.

East Bay's enormous parkland is connected by 106 miles of trails.

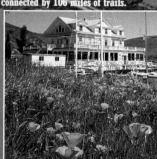

Pastoral charm pervades the waterways near Glen Cove, Vallejo.

Bacterial growth in Leslie Salt Company's concentrating ponds creates an impressive color show for air travelers approaching Oakland International Airport.

Oakland Museum traces California art from the 1600s to present.

Lifestyles of the past are preserved in Oakland Museum's history section.

From April to October, Concord Pavilion stages open-air entertainment.

Grateful Dead performance, an annual Bay Area happening

Thoroughbreds race 100 days a year at Golden Gate Fields.

Lawrence Hall of Science at Berkeley mixes beauty and education.

Paramount Theater, restored survivor of the art deco era

With an eye towards the past, tour the Camron-Stanford House (erected in 1876) and the Dunsmuir House and Gardens, built by a Scotch-Canadian coal miner for his paramour in 1879.

Literary history buffs, lovers of the sea, shoppers and diners will find their fill at Jack London Square and Village, encompassing six blocks on the Oakland Estuary. For boaters, there are marina berths and a yacht club. Aficionados of the printed page can tread in the footsteps of Robert Louis Stevenson, Bret Harte, Joaquin Miller, and of course, Jack London, Oakland's most famous adopted son. Remains of the London connection include the reconstructed log cabin where he weathered the Klondike winter of 1898, and the First and Last Chance Saloon, built from the deckhouse of an old sailing vessel, where young Jack would sit for hours studying owner Johnny Heinhold's dictionary. Now under new management, the saloon still serves a healthy drink with a friendly smile. The import stores, boutiques, and knickknack shops will provide hours of enjoyment, and over a dozen restaurants will cater to every taste and appetite.

But for the truest picture of what the East Bay area was like "in the old days," you need only drive up to Skyline Boulevard, park at any marked entrance on the east side of the street, and walk a few paces into the Skyline National Trail. There a broad expanse of redwood-studded land will unfold before your eyes, and you will see things much as Don Luis Maria Peralta saw them when Oakland and the entire East Bay region was his Rancho San Antonio.

Today the East Bay Regional Park District preserves the land east of Oakland in a network of 41 regional parks. Ingeniously divided into smaller acreages serving distinct functions, the East Bay parks make available every conceivable outdoor activity. Beyond the usual backpacking, camping, picnicking,

Built in time for the Panama Pacific International Exposition of 1915, painted pure white in 1940, the Claremont Resort Hotel and Tennis Club has long catered to world-famous guests.

Once a railroad depot, Santa Fe Bar & Grill serves *new California cuisine.*

Gourmet Creole is the Gingerbread House specialty.

T.J. Robinson's Gingerbread House is a family-run operation.

The ultimate in elegance—Mirabeau Restaurant, Kaiser Center

Christmas glitter sparkles at Jack London Square.

boating, fishing, and swimming, visitors here can rent a horse at the Equestrian Center for an escorted trip along the trails, take a guided tour of the 2,300-year old protected Indian shellmounds, ride a scale-model steam locomotive, a restored merry-go-round, and a giant rapids waterslide. Perhaps your interests extend to archery, bocce ball, or radio-controlled model glider flying. You'll find it all here, in a setting of tranquil grandeur.

While out and about, head up to Berkeley and spend an afternoon at the University of California. Chartered in 1868, focused upon during the 1960s student revolts, UC-Berkeley continues to be one of America's finest academic institutions and most impressive campuses. Arrive around noon and you'll find the Common swarming with students between classes. After getting a feel for the campus atmosphere, stroll along the wooded walkways, through the Botanical Garden (with more than 8,000 species of plants), and stop at the University Art Museum. Finally, spend some time at the Lawrence Hall of Science, a massive concentration of hands-on exhibits covering topics from radio astronomy to probability.

As with every other section of the Bay Area, the East Bay has more than its share of distinctive dining choices. Those in the know consider Chez Panisse on Shattuck Avenue to be perhaps the finest French restaurant in the Bay Area. Located on the ground floor of a renovated old house, Chez Panisse specializes in *California nouvelle cuisine,* which uses fresh ingredients indigenous to the region to create simple but elegant dishes. The Cafe upstairs features Italian fare (fold-over pizza and home-made pastas) of equal distinction. Deep appetites can be satisfied royally at Warszawa in Berkeley, which prepares home-cooked Eastern European meals of roast duckling, Polish stew, pea soup, borscht and black bread. For four-star dining go to the Mirabeau Restaurant

The physical and spiritual heart of modern Oakland, Lake Merritt is the largest salt water tidal lake within any city in the world. Its shimmering waters smooth the rough edges of city life.

Fishing is one of many outdoor activities enjoyed at Lake Temescal. Leisure seekers also partake of boating, swimming and sunbathing

at Oakland's Kaiser Center. The Mirabeau's offering changes with the passing of seasons and is classic French , with a dash of Creole, served on sparkling china and crystal.

On Fifth Street in Oakland you'll find an adorable restaurant called the Gingerbread House, decked out in antiques, dolls, toys, and greeting cards. Owner T.J. Robinson terms her cooking style "Louisiana Fancyfare," which includes such appetite-provoking creations as "Eat Your Heart Out Chicken," "Spoon" Jambalaya, Sauteed Quail, and Whiskey Stuffed Lobster.

And, finally, for fantastic dining at a reasonable price, head directly to the Santa Fe Bar & Grill where the incomparable Jeremiah Tower (formerly of Chez Panisse) presides over the kitchen. Again you will be treated to the new California cuisine with special emphasis on mouth-watering fish and poultry concoctions.

Oakland's cultural heritage is graphically embodied in the Paramount Theater of the Arts, a national hitoric landmark. A rare survivor of the 1930s art deco style of architecture and decor, the newly renovated Paramount combines rich carpets, softly lit ceilings and carved golden walls in tropical and botanical motifs. The Paramount houses the world-acclaimed Oakland Symphony and the up-and-coming Oakland Ballet and Oakland Opera.

Sports fans will find year-round professional action at the Oakland/Alameda County Stadium. The city that produced such sports notables as Frank Robinson, Bill Russell, and John Brodie is home to baseball's A's, basketball's Golden State Warriors, and the Invaders of the United States Football League.

Before leaving the East Bay, don't pass up trips to such interesting spots as Walnut Creek, Orinda, Danville, and Pleasanton. Then it's on to the state capital, Sacramento, and nature's wonder, Yosemite National Park.

Railroads, steamboats, stagecoaches—the lifeblood of the West and long-time servants of the city of Sacramento. A city located in the heart of Gold Rush country, a city surrounded by the American and Sacramento rivers, a city which was home to the first railroad west of the Rockies, Sacramento has a boomtown heritage which continues on into the present.

Sacramento has much to offer the Northern California traveler, beginning with 1500 miles of waterways and accompanying water recreation. Moreover, the climate here is appealing, with little humidity and plenty of sunshine. Combine these pluses with easy access to all of Northern California and many unique attractions steeped in history, and you have no excuse to stay away.

Certainly one of Sacramento's claims to fame must be Sutter's Fort, the reconstructed site of the original settlement founded by Captain John A. Sutter in 1839. Then there's Old Sacramento, once the main riverboat landing for Sutter's Fort and gateway for gold seekers, preserved on a 28-acre site rich with history, museums, points of interest, restaurants and shops.

Sacramento has all manner of tour possibilities to offer the eager visitor. For an out-of-the-ordinary trip, venture to Locke, California, previously the home of over 1500 Chinese immigrants who helped construct the Delta levees. Visit the Gold Country, which stretches from Downieville and Sierra City in the North to Mariposa/Yosemite in the South, where beautiful scenery, camping, and backpacking possibilities are endless. For an insider's look at almond processing and perpetuating the American River salmon, tour the California Almond Growers Exchange and the Nimbus Fish Hatchery.

Dubbed the "Williamsburg of Jazz," Sacramento annually hosts

SACRAMENTO:
The Golden Heritage

The newly restored California State Capitol is open for tours.

A blacksmith is a permanent fixture at Sutter's Fort.

Fifth graders pan for gold with piepans at Coloma in the Sierras.

Catch a glimpse of what life was like during pioneer days at Sutter's Fort.

An old-fashioned wedding takes place in Coloma—famous gold discovery site.

The Port of Sacramento is the newest, most up-to-date port on the West Coast.

Prune orchards abound in the Marysville/Yuba City region.

Sports-minded Sacramento residents participate in the city's marathon.

Hot-air ballooning is a popular sport in the Sacramento Valley.

The California State Fair is the largest agricultural fair in the U.S.

Tourists admire Sacramento's thriving downtown mall area.

The California State Railroad Museum displays 21 restored locomotives/cars.

the Dixieland Jazz Festival, the biggest jazz conclave in the country, on Memorial Day weekend. Another annual event, the California State Fair, has been held in Sacramento since 1861. The University of California at Davis, the third largest UC campus, is located just 13 miles west of Sacramento. The Guy West Bridge is a miniature copy of San Francisco's Golden Gate Bridge at California State University in Sacramento.

Sacramento abounds with parks and lakes. Explore the American River Parkway, which extends from Folsom Lake State Park downstream to the Sacramento River. The Sacramento Delta is often called the Everglades of the West, and here you can find two popular pastimes, houseboating and rafting. Better yet, take a riverboat cruise between Sacramento and San Francisco.

If you enjoy shopping, Sacramento offers many special shopping spots: The Building, the Sacramento Antique Center, Old Sacramento, Folsom Historical Shopping Area in Folsom, Fountain Square in Citrus Heights, and Town & Country Village—the oldest shopping center west of the Rockies.

For unusal dining, you needn't look far. Period restaurants located in Old Sacramento, like the Firehouse, Fat City Bar & Cafe and China Camp, offer unique atmosphere and fine food. Other noted spots include The Rusty Duck Restaurant & Saloon and the TajMahal. If you're willing to travel a ways, try Al's Place in Locke, the first Caucasian business in town, featuring just one entree—steak. For a safari atmosphere visit Foster's Bighorn Restaurant in Rio Vista, displaying over 250 wild animals from all over the world, 95 percent of which were shot by Foster himself.

When it's time to turn in, consider Sacramento's fine bed-and-breakfast inns—Amber House Bed and Breakfast, Aunt Abigail's Bed and Breakfast or The Briggs House.

Los Angeles has a Rose Bowl, Miami an Orange Bowl and Sacramento—well, it has a Pig Bowl, where local police and county sheriffs hog the limelight once each year.

WaterWorld USA, a 14-acre theme park on California State Fairgrounds

Locke, Calif.—the only city in the nation founded and settled by Chinese

Fat City Bar & Cafe houses a historic 19th century mahogany bar.

The Cal State Fair brings early fair-going days to life.

Sacramento in the fall—a city of trees bursting with color

State
of
the
Art

Photo courtesy of Batton/Dysan and Carl N. Swenson Co., Inc.

Sites to meet today's requirements.
Designed for tomorrow's technology.

You want a home for your company that's as state-of-the-art as your product...one that will satisfy your current requirements *and* keep up with you while you keep up with technology.

Chevron Land and Development Company understands the special needs of growing companies. We offer quality business and industrial environments designed to help you stay ahead of your competition--plentiful labor markets to improve your productivity-- and low land prices to enhance your bottom-line.

No matter what the size of your company--whether you need space to lease or land to purchase--Chevron Land has a state-of-the-art answer. Call us today.

HILLTOP 950 Acres Richmond, CA (415) 223-5872

VACA VALLEY CORPORATE CENTER
1,700 Acres Vacaville, CA (707) 446-1374

BAKERSFIELD INDUSTRIAL AND BUSINESS CENTERS
840 Acres Bakersfield, CA (805) 392-3313

Chevron

Chevron Land and Development Company

*The Governor's Mansion housed thirteen
governors between 1903 and 1967.*

Roughly the size of Rhode Island, well over 760,000 acres, and drawing more than two and one-half million visitors a year, Yosemite National Park is one of nature's finest achievements. Located only hours from San Francisco and surrounding areas, this wonderland of granite peaks and domes, waterfalls and forests, meadows, streams and crystal lakes was formed by glaciers thousands of years ago.

Access to Yosemite is ample. Fly into the Fresno Air Terminal or Merced Airport, each two and a half hours from the Yosemite Valley, then proceed by car or bus. Amtrak, Greyhound and Trailways can whisk you as far as Merced, and the Yosemite Transportation System takes you the rest of the way. If you're driving from San Francisco, take Interstate 580 to Highway 120 straight through to the Valley. Access from other areas in California is just as direct. Once you're in Yosemite Valley, free shuttles provide transportation to the Ahwahnee Hotel, Yosemite Lodge, Curry Village, Yosemite Village and the Chapel.

For the winter enthusiast, Badger Pass, which first opened to skiers in 1935, provides downhill skiing for the whole family as well as the renowned Yosemite Ski School. Ice skating is another favorite pastime. Curry Village offers rental skates and lessons. For a trip along the edge of the five ski runs, take the open-air Snowcat Tour. Snowshoeing or Nordic Ski Touring through 90 miles of marked cross-country ski trails is available through the Yosemite Mountaineering School, as is mountain climbing.

What better way to spend an afternoon than horseback riding through the Valley! Fine facilities and expert wranglers await you. Or, you can peddle your way through the park, Bicycle rentals are available at Yosemite Lodge and Curry Village.

YOSEMITE
Awesome Result Of Nature's Artistry

And for an even more thrilling ride, go river rafting down the Merced.

The best way to see Yosemite's major attractions is to take one of the guided bus tours. Yosemite Tours provides expert guides versed in the lore of the area who can enhance spectacular views such as Half Dome, El Capitan, Yosemite Falls, the Mariposa Grove of Big Trees, and Glacier Point, among others.

Fine lodging is available at the Ahwahnee Hotel, which was built in the mid-1920s in response to the lack of adequate accommodations for visiting nobility. The grandeur of the building is not surprising considering the cost at the time—$1 million to build and $250,000 to furnish. The food offered at the dining room is worth a trip alone. The Hotel Wawona, a Victorian resort hotel built in 1856, is listed in the National Register of Historic Places and boasts, on a smaller scale, equally fine amenities. Yosemite Lodge and Curry Village provide hotel rooms and cottage rooms, and housekeeping camp units along the Merced River are the closest thing to roughing it without a tent. High Sierra accommodations are also available.

No matter where you stay, however, chances are you will be lulled to sleep by the sound of the great falls in the distance and the peacefulness of Yosemite will envelop you as it did John Muir:

"Oh, these vast, calm, measure-less mountain days, inciting at once to work and rest! Days in whose light everything seems equally divine, opening a thousand windows to show us God. Never-more, however weary, should one faint by the way who gains the blessings of one mountain day; whatever his fate, long life, short life, stormy or calm, he is rich forever."

The Ahwahnee Hotel in Yosemite National Park is included in the National Register of Historic Places for its architectural significance. Cathedral ceilings, stone hearths, and rich Indian and Oriental rugs grace this American castle.

Yosemite affords explorers a wealth of beauty and challenge.

Bridalveil Fall—the first of the great waterfalls visitors to Yosemite see

The backwoods of Yosemite Valley accommodate even the most avid hikers.

photo: Rick Bernard

The most popular form of lodging at Yosemite is the tent.

photo: Rick Bernard

One of Yosemite's spectacles, Half Dome rises a mile high.

Yosemite's lakes and streams are bountiful and offer hours of relaxation.

There's no finer place to learn rock-climbing fundamentals than Yosemite.

From the vantage point of a bicycle, the glory of Yosemite is more apparent.

"The air is delicious, tangy, and when you return after a stint in a place like New York you can eat it."

John R. Coyne, Jr.,
The Kumquat Statement, 1970

ne reason for the San Francisco Bay Area's enormous popularity is its close proximity to a wide range of scenery, weather conditions, and leisure activities. Driving east from the city, the traveler passes from cool sea breezes and gentle hills, through an agricultural valley fed by waterways and the sun's heat, to the gradual ascent of glorious mountain peaks.

Nestled in the center of the range is Lake Tahoe, geographically divided between Nevada and California. Fringed by sandy beaches and magnificent homes, this shimmering body of emerald water reflects the mountainous beauty climbing to the sky.

Summertime offers the smell of pine and evergreen, suntan lotion and barbecues, the sounds of children laughing, motorboats towing skiers, and sails flapping against the breeze.

In winter, the roads become edged with a wall of packed snow which deepens as the elevation increases. Summer noises are replaced by stillness, broken only by the swooshing of skis across the slopes or toboggans plummeting downhill and across a clearing. Crackling fires and hot toddies replace summer's wine coolers.

For those who can relax for only so long, the Nevada side provides extravagant floor shows, night spots, dancing, and a full array of enticing gaming tables in the glittering casinos.

Tahoe is a year-round playground catering to every taste and fancy. But it is also a place for regeneration of body and spirit, a place to soften the rough edges of the fast-paced city life.

Lake Tahoe, the second largest mountain lake in the world, was formed by earthquakes and volcanic action and filled with the water of melting glaciers. For generations, the region was inhabited by tribes of Washoe Indians who believed the basin to be spiritual.

LAKE TAHOE
Lake Of The Sky

It was not until 1844 that white men first glimpsed this scenic wonder.

Captain John Fremont, leading an expedition guided by Kit Carson, discovered the lake as his group climbed over Echo Pass. In his writings, Fremont referred to it as Lake Bonpland, after a fellow explorer. But on resulting maps, it was given the name "Mountain Lake" and remained so until the early 1900s, when the Washoe Indian word for lake, "tahoe," became firmly established.

Reports of Tahoe's splendor circulated quickly. Mark Twain, in his book *Roughing It*, admitted uncharacteristic amazement when he first laid eyes on Tahoe. "The lake burst upon us — a noble sheet of blue water lifted 6,300 feet above the level of the sea, and walled in by a rim of snow-clad mountain peaks that flowered aloft full 3,000 feet higher still! It was a vast oval, and one would love to use up eighty or a hundred good miles in traveling around it. As it lay there with the shadows of the mountains brilliantly photographed upon its still surface I thought it must surely be the fairest picture the whole earth affords."

As with most of Northern California, Lake Tahoe's development is closely linked to the 1800's Gold Rush. The verdant mountains surrounding the lake were picked clean to supply timber for use in the railroads and mines.

During this colorful period in history, hunters, gamblers, explorers, miners and the Pony Express were fixtures around the lake — contributing to the area's rich folklore. But the development of a railroad between Truckee and Tahoe enabled "tourists" from San Francisco to experience the beauty of the area. A brochure encouraging visitors stated that one could "make the entire trip from San Francisco with all the luxuries afforded by the best-equipped and modern railroad." The roundtrip excursion, including a steamer trip around the lake, was $16.50. A

"The main body of the [Emerald] bay is a deep blue our eyes have already become accustomed to, but the shoreline is a wonderful combination of jade and emerald that dances and scintillates as the breeze plays with the surface of the water."

George Wharton James
Lake of the Sky, 1915

room at the Tahoe Tavern was listed at $3.00 a night.

Today, Lake Tahoe remains a haven of relaxation, a splendid retreat from urban stress. Its wide assortment of winter sports and recreational facilities was brought about in large part by the 1960 Winter Olympics at Squaw Valley. With an average snowfall of over 200 inches per year (300 to 500 inches at higher elevations), the area boasts some of the world's finest powder and most challenging slopes, attracting beginners and seasoned skiers alike.

The northern area around Donner Summit off Interstate 80 contains five ski resorts and lodging nearby. Among North Shore's eight resorts, special attention should be paid to Alpine Meadows and Squaw Valley. Both locations have outstanding amenities, ski schools, class-A lodging and dining. Of special note are the dogsled races held in Truckee each February. This fun-packed weekend draws teams and spectators from throughout the West and benefits the Guide Dogs for the Blind program.

North Shore also hosts the annual Snowfest, a nine-day carnival commencing the first Saturday in March. The celebrations begin with fireworks and a torchlight parade on the slopes. Street-dancing, the Great Ski Race, Camel Ski Days, a celebrity race, and special parties and contests make Snowfest a not-to-be-missed week of good times for every interest.

Incline Village and neighboring Ski Incline form the hub of the eastern shore. Many people stay in the luxurious condominiums abundant here. Others opt for Hyatt Lake Tahoe, a stylish hotel towering above the shoreline with 460 rooms, a casino, and resort accommodations for the entire family.

Finally, four more ski areas on the South Shore complete this vast winter sports wonderland. Visitors can take advantage of distinctive winter diversions such as Nordic skiing, sledding, snowmobiling, hiking, and sleigh riding.

Tahoe is not just hushed snow-fall, winter sports and hot buttered rum by a blazing fire. The lure of this, one of Mother Nature's most favored spots, endures twelve months a year. According to a journalist in the 1800s, "People who have heretofore sought the seashore for summer recreation may have become alive to the fact that at Lake Tahoe they can enjoy a combination of both marine and mountain advantages."

Even Twain had cause to observe that "three months of camp life on Lake Tahoe would restore an Egyptian mummy to his pristine vigor and give him an appetite like an alligator. I do not mean the oldest and driest mummies, of course, but the fresher ones."

Towards May, the sun dries the earth and warms the lake's crystal waters. Temperatures in the area never get too hot or too cold. The altitude creates a glowing warmth to bronze the skin and keep clothing to a minimum.

With the passing of winter, the lake comes alive with laughter, traffic, bright colors and effervescence. The air fills with music and the aroma of budding flowers, a true joy to the senses. According to a veteran of Tahoe's pleasures, "If I only had one year to live, it would most assuredly include at least two trips to Lake Tahoe!"

The lake beckons water-sport fanciers and, lest you worry about being crowded out, remember that there is enough water in the lake to supply every person in the United States with 50 gallons each day for five years.

Between May and October, the majesty of the lake attracts sailing, water-skiing, and swimming enthusiasts. Excellent fishing can be had for the drop of the line, since the lake teems with brook trout, kokanee salmon, rainbow and mackinaw trout. Further recreational activities exist independent of the lake. Hiking, horseback riding, golf, tennis, and biking all abound.

One of the most enjoyable ways

The lake is dotted with many palatial estates. Pictured here is a mansion featured in "Godfather II."

to spend a summer day is to pack a gourmet lunch, rent a motorboat, and go exploring. Traveling close to shoreline, you moor in one of the dozens of coves, wade ashore, spread out the blanket, and picnic. The trees and sand, the calm and tranquility call for a good book and a classical music tape.

If sports and relaxation bore you, consider other pursuits to fill the daytime hours. Sightsee at such historically significant locations as the Gatekeeper's Log Cabin Museum (housing an extensive array of artifacts from Tahoe's early days); Erhman Mansion; the Doll and Toy Museum in Tahoe City; Ponderosa Ranch (a western theme park made famous by the "Bonanza" TV series); Vikingsholm (a 38-room Swedish castle, once the summer home of heiress Laura Knight); and Harrah's Automobile Collection (over 1,110 restored or preserved vintage vehicles) located near Reno, Nevada.

Shopping your bag? Dozens of unique shopping complexes surround the lake. Many of the stores feature goods and crafts made by residents. To frequent visitors, favorite spots include the Boatworks, the Roundhouse Center, Incline Village, and Cobblestone, each one filled with quaint gift shops and distinctive boutiques.

A truly unusual spot for browsing and outdoor luncheons is the Squirrel's Nest, a fantasy land of art, clothing, crafts, and kitchenware. Since dining is alfresco in its fanciful gardens of flowers and pop art, the Squirrel's Nest is open only in the summer months. Take Highway 89 to the west side of the lake to Homewood and plan on spending an afternoon. The food alone is worth the trip.

Environment and lifestyle differ greatly between the North and South shores, partly due to terrain, partly because the South houses the bulk of the major hotels and casinos.

On the northern end, scores of luxury condominiums have been

"If the philosophers had lived among your mountains their systems would have been different from what they are."

George Santayana, 1911

built over the past decade, and condo-living has become the most prevalent form of lodging there. Motels dating back to the '30s and '40s remain along the northeastern shore, now modernized and converted to "timeshare" units. During the past 15 years, Tahoe time-sharing has increased in popularity, with people from all over the country taking advantage of its value and convenience.

But for the ultimate in living conditions, rent a cozy cabin in the woods or near the lake. Most realtors in the area can make rental arrangements. Don't overlook this opportunity to live in the fashion of the Tahoe townies of days gone by.

At South Shore, high-rise hotels line both sides of the highway, flanked by an abundance of smaller motels and inns. Outstanding among them is Inn By The Lake, a brand new hotel catering to the most discriminating tastes. For those who wish to be in the thick of the action, Harrah's and Caesar's afford luxury rooms, floor shows and full casinos, and a bevy of shops and restaurants from which to choose.

Certainly, every holiday centers around dining, and here again Lake Tahoe can hold its own with any world-class resort. Each locale features a sophisticated assortment of dining motifs—from casual meals on outdoor patios to gourmet dinners in elegant settings.

Naturally, certain restaurants stand out for the quality of their food, service and ambience. In South Lake Tahoe, the Summit atop Harrah's Tahoe Hotel and Casino is as romantic as it is chic. If you're planning that special night on the town, don tuxedo or evening gown and head for the Summit. No other place at the lake can match it for view, decor, and service.

Several superior dining houses can be found between Tahoe Vista and Kings Beach. La Cheminee serves excellent French cuisine in warm, comfortable surroundings. The fare at such places as Chez

Nightfall brings people together at the gaming tables of casinos on the Nevada side of the lake for everything from Baccarat to bingo, roulette to the nickel slots.

photo: Vance Fox

The summer season affords unlimited opportunities to participate in all manner of sports, with an emphasis on water sports

Lyliane, Le Petit Pier, and Steven by the Lake are well worth sampling.

For a change of pace, try the more casual atmosphere available at Cantina Los Tres Hombres, the Chinese Village (Tahoe City), and Swiss Lakewood on the west shore. Nearby restaurants of special note include C.B. Whites and La Vielle Maison, both located in charming Victorian homes in Truckee.

If time permits, plan an outing to the old mining towns of Virginia City and Carson City, where the Gold Rush lifestyle of the 1800s endures. While in Carson City, be sure to eat at Adele's, an award-winning restaurant devoted to creative dining.

An easy drive to Reno avails the added excitement of casinos and cabarets, floor shows and discos. Unlike Las Vegas with its famed "Strip," Reno's hotels and casinos are scattered throughout three square miles downtown.

Proudly proclaiming itself "The Biggest Little City in the World," Reno shuns the Vegas glitter in favor of blue jeans and cowboy hats. A century and a half after the Gold Rush, Reno remains a wide-open town where folks come from far and wide to whoop it up. Whatever your gambling pleasure, you'll find ample opportunities to place a wager in Reno.

Away from the tables, Reno hosts a wide array of stage acts. For openers, see Donn Arden's magnificent "Hello, Hollywood, Hello" at the MGM Grand Hotel. Other hotels feature headline performers like Don Rickles, Debbie Reynolds, Wayne Newton and Mickey Gilley.

To Californians, Lake Tahoe has long been an oasis rather than a playground. But without a doubt, there are few places in the world that offer more scenic beauty, more recreational activities and dining choices than Lake Tahoe. Whether it's boating, baccarat, boogying or basking in the sun, the visitor will come away refreshed and ready to return to the rigors of city life.

Entertainment at Reno runs the gamut from intimate bar shows to bawdy burlesque to headliners and stage productions. The most lavish of them all, "Hello, Hollywood, Hello" at the MGM Grand, combines waterfalls, a giant airplane, circus acts and scores of performers.

Originating in Alaska in 1908, dog sled racing has become a spirited winter sporting event in Truckee. The race draws teams of all ages from throughout North America.

photo: Vance Fox

The Great Ski Race, the largest cross-country race in California, attracts over 700 entrants and is a focal point of the North Tahoe annual Snowfest celebration, one of many such festivals taking place throughout the winter season.

Five hours south of the Bay Area lies the Danish-style village of Solvang, with imports, clogs, thatched roofs and Ableskiver pastry. Located in Santa Inez Valley, the village is surrounded by a burgeoning wine industry, horse-breeding ranches, and the Alisal working dude ranch. Nearby is Lompoc and the Valley of Flowers. This charming region is within one hour of Santa Barbara.

Fickle fortune sometimes smiles on patrons of the "one-arm bandits" at Lake Tahoe's casinos.

ost people travel to the North Bay by way of the Golden Gate Bridge, past Vista Point, the Marin Headlands, and through the Waldo Tunnel, emblazoned with a brightly colored rainbow. Marinites believe their land to be full of riches and promise. There can be no denying the scenic beauty of the hills generously sprinkled with trees, the fields of billowing wheat and grazing cattle, and the quaint villages scattered throughout the county. Few people visiting here are prepared for such pastoral majesty within a twenty-minute drive from San Francisco, one of the world's more cosmopolitan cities.

Marin appears to be an area of conservative lifestyles and values rooted in the land, of families and simple pleasures. Often characterized by the media as a mecca for hedonists, dopers, flakes, and laid-back living, Marin shrugs off the critcism and settles into a life somewhere in between.

This middle ground is as full of contradictions as it is lovely. Perhaps nowhere is this so true as in Sausalito, a tiny village with Mediterranean ambiance just beyond the Golden Gate.

Built on a history of seafaring captains and artists, Sausalito was a quiet fishing village well into this century, accessible only by ferry boat. The grand homes along the hillside were built by affluent businessmen in San Francisco, who longed for the tranquility, open space, and verdant surroundings not available in the city.

During World War II, southern Marin was a hub of activity as ship-building demands swelled the local work force and caused serious housing shortages. Many of the magnificent old homes were divided into apartments to add much-needed dwelling space. Over the decades after the war, factories closed and the communities reverted to sleepy villages.

MARIN COUNTY
Marvelous Mixture of Country and Cosmopolitan

Today Sausalito is a thriving community with tourism as the foundation of its economic stability. The waterfront, once seedy and decayed, is now a bustling marina amid a parklike setting, surrounded by shops and restaurants. The abandoned landing-craft hulls and lifeboats from WWII have been jerry-built to serve as bases for dozens of houseboats. Other floating homes range from makeshift craft to a floating "island" complete with beach, palm trees and waterfall, for sale at a cool $1.5 million.

The tradition of blending artists, seamen, residents and visitors continues, if with a struggle. The quaint European charm that once lured poets, sculptors, and wealthy San Franciscans stubbornly persists, despite growth and a steady stream of traffic.

Arriving by boat or by car, one is instantly embraced by Sausalito's beauty mixed with an undercurrent of excitement. Here you can wander for hours amid shops and galleries, dine at cafes or elegant restaurants. Foremost among the many dining spots are Ondine's overlooking the Bay, serving continental cuisine; Alta Mira for outdoor brunch and breathtaking views; and Christophe for a romantically French rendezvous.

Exploring the varied areas of Marin County is both fun and informative and easily accommodates a one-day outing. While in Sausalito, be sure to visit the Bay Model, a laboratory for engineers to study the effects of man's interaction with nature in the Bay Area and the Delta regions. The model, located in the Visitor Center, replicates our environment and operates on 250,000 gallons of water to simulate tides and currents.

North of Sausalito lies the tiny village of Tiburon. A stop for juicy hamburgers and spicy Bloody Marys is a local tradition at Sam's Anchor Cafe, which combines hearty food with a marina setting and a city skyline backdrop. While in the area, don't miss China Cabin,

Marin's annual Renaissance Fair held each weekend throughout August features jesters and jugglers, mimes, Elizabethan architecture, jolly games of merry old England such as tossing tokens into bosoms, and scrumptious food stalls manned by serving wenches. Heralds announce daily events including Shakespearean plays and Queen plays and Queen Elizabeth's arrival.

photo: Dick Cummings

An exotic, albeit untraditional living style in Sausalito encompasses a vast array of houseboats. They range in size and comfort from rustic, one-room clapboard affairs to palatial multiroom boats, some with decks, skylights, and fully equipped kitchens.

a luxurious Victorian saloon restored for use as a maritime center. This national treasure dates back to 1866 when it was part of the side-wheeler, S.S. China.

Venturing west to the ocean, you encounter miles of smooth beach, state parks, and wind-swept cliffs for hiking and relaxing. Audubon Canyon Ranch, north of Stinson Beach, is a 1,000-acre bird sanctuary and treasured national landmark.

To the northeast is Muir Woods National Monument, a forest of towering redwoods and a constant reminder of man's insignificance in nature's realm. Of these soaring giants, John Steinbeck wrote, "From them come silence and awe. It's not only their unbelievable stature, nor the color which seems to shift and vary under your eyes, no, they are not like any trees we know, they are ambassadors from another time."

Nearby, Mount Tamalpais proudly watches over the lands below and avails itself to visitors for camping, hiking, and vista viewing in all directions.

In the surrounding lowlands are the villages of Ross, Kent, Fairfax, San Anselmo, Larkspur and San Rafael. Larkspur is home to the Ferry Terminal (gateway to San Francisco via ferry), Larkspur Landing (a Cape Cod-styled shopping and dining complex), and one of Marin's most innovative restaurants, 464 Magnolia, featuring French country cooking.

Largest of the Marin communities, San Rafael is the site of the Marin County Civic Center. Built by Frank Lloyd Wright, it resembles the Starship Enterprise resting on a tree-covered knoll. The town boasts one of the Bay Area's most noted restaurants, Maurice et Charles, serving creatively classic French cuisine with prices to match.

For an unabashedly romantic getaway, consider East Brother Light, a tiny one-acre island upon which rests an 1873 lighthouse. The station still guards the straits

Brunch on the deck at Sam's Cafe, Tiburon, is a favorite weekend pastime for local residents. Be it January or July, the weather is divine. Tiburon lies on the peninsula that juts into Richardson Bay, and neighboring Belvedere is home to the county's more affluent. Tiburon Cove is a major stopping point for ferries and pleasure boats.

Mother Nature creates billowy fog that cools the western side of the Bay. Some say that the fog was responsible for Sir Francis Drake mistaking a cove on the Marin shoreline for San Francisco Bay.

"In other parts of the world, youth lasts a reasonable period of time; in California it lasts a lifetime."

Ashley Montagu
The American Way of Life, 1967

for ships but has been lovingly restored to include one of the country's most unusual bed-and-breakfast inns. Phone 233-2385 for details.

If your excursion calls for overnight accommodations, try Casa Madrona, sitting precariously on the hillside in Sausalito. Recently renovated and enlarged, it offers fine continental dining, magnificent views and luxurious lodging. Another excellent choice is the Sausalito Hotel, resplendent with antiques and charm and conveniently located in the center of this Riviera-like setting.

Once you've explored the villages and vast acres of land preserved for human enjoyment, it is time to move on to the last leg of the journey.

Northward lies a land where privacy is cherished, where the sun is never more perpetually bright, and where man and nature have conspired to produce one of life's great pleasures—WINE.

art by Terry Mollenauer

233

Point Reyes Seashore offers an array of picnic spots and hiking trails.

Inverness Library—for history buffs and browsers

A plethora of shops and restaurants surrounds Sausalito's village square.

Skywalker Ranch, home of the George Lucas empire

A trail at Point Reyes—horseback riding is a favorite sport of Marinites.

Beniamino Bufano sculpture arouses shoreline interest in Sausalito.

"The flashing and golden pageant of California, the sudden and gorgeous, the sunny and ample lands..."

Walt Whitman
"Song of the Redwood Tree," 1881

For centuries, poets and scribes have extolled the lure of the grape and its heady stature when combined with "a loaf of bread ... and thou." Indeed, wine is synonymous with the good things in life. Since the early 1800s, it has played an integral role in the development of the land stretching north from San Francisco Bay.

When gold was discovered in 1848, the local population swelled with wealth-seekers from all over the world. As the search for gold lost its glitter, some immigrants turned their attention to viticulture (winemaking). Many such growers imported vines from their native lands in Europe.

The legacy of their efforts is displayed today along the golden hills of the North Bay territory. A leisurely drive from San Francisco through Marin, Napa, and Sonoma counties fills the traveler with a sense that Mother Nature has rarely dispensed her favors to a greater degree.

Glimpse the beauty of the rolling landscape, the forests, rivers and streams, the verdant acreage, and perpetual sun. Savor the warmth, the smells of wild flowers in the fields and the grapes awaiting harvesting. Let your eyes languidly survey nature's beauty, at once stark and sumptuous. Let your mind pause from the pressures of the day and reflect on how good life can really be.

Charming cafes and garden restaurants dot the highways and byways to maintain your strength for one more glass of liquid velvet. As the sun falls behind the hills, a splendid array of country inns, luxury spas, resorts and retreats is available to restore you for yet another day.

The diversity of wonders in the North Bay will keep you happily occupied. Begin in Marin County with its national parks and seashore, the massive redwood trees in Muir Woods, the picturesque

WINE COUNTRY:
Kiss Of The Sun, Fruit Of The Field

waterside villages of Sausalito and Tiburon, and scenic Mount Tamalpais.

Continue to Napa and Sonoma counties where you will be greeted by an inspiring contrast of the old and new. Victorian gingerbread houses and wineries resembling European castles stand proudly next to sleek modern buildings. Guided tours encompass cool dark caves carved into hillsides and wine production plants filled with the most advanced viticulture equipment in the world. A number of one-day wine country tours will accommodate time constraints.

If your interests include golf, auto racing, water-skiing, gliding, ballooning, camping and sightseeing, you are sure to find a complete menu in North Bay to fill your days with enjoyment.

Taking our own advice, we organized a series of excursions to explore the back roads of the Wine Country. For maximum comfort and travel ease, we retained the services of Carey Nob Hill Limousine for an early-morning departure from San Francisco.

DAY ONE: Our first stop was Korbell Champagne Cellars. The picturesque setting and tour of the cellars was both informative and interesting, since old-world methods for producing sparkling wines have been used here for over a hundred years. After a jolly round of tasting, we journeyed over country lanes to Hop Kiln, where ducks wander the grounds and splash in a pond adjacent to the tasting room. It was too early in the day for a picnic, but this would have been a lovely spot for one.

Continuing on the same road, we discovered a stunning inn, The Madrona Manor, owned and operated by descendants of John Muir, the noted ecologist of the early 1900s. Although our plans were set for lodging that night, we prevailed upon the manager to show us around. Each room was immaculate and furnished with museum-quality antiques. We vowed to return and avail ourselves of the charm, hospitality, and cuisine.

The champagne piqued our appetites and encouraged our speedy arrival at Souvereign Winery and Restaurant. We were greeted with a sunny dining room overlooking the vineyard in a building resembling a sleek French chateau. The food was delightful, the service attentive, making for a pleasant midday respite. The tour and tasting at Simi Winery that followed was a perfect conclusion to our first day's journey.

There is a magic in this land of vineyards and warming sun that melts away the tensions of city life. As we drove to Calistoga, our eyes languidly surveyed the gentle rolling foothills, redwood forests and manicured vineyards. It didn't take long to fall in love with our surroundings.

The combination of sun and wine is a heady one. Although we resented the day's quick passage, we were eager to check into our hotel and join friends who had driven from the South Bay. Our arrival at the Mount View Hotel in Calistoga was a welcome relief and the art deco interior was inviting. The minisuite was cozy and comfortable and the large, footed tub offered a soothing soak before dinner. The country-French dining room was spacious and attractive, and the menu offered a limited but well-rounded, creative selection. After a leisurely dinner we adjourned to the lively bar for a nitecap.

DAY TWO: Bleary-eyed, we greeted the still-blackened sky for our drive southward to join other early-rising adventurers for hot air ballooning. The drive was peaceful and serene as the morning dew sparkled under the rising sun. Balloon Aviation of Napa was our host and as they readied our craft for takeoff, we enjoyed a picnic brunch. Except for the bursts of flame releasing hot air into the balloon, it was incredibly peaceful. What a beautiful sight—a "must"

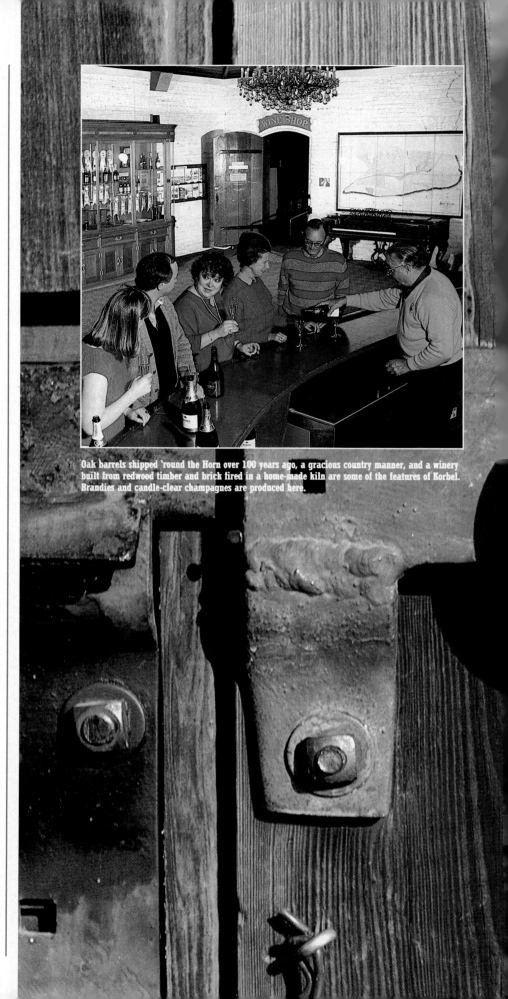

Oak barrels shipped 'round the Horn over 100 years ago, a gracious country manner, and a winery built from redwood timber and brick fired in a home-made kiln are some of the features of Korbel. Brandies and candle-clear champagnes are produced here.

Founded by Agoston Haraszthy, the father of California wine, Buena Vista Winery was the first to make sparkling wine in California. Haraszthy' dramatic contribution to the California wine industry included the acquiring of cuttings of fine grape varieties from Germany, France and Italy. The resulting nursery stocks provided extensive vineyards for his own use and dozens of other growers throughout the North Coast Counties. It is quite possible that some of the winery's Zinfandel vines are originals planted by Haraszthy between 1860 and 1880.

for any visitor.

Within walking distance of the ballooning office, we discovered a special bed-and-breakfast inn, Beazley House, one of the most delightful inns in the Wine Country and a perfect spot to stay prior to ballooning.

Time did not permit us to enjoy a carriage ride and tour of neighboring wineries. Instead, we drove to Inglenook for a most memorable winetasting. This imposing structure, whose name translates to "cozy corner," was built a century ago by Captain Niebaum, whose lavish care of his vineyard is now legendary.

Wine does stimulate the appetite. Famished, we moved on to one of Northern California's most honored restaurants, Auberge du Soleil. Having glimpsed Auberge on TV's *Falcon Crest*, we were eager to sample food which critics consistently give top honors. The atmosphere was sublime and the food was poetry—each dish demanding superlatives and raves. If you're to have only one grand meal while visiting, let it be here. It is worth every drachma!

After such a repast, we were tempted to nap beneath a nearby oak tree but devotedly pressed on in our quest for perfection.

Joseph Phelps is one of many outstanding boutique wineries, producing superior wines. This facility was striking, the Chardonnay superior.

A stop at Beringer gave us a chance to tour the cool dark caves where wines are aged. The aromas were maddeningly tantalizing but not fullfilling until we sampled a supreme port in the attractive tasting room.

The last stop of the day was Silverado Country Club. This grand dame of resorts reposes in a majestic setting of manicured grounds lush with flowers and towering trees. Its grandeur befits the tastes of the most affluent, and the resulting atmosphere is restrained and hushed. Our meal was on a par with Auberge and the dining

For the serious gourmet and gourmand, Auberge du Soleil offers world-class French cuisine. Opened less than two years ago, Auberge is one of the dining highlights of the Wine Country. Reservations should be made well in advance.

DID YOU KNOW THAT STANFORD PLAYED IN THE FIRST ROSE BOWL GAME?

Painting by Robert Childress

STANFORD VS. MICHIGAN, PASADENA, JANUARY 1, 1902.

Who would have dreamed at that small 1902 event that one day another football classic, Super Bowl XIX, would be played in Stanford's own stadium, before 85,000 spectators and more than 100 million television-watchers?

As you can see, football is a long and cherished tradition at Stanford, along with an academic tradition that ranks Stanford as one of the world's great universities.

A super setting for Super Bowl XIX.

INVITATION FROM A STANFORD NEIGHBOR.*

During your Bay Area stay, come and visit the home and colorful gardens of Sunset Magazine, Books, and Films, just a few blocks east of Stanford Stadium.

Sunset is the popular Magazine of Western Living for more than 5 million discriminating Westerners, and Sunset Books are read by millions more around the world.

*Actually, Stanford and Sunset are more than neighbors. They are related by heritage. Leland Stanford, who founded the University, was one of the Big Four who built the Southern Pacific Railroad. The railroad, in turn, founded Sunset Magazine (in 1898) to encourage travel to the West.

Later, Sunset employees bought the publication, and in 1928, with its purchase by the Lane family, Sunset became the Magazine of Western Living.

SUNSET

NOVEMBER 1903
Thanksgiving Number

Lane Publishing Co., Menlo Park, California 94025

Magazine ◆ Books ◆ Films

Visitors are welcome every weekday (except holidays) from 10:30 to 3:00

Hacienda Winery's delectable wines on display

Hanns Kornell—one of two original champagne specialists in the Napa Valley

Gracious estate living at Spring Mountain Winery

Buena Vista's large tasting room features ever-changing art exhibits.

Every day for weeks a riddler turns each bottle to coax the yeast into the neck.

At Domaine Chandon you'll be treated to ambiance, good food and champagne.

A Sterling introduction for wishful oenophiles

Courtyard and fountain frame the historic Chateau St. Jean.

room with grand piano and twinkling chandeliers was resplendent. Others in our group stayed at Holiday Inn Napa, where every amenity was provided and the decor was lovely.

DAY THREE: After a hearty country breakfast we rendezvoused at Sterling, an imposing hilltop structure often mistaken for a monastery. To traverse the hillside, we boarded a tram for a picturesque ride to the top. The views were breathtaking and the building's arrangement permitted self-guided tours.

Though it was closed, we were anxious to see the home and grounds of Schramsburg, where highly respected champagne is produced and aged in a catacomb of tunnels burrowed into the hillside.

That night we opted to stay at the new Harvest Inn, an English Tudor complex nestled amid a working vineyard. Our rooms were charming, decorated with antiques and a fireplace—a perfect end to a perfect day. Dinner at Le Rhone in St. Helena proved to be another extraordinary dining experience. The prix fixe menu tantalized our tastebuds and the service was impeccable.

DAY FOUR: On this morning we leisurely drove north and stopped at Oakville Grocery to browse among displays brimming with delicacies from around the world. This is one of *the* spots for assembling picnic fare, and picnics are a Wine Country tradition. From truffles to pastries, quail eggs to pate, cheeses to pasta salads—it's all here, and more. But this day we dined alfresco at Meadowood Country Club, which has it all in the way of accommodations and cuisine. This is a popular spot with local residents as evidenced by the presence of Robert Mondavi and guests. However, since our visit, a fire destroyed much of the lodge and it is now closed for rebuilding.

After lunch we toured Hanns Kornell Cellars where racks of

Limousines and exotic cars are commonplace at the Sonoma Mission Inn, one of Northern California's most luxurious resorts.

Above and *below:* The majestic Madrona Manor, built in 1881, now serves as an elegant country retreat for visitors to Sonoma County. Few inns offer such pristine charm and atmosphere.

bottles are "riddled" (a process of systematic turning) by hand during the final stages of aging.

For four days we were "flying high," so it is fitting that we visited Calistoga Soaring Center for a first-time flight in a sailplane. Towed aloft by a small plane, sweaty palms were replaced by exhilaration and joy as we soared and circled above the hills and became one with the environment. It's a thrill we hope to recapture again and again.

From lofty heights to depths of rejuvenating mud, and all in one hour! The Golden Haven Spa ushered us into mud baths where we submerged for the "cure". It was a most unusual experience that left the skin silky smooth. We moved from mud to a steamy mineral jacuzzi pool and then to a table where strong, skilled hands tugged and kneaded every last ounce of tension from our bodies. We collapsed into our limousine, grateful that we had left the driving to someone else. Before long we arrived at the chic Sonoma Mission Inn, a resort and spa attracting the beautiful people from throughout the country.

After removing the last vestiges of mud and minerals, we dined sumptuously at Provencal, the inn's splendid restaurant. Others in our party stayed at the Sonoma Hotel and reported good food and Victorian elegance. Their special find was Fantasie au Chocolat, a dessert establishment of decadent and caloric proportions.

DAY FIVE: Sonoma Cheese Factory was the perfect introduction to cheesemaking and sampling, and owner Dave Viviani was a most cordial host.

Nearby, Hacienda Winery produces wonderful premium wines. The lone picnic table in the lovely garden gave us the perfect excuse to pause and sample our cheese and an aromatic, velvety Cabernet.

When we arrived at Buena Vista, we had no idea we were in for an outrageously good time. It proved to be the absolute highlight of our

Sonoma Cheese Factory is one of California's leading makers of Jack cheese. The cheese is made by scooping curds into muslin, then shaping the curds into wheels for several weeks of aging. The factory dates back to the 1940s and boasts a complete deli for picnic fare.

Outdoor wine-tasting at Sterling Vineyards becomes a companionable interlude of leisurely conversation and quiet contemplation of the gracious countryside.

Three-pound and ten-pound wheels of Jack cheese are stored in a refrigerated room where they are systematically turned to maintain their shape throughout aging. The Sonoma Cheese Factory has a ten-minute slide show on their cheese making process.

Wealthy bon vivant and man about town lands in Napa in his private craft and is met by his waiting limousine. Many visitors travel to the Wine Country by private planes.

tasting room experiences.

The afternoon was spent touring Jack London Park where London lived and worked at the turn of the century. The old ranch house has been turned into a museum offering a glimpse of the author's life.

In the evening we joined our new friends from Buena Vista for a mesquite-grilled dinner at Mustards, a popular new establishment in the Napa Valley.

Additional dining recommendations include Au Relais (Sonoma), La Belle Helene and Rose Et Le Favour (St. Helena), La Boucane (Napa) and Las Parrillas (Cotati).

Our trip had been a series of days filled with pleasure, relaxation, beauty and fun. And yet, we had only scratched the surface. One thing is certain, you can successfully improvise in your touring plans and be confident that your discoveries will be a marvelous adventure. But if a private customized tour is more to your liking, contact Linda Viviani Touring Company (707)938-2100.

Either way, a visit to the wine country—though last in our sequence of scenic tours—will be a long-remembered highlight of your travels.

Whether you come to Super Bowl XIX or postpone the pleasures of Northern California to some later time, we hope our words and pictures will help make your visit a memorable experience.

Meanwhile, when the blizzards blitz New England or heatwaves hug the Midwest, return to these pages for a refreshing breath of San Francisco salt air, a swish of skis on sunny Sierra slopes, a sense of history at Sutter's Fort in Sacramento.

Anticipate the unique grandeur of Yosemite's peaks and valleys, the heady mixture of show biz and luck-busting at Lake Tahoe's busy casinos, the surfside flight of a well-aimed drive up the 18th fairway at Pebble Beach.

It's all here, waiting, just as we've promised you!

Simi Winery has been restored to its ancient prominence.

For small groups, the private tasting room at Buena Vista is superior.

Sonoma-Mission Inn is home to one of California's newest up-and-coming spas.

The spa offers every amenity for men and women.

Restored to its original splendor, the Sonoma Hotel is a little-known gem.

The Harvest Inn, an English Tudor-style collection of cottages in a vineyard

Meadowood is both a residence and vacation spot with an emphasis on sports

Mesquite-grilling is Mustard's specialty.

Souvereign is one of the few wineries where one can dine in a vineyard.

Beringer features caves dating back to 1877 and a lovely tasting room.

Calistoga's Mount View Hotel oozes art deco charm and excellent cuisine.

The Bale Grist Mill is a historical landmark dating back to 1846.

An outstanding boutique winery—Joseph Phelps

Delicacies from throughout the world are available at the Oakville Grocery.

TRAIL OF THE GRAPE

Robert Louis Stevenson Park

29

Chateau Montelena

Aetna Springs

Pope Valley

Lake Berryessa

Robert Pecota

Calistoga Mud Baths

Calistoga

Pope Valley

Sterling

Cuvaison

Burgess Cellars

Schramsberg

tony Hill

St. Helena Wine Co.

Deer Park
Road

Angwin

Pope Valley Road

Freemark Abbey

Round Hill

Burnham

Green and Red

Chaslen Bros.

Rustler

Christian Brothers

Chaffes Pope Valley Road

Lower Chiles
Valley Road

Mirinini

Joseph Phelps

St. Helena

Napa Creek

Sutter Home

Louis Martini

Nichelini

Raymond

128

Franciscan

Beaulieu

Grgich Hills Cellars

Long

Inglenook

Niebaum Coppola

Chappellet

Rutherford

Robert Mondavi Winery

Lakewood

128

Silver Oak

Oakville

Oakville Grade

Napa Wine Cellars

Hacienda
Sonoma Vista

Napa Balloon Rides

S. Ishikawa '84

DINING DIRECTORY

American

Bette's Ocean View Diner
1807A Fourth Street (415)644-3230
Berkeley
Reservations not accepted
WA B/L/D Inexpensive

British Banker's Club
1090 El Camino Real (415)327-8769
Menlo Park
V MC AE DC CB Reservations rcmd
BAR L/D Moderate

Cafe Americain
317 Columbus Avenue (415)981-8266
San Francisco
V MC Reservations recommended
WA L/D Moderate

Campton Place Restaurant
90 Campton Place (415)781-5155
San Francisco
V MC AE DC CB Reservations accepted
WA BAR B/L/D Expensive

Casa Madrona Hotel & Restaurant
801 Bridgeway (415)331-5888
Sausalito
V MC AE DC Reservations accepted
D Moderate to expensive

Chez Panisse
1517 Shattuck Avenue (415)548-5525
Berkeley
Reservations required
WA D Expensive

Christy Hill Restaurant & Inn
1650 Squaw Valley Road (916)583-8551
Squaw Valley
V MC AE Reservations accepted
WA D/Br Expensive

The Courtyard Bar & Restaurant
2436 Clement (415)387-7616
San Francisco
V MC AE DC CB Reservations accepted
WA BAR L/D Inexpensive to moderate

Doidge's Kitchen
2217 Union Street (415)921-2149
San Francisco
V MC Reservations accepted
WA B/L Inexpensive

Fatapple's
1346 Martin Luther King Blvd.
Berkeley (415)526-2260
Reservations not accepted
WA B/L/D Moderate

Fat City Bar & Cafe
1001 Front (916)446-6768
Sacramento
V MC
WA BAR D/Br Moderate

JoAnn's
1131 El Camino Real (415)872-2810
South San Francisco
Reservations not accepted
B/L/Br Inexpensive

Lehr's Greenhouse Restaurant
740 Sutter (415)474-6478
San Francisco
V MC AE Reservations accepted
WA BAR L/D/Br Moderate

Madrona Manor
1001 Westside Road (707)433-4231
Healdsburg
V MC AE Reservations accepted
WA D/Br Expensive

Mustard's Grill
7399 Saint Helena's Highway
Yountville (707)944-2424
V MC Reservations accepted
WA L/D Moderate

Perry's
Mill Valley (415)383-9300
San Francisco (415)922-9022
V MC AE Reservations accepted
WA BAR B/L/D Moderate

Provencal Bar & Grill
18140 Sonoma Hwy (707)938-4953
Boys Hot Springs
V MC AE DC CB Reservations rcmd
WA BAR ENT L/D Moderate

Royal Oak
Silverado Country Club & Resort
1600 Atlas Peak Road (707)257-0200
Napa
V MC AE Reservations required
WA BAR L/D Expensive

San Benito House
356 Main Street (415)726-3425
Half Moon Bay
V MC Reservations recommended
WA BAR L/D/Br Moderate

Santa Fe Bar & Grill
1310 University Avenue (415)841-4740
Berkeley
V MC AE Reservations accepted
WA BAR ENT L/D Moderate to expensive

Skywood Restaurant
Skyline Blvd. & Woodside Road
Woodside (415)851-7444
V MC AE DC Reservations required
WA BAR ENT D Moderate

The Squirrel's Nest
Highway 89 (916)525-7944
Homewood
Reservations accepted
WA L Summer only Moderate

Steven Lake Tahoe
341 Ski Way (702)832-0222
Incline Village
V MC AE DC CB Rsvns accepted
WA BAR ENT D/Br Moderate

Ventana Restaurant
Highway 1 (408)667-2332
Big Sur
V MC AE DC Reservations rcmd
WA BAR ENT L/D Moderate to expensive

Vintner's Court
Silverado Country Club & Resort
1600 Atlas Peak Rd. (707)257-0200
V MC AE Reservations required
WA BAR ENT D/Br Expensive

Zuni Cafe
1658 Market (415)552-2522
San Francisco
Reservations accepted
WA BAR L/D Moderate

Chinese

China Camp
1015 Front, (916)441-7966
Sacramento
V MC Reservations accepted
WA BAR L/D Moderate

China Moon
(415)863-6666
San Francisco
To open in 1985

The Chinese Village
950 North Lake Boulevard
Tahoe City (916)583-1895
V MC Reservations accepted
L/D Moderate

B - Breakfast L - Lunch D - Dinner Br - Brunch V - VISA MC - MasterCard AE - American Express DC - Diners' Club
CB - Carte Blanche WA - Wheelchair Access BAR - Full Service Bar ENT - Entertainment Rsvns - Reservations rcmd - recommended

The Mandarin
900 North Point Street
San Francisco (415)673-8812
V MC AE DC CB Rsvns accepted
WA BAR L/D Expensive

Red's
1475 Polk (415)441-7337
San Francisco
V MC AE Reservations accepted
WA BAR ENT L/D Moderate

Szechuan Flower
180 E. 4th Avenue (415)344-6831
San Mateo
V MC AE DC Reservatins rcmd
WA BAR L/D Moderate

Tien Fu
1395 Noriega (415)665-1064
San Francisco
V MC Reservations accepted
L/D Inexpensive

Tsing Tao
3107 Clement (415)387-2344
San Francisco
V MC DC Reservations accepted
WA L/D Inexpensive

Yank Sing
427 Battery (415)362-1640
San Francisco
V MC AE DC CB Rsvns accepted
WA BAR L/D Moderate

Continental

Adele's Restaurant & Lounge
1112 N. Carson (916)882-3353
Carson City
V MC Reservations not accepted
WA BAR L/D Expensive

Ahwahnee Hotel
Yosemite (209)372-1488 or 1489
Yosemite National Park
V MC AE DC CB Rsvns required
WA BAR ENT L/D/Br Moderate to exp

Alta Mira Hotel
Bulkley Avenue (415)332-1350
Sausalito
V MC AE DC CB Rsvns accepted
BAR B/L/D/Br Moderate to expensive

Andre's Restaurant of Carmel
3770 The Barnyard (408)625-0447
Carmel
V MC AE Reservations recommended
WA BAR ENT L/D Moderate to exp

The Blue Fox Restaurant
659 Merchant (415)981-1177
San Francisco
V MC AE DC CB Rsvns accepted
BAR D Expensive

Calcutta Cricket Club
1380 Old Bayshore Hwy.
Burlingame (415)347-5444
V MC AE DC CB Reservations rcmd
WA BAR L/D Moderate to expensive

Caprice Restaurant
2000 Paradise Drive (415)435-3400
Tiburon
V MC AE DC CB Reservations rcmd
WA BAR L/D Moderate to expensive

The Castaway
Coyote Point Drive (415)347-1027
San Mateo
V MC AE DC CB Rsvns accepted
WA BAR L/D/Br Moderate to expensive

C.B. Whites
Commercial Row—West End
Truckee (916)587-4364
V MC AE DC CB Rsvns accepted
WA D/Br Moderate

The Covey (at Quail Lodge)
8205 Valley Greens Drive
Carmel (408)624-1581
V MC AE DC CB Rsvns required
WA BAR ENT D Expensive

Dartanian's
1655 Saratoga-Sunnyvale Road
Cupertino (408)257-1120
V MC AE Reservations recommended
WA BAR ENT L/D Moderate to expensive

Fandango Restaurant
223 17th Street (408)373-0588
Pacific Grove
V MC Reservations accepted
WA ENT B/L/D/Br Moderate

The Firehouse
1112 2nd Street (916)442-4772
Sacramento
V MC AE Reservations rcmd
WA BAR L/D Moderate to expensive

Fournou's Ovens
905 California (415)989-1910
San Francisco
V MC AE DC CB Rsvns accepted
WA BAR ENT L/D Expensive

Gregory's Stonehouse Restaurant
2999 Highway 68 (408)373-3175
Monterey
V MC AE DC CB Reservations rcmd
BAR L/D/Br Expensive

Josephine's
924 Presidio Avenue (415)495-0457
San Francisco
V MC AE DC Reservations accepted
WA ENT L/D/Br Moderate

Lark Creek Inn
234 Magnolia (415)924-7766
Larkspur
V MC AE DC CB Reservations rcmd
BAR L/D/Br Moderate

Mama's of San Francisco
1177 California Street (415)928-1004
San Francisco (7 other locations)
V MC AE Reservations accepted
WA BAR ENT B/L/D Moderate

Nathan's Restaurant
1100 Burlingame Ave. (415)347-1414
Burlingame
V MC AE DC CB Rsvns accepted
WA BAR L/D Moderate

Old Bath House Restaurant
620 Ocean View Blvd. (408)375-5195
Pacific Grove
V MC AE DC CB Reservations rcmd
BAR D/Br Expensive

Paolo's Restaurant
520 E. Santa Clara (408)294-2558
San Jose
V MC AE DC CB Reservations rcmd
WA BAR L/D Moderate to expensive

Ruby's
500 Brannan (415)495-0457
San Francisco
V MC AE DC Reservations accepted
WA ENT L/D/Br Moderate to expensive

The Sardine Factory
701 Wave Street (408)373-3775
Monterey
V MC AE DC CB Reservations rcmd
WA BAR L/D Expensive

Scotty Campbell's
2907 El Camino Real (415)369-3773
Redwood City
V MC AE DC CB Rsvns accepted
WA BAR ENT D Moderate

The Summit
18th Floor of Harrah's (702)588-6611
Stateline Nevada
V MC AE DC CB Rsvns accepted
BAR ENT D Expensive

Swiss Lakewood Lodge
5055 West Lake Blvd.
Homewood (916)525-5211
V MC AE Reservations accepted
WA BAR D Expensive

Tuba Garden
3634 Sacramento (415)921-8882
San Francisco
V MC AE DC CB Rsvns accepted
L Moderate

Villa Chartier Restaurant
4060 S. El Camino Real
San Mateo (415)341-3456
V MC AE DC CB Rsvns accepted
WA BAR ENT L/D Moderate

Creole

The Elite Cafe
2049 Filmore (415)346-8668
San Francisco
Reservations not accepted
WA BAR D/Br Moderate

The Gingerbread House
741 Fifth Street (415)444-7373
Oakland
V MC AE DC CB Rsvns required
ENT L/D Moderate to expensive

B - Breakfast L - Lunch D - Dinner Br - Brunch V - VISA MC - MasterCard AE - American Express DC - Diners' Club
CB - Carte Blanche WA - Wheelchair Access BAR - Full Service Bar ENT - Entertainment Rsvns - Reservations rcmd - recommended

Delis, Groceries, Cafes

De Young Museum Cafe
Golden Gate Park (415)752-0116
San Francisco
Reservations not accepted Wed-Sun 10-4
WA L Inexpensive

**G.B. Ratto and Company,
International Grocery**
821 Washington St. (415)832-6503
Oakland M-F 11am-2pm
WA Inexpensive

Oakville Grocery
San Francisco (415)885-4411
Oakville (707)944-8802
V MC VA
M-F(10-7)Sat(10-6)Sun(10-5)Moderate

Vivande Porta Via
(gourmet carryout)
2125 Filmore (415)346-4430
San Francisco
V MC AE DC CB
M-F(10-7)Sat(10-6)Sun(10-5)Moderate

Desserts

Cocolat
1481 Shattuck Ave. (415)843-3265
*Berkeley (other locations in SF, Stanford
Oakland) V MC*
WA M-Sat (10-6) Sun (11-5) Moderate

Fantasie au Chocolat
40 West Spain St. (707)938-2020
Sonoma (Yountville location also)
V MC Reservations not accepted
WA M-Sun (10-5:30) Moderate

Gelato Ice Cream
7 locations
San Francisco
WA 12pm to 11 pm

English

Tuck Box English Tea Room
Dolores between Ocean and 7th
Carmel (408)624-6365
Reservations not accepted
B/L/Tea Moderate

The Village Green
89 Avenue Portola (415)726-3690
El Granada
V MC
WA B/L/Saturday dinner Inexpensive

French

Alouette French Restaurant
401 Lytton Avenue (415)327-4187
Palo Alto
V MC Reservations recommended
WA L/D Moderate

Auberge du Soleil
180 Rutherford Hill Road
Rutherford (707)963-1211
V MC AE Reservations required
WA BAR L/D Expensive

Au Chambertin Restaurant
170 State Street (415)948-8721
Los Altos
V MC AE DC CB Reservations rcmd
WA BAR L/D Moderate to expensive

Au Relais Restaurant
691 Broadway (707)996-1031
Sonoma
V MC AE Reservations rcmd
WA BAR L/D/Br Moderate to expensive

Cafe Mozart
708 Bush (415)391-8480
San Francisco
V MC AE Reservations accepted
WA D Expensive

**The California Culinary Academy
Restaurant,** *215 Fremont*
San Francisco (415)546-1316
V MC AE Reservations required
WA L/D Expensive

Camargue Grill et Rotisserie
2316 Polk (415)776-5577
San Francisco
V MC
WA D Moderate

Casanova
5th between San Carlos & Mission
Carmel (408)625-0501
V MC
WA B/L/D/Br Moderate to expensive

Chez Lyliane
6731 North Lake Blvd. (916)546-2766
Tahoe Vista
V MC Reservations recommended
D Moderate

Chez Michel
804 North Point (415)771-6077
San Francisco
V MC Reservations recommended
BAR D Expensive

Chez Serge
3670 The Barnyard (408)625-5011
Carmel
V MC AE Reservations accepted
WA L/D/Br Moderate

Christophe Restaurant Francais
1919 Bridgeway (415)332-9244
Sausalito
V MC DC Reservations required
L/D Expensive

Coquelicot
23 Ross Common (415)461-4782
Ross
V MC Reservations accepted
WA L/D Moderate to expensive

Emile's
545 S. 2nd Street (408)289-1960
San Jose
V MC AE DC CB Rsvns required
WA BAR L/D Expensive

464 Magnolia
464 Magnolia (415)924-6831
Larkspur
V MC AE DC CB Reservations rcmd
WA L/D/Br Moderate

The French Room
Four Seasons Clift Hotel, Geary & Taylor
San Francisco (415)775-4700
V MC AE DC CB Reservations rcmd
WA BAR ENT B/L/D/Br Expensive

Fresh Cream Restaurant
100 Pacific Street at Heritage Harbor
Monterey (408)375-9798
V MC Reservations required
WA D Expensive

La Belle Helene
1345 Railroad Avenue (707)963-9984
St. Helena
V MC AE Reservations accepted
L/D Moderate to expensive

La Bonne Auberge
2075 S. El Camino (415)341-2525
San Mateo
V MC Reservations required
D Moderate

La Boucane
1778 2nd Street (707)253-1177
Napa
V MC AE Reservations recommened
D Closed January Moderate to expensive

La Bourgogne
330 Mason (415)362-7352
San Francisco
V MC AE DC CB Rsvns accepted
WA BAR D Expensive

La Cheminee Restaurant
8504 North Lake Blvd. (916)546-4322
Kings Beach
V MC AE Reservations required
D Expensive

La Reserve
60 E. 3rd Avenue, 2nd Floor
San Mateo (415)348-1881
V MC AE DC CB Rsvns accepted
WA BAR L/D Moderate to expensive

La Vieille Maison
Highway 267 at River Street
Truckee (916)587-2421
V MC AE Reservations recommended
D Moderate to expensive

Le Castel
3235 Sacramento (415)921-7115
San Francisco
V MC AE Reservations required
WA D Expensive

Le Chardonnay
6534 Washington Street (707)944-2521
Yountville
V MC AE Reservations recommended
WA l/D Closed Jan Moderate to exp.

Le Club
1250 Jones (514)771-5400
San Francisco
V MC AE DC CB Rsvns accepted
WA BAR D Expensive

Le Petit Pier
7250 North Lake Blvd. (916)546-4464
Tahoe Vista
V MC AE DC CB Rsvns required
WA BAR D Expensive

Le Rhone
1234 Main (707)963-0240
St. Helena
Reservations required
WA D Expensive

L'Escargot
Mission & 4th (408)624-4914
Carmel
V MC AE Reservations recommended
WA D Moderate

Le St. Tropez
126 Clement (415)387-0408
San Francisco
V MC AE Reservations accepted
WA BAR D Moderate to expensive

Le Vaudville
39 A Grove (415)861-0788
San Francisco
V MC Reservations accepted
WA L/D Expensive

Marquis Restaurant
San Carlos & 4th (408)624-8068
Carmel
V MC AE Reservations recommended
D Moderate

Masa's
648 Bush (415)989-7154
San Francisco
V MC AE Reservations required
WA BAR D Expensive

Maurice et Charles Bistrot
901 Lincoln Avenue (415)456-2010
San Rafael
V MC AE Reservations required
WA D Expensive

Mirabeau Restaurant
344 20th Street (415)834-6575
Oakland
V MC AE DC CB Rsvns accepted
WA BAR ENT L/D Expensive

Miramonte
1327 Railroad Avenue (707)963-3970
St. Helena
Reservations required
WA D Expensive

Mount View Hotel
1457 Lincoln Avenue (707)942-6877
Calistoga
V MC Reservations accepted
WA BAR B/L/D Moderate to expensive

Ondine
558 Bridgeway (415)332-0791
Sausalito
V MC AE DC CB Reservations rcmd
BAR D Expensive

Pear William's
150 Middlefield Rd. (415)323-8445
Menlo Park
V MC DC Reservations accepted
WA L/D/Br Moderate

The Plumed Horse
14555 Big Bason Way
Saratoga (408)867-4711
V MC AE DC CB Rsvns accepted
WA BAR ENT D Expensive

Rose et LeFavour
1420 Main Street (707)963-1681
St. Helena
Reservations required
WA L/D Expensive

Sans Souci Restaurant
Lincoln between 5th and 6th
Carmel (408)624-6220
V MC AE Reservations recommended
D Moderate

Souverain Restaurant
400 Souverain Rd. (707)433-3141
Geyserville
V MC AE Reservations accepted
WA L/D/Br Moderate to expensive

Triples
220 Olivier Street (408)372-4744
Monterey
V MC AE DC CB Rsvns accepted
L/D Moderate to expensive

Victoria Emmons Restaurant
2699 Middlefield Road
Palo Alto (415)325-4721
V MC Reservations accepted
WA L/D Moderate

German

The Pine Brook Inn
1015 Alameda de Las Pulgas
Belmont (415)591-1735
V MC Reservations recommended
WA BAR ENT L/D/Br Moderate

Indian

Gaylord India Restaurant
317 Stanford Shopping Center
Stanford (415)326-8761
V MC AE DC CB Reservations rcmd
WA BAR L/D/Br Moderate to expensive

The Peacock Restaurant
2800 Van Ness Avenue (415)928-7001
San Francisco
V MC AE DC DB Reservations rcmd
WA BAR L/D Moderate

Taj Mahal
2355 Arden Way (916)924-8378
Sacramento
V MC AE DC
ENT L/D Moderate

Italian

Avanti Pasta Cafe
397 Main (415)941-4256
Los Altos
V MC AE Reservations accepted
WA BAR L/D Moderate

Caffe Sport
574 Green (415)981-1251
San Francisco
BAR D Moderate to expensive

Ciao
230 Jackson St. (415)982-9500
San Francisco
V MC AE Reservations required
BAR L/D Moderate

Donatello Ristorante
501 Post at Mason, Pacific Plaza Hotel
San Francisco (415)441-7182
V MC AE DC CB Reservations required
WA BAR B/L/D Expensive

Giramonti Restaurant
655 Redwood Hwy (415)383-3000
Mill Valley
V MC Reservations required
WA D Moderate to expensive

Gold Street Restaurant & Bar
56 Gold Street (415)397-4653
San Francisco
V MC AE DC CB Reservations rcmd
WA BAR ENT L/D Moderate

La Pergola Ristorante
2060 Chestnut (415)563-4500
San Francisco
V MC Reservations recommended
D Moderate to expensive

Modesto Lazone's
601 Van Ness, Opera Plaza
San Francisco (415)928-0400
V MC AE DC CB Rsvns accepted
WA BAR L/D Expensive

Raffaello Restaurant
Mission between Ocean & 7th
Carmel (408)624-1541
V MC Reservations recommended
WA D Moderate to expensive

B - Breakfast L - Lunch D - Dinner Br - Brunch V - VISA MC - MasterCard AE - American Express DC - Diners' Club
CB - Carte Blanche WA - Wheelchair Access BAR - Full Service Bar ENT - Entertainment Rsvns - Reservations rcmd - recommended

Vercelli's
331 Hacienda (408)374-3400
Campbell
V MC AE DC CB Reservations rcmd
WA BAR ENT L/D Expensive

Washington Square Bar & Grill
1707 Powell (415)982-8123
San Francisco
V MC AE Reservations accepted
BAR L/D Moderate

Japanese

Benihana of Tokyo
1496 Old Bayshore Hwy (415)342-5202
Burlingame (2 locations in San Francisco)
V MC AE DC CB Rsvns accepted
WA BAR ENT L/D Moderate to expensive

Isobune Sushi (sushi bar)
San Francisco (415)563-1030
Burlingame (415)344-8433
V MC Reservations not accepted
WA L/D Moderate

Koharu Japanese Cuisine
47 East 4th Ave. (415)348-0654
San Mateo
V MC AE DC Reservations accepted
L/D Moderate

Nikko Sukiyaki (sushi)
Van Ness at Pine (415)474-7722
San Francisco
V MC AE DC CB Reservations rcmd
WA BAR L/D Moderate

Yoshida-Ya
2909 Webster (415)346-3431
San Francisco
V MC AE DC Reservations accepted
BAR D Expensive

Korean

Seoul Garden
372 Grand Ave. (415)563-7664
San Francisco
V MC AE DC CB Reservations rcmd
WA BAR L/D Moderate

Sorabol Restaurant
372 Grand Ave. (415)839-2288
Oakland
V MC AE DC CB Reservations rcmd
WA BAR L/D Moderate

Mexican

Cadillac Bar & Restaurant
1 Holland Court (415)543-8226
San Francisco
V MC AE DC CB
WA BAR ENT L/D Moderate

Cantina Los Tres Hombres
8791 North Lake Boulevard
Kings Beach (916)546-4052
V MC Reservations not accepted
WA BAR D Inexpensive

El Tapatio
475 Francisco Street (415)981-3018
San Francisco
V MC AE Reservations accepted
WA BAR ENT L/D Inexpensive to mod.

Jalapeno's
2033 Union Street (415)921-2210
San Francisco
V MC AE Reservations accepted
BAR L/D Inexpensive

Las Mananitas
850 Montgomery (415)434-2088
San Francisco
V MC AE DC Reservations required
BAR ENT L/D Moderate to expensive

Las Parrillas
7600 Commerce Blvd. (707)795-7600
Cotati
V MC
WA BAR ENT L/D Moderate

Pedro's
Palo Alto (415)324-1510
Santa Clara (408)496-6777
Los Gatos (408)354-7570
V MC WA BAR L/D Inexpensive

Seafood

Borel's
2951 Campus Drive (415)341-7464
San Mateo
V MC AE DC Reservations rcmd
WA BAR ENT L/Br Moderate

Ferry Plaza
1 Ferry Plaza (415)391-8403
San Francisco
V MC AE DC CB Reservations required
WA BAR L/D Moderate

Ketch Joanne
Johnson Pier, Pillar Point Harbor
Princeton-by-the-Sea (415)728-3747
V MC Reservations accepted
BAR ENT B/L/D Moderate

The Moss Beach Distillery
Beach and Ocean (415)728-5434
Moss Beach
V MC AE DC Rsvns not accepted
BAR ENT D/Br Moderate

Paul & Barbara's Fish Trap
130 Capistrano Road (415)728-7049
Princeton-by-the-Sea
Reservations not accepted
WA L/D Inexpensive to moderate

Princeton Inn
Capistrano Road & Prospect Road
Princeton-by-the-Sea (415)728-7311
V MC AE DC CB Reservations accepted
WA BAR ENT L/D Moderate

The Rusty Duck Restaurant & Saloon
500 Bercut (916)441-1191
Sacramento
V MC AE DC Reservations accepted
WA BAR ENT L/D/Br Moderate

Sam's Anchor Cafe
27 Main Street (415)435-4527
Tiburon
V MC Reservations not accepted
WA BAR L/D/Br Moderate

The Seafood & Beverage Company
Cliff House, 1090 Point Lobos Avenue
San Francisco (415)386-3330
V MC AE Reservations not accepted
BAR L/D/Br Moderate

The Waterfront Restaurant
Pier 7 on Embarcadero Blvd.
San Francisco (415)391-2696
V MC AE DC CB Rsvns accepted
WA BAR L/D/Br Moderate

Steak

Al's Place
Main Street (916)776-1800
Locke
Reservations not accepted
WA BAR L/D Moderate

The Cellar
4926 El Camino Real (415)964-0220
Los Altos
V MC AE DC Reservations accepted
WA BAR ENT L/D Moderate

Foster's Bighorn
143 Main (707)374-2511
Rio Vista
V MC
WA BAR L/D Inexpensive to moderate

The Garden City
360 South Saratoga Avenue
San Jose (408)244-3333
V MC AE DC CB Reservations accepted
WA BAR ENT L/D Moderate to expensive

Harris'
2100 Van Ness (415)673-1888
San Francisco
VA MC AE Reservations requested
WA BAR ENT L/D Moderate to expensive

Etc.

Alejandro's (Spanish)
1840 Clement Street (415)668-1184
San Francisco
V MC AE DC CB Reservations rcmd
WA BAR D Moderate

Archil's Restaurant (Russian)
3011 Steiner (415)921-2141
San Francisco
V MC Reservations recommended
WA D Moderate

Greens (Vegitarian)
Fort Mason Bldg. A (415)771-6222
San Francisco
V MC Reservations required
L/D/Br Moderate to expensive

Jack London's Bar & Bistro
San Carlos between 5th and 6th
Carmel (408)624-2336
V MC AE Reservations not accepted
WA BAR L/D Inexpensive

Khan Toke Thai House
5937 Geary Blvd. (415)668-6654
San Francisco
V MC AE Reservations accepted
ENT D Moderate

Mamounia (Moroccan)
4411 Balboa (415)742-6566
San Francisco
V MC Reservations recommended
WA D Moderate to expensive

Manka's Inverness Lodge (Czech.)
30 Callendar Way (415)669-1034
Inverness
V MC AE DC CB Reservations rcmd
B/D/Br Moderate to expensive

Mary Gulli's (Australian)
3661 Sacramento (415)931-5151
San Francisco
V MC AE Reservations accepted
WA D Moderate

Pasha (Moroccan)
1516 Broadway (415)885-4477
San Francisco
V MC AE DC Reservations accepted
WA BAR ENT D Moderate

Warszawa (Polish)
1730 Shattuck Ave. (415)841-5539
Berkeley
V MC Reservations accepted
D Moderate

B - Breakfast L - Lunch D - Dinner Br - Brunch V - VISA MC - MasterCard AE - American Express DC - Diners' Club
CB - Carte Blanche WA - Wheelchair Access BAR - Full Service Bar ENT - Entertainment Rsvns - Reservations rcmd - recommended

257

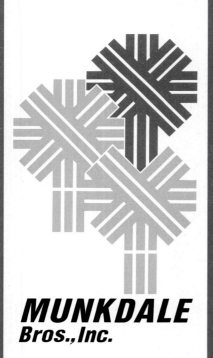

San Francisco is literally loaded with sushi bars. Among the best known is Isobune Japanese Restaurant.

photo: Gerald French

PERFECTION!
TOBACCO, CLOVES
HAND~ROLLED

NOW
AVAILABLE
IN
AMERICA

CREATED BY

 THE HOUSE OF SAMPOERNA

INDONESIA

Imported by:
George Bensen & Son, 1350 Van Dyke Ave. San Francisco Calif. 94124

260

"One of those lovely mist mornings of late spring when every flower in New Orleans seems to melt and mix with the air."

Lillian Hellman
An Unfinished Woman, 1969

teeped in a restless and mysterious past, New Orleans sprawls along the banks of the Mississippi River and remains a hub of shipping, economic and social growth in the South. The ambience and excitement present here have proven to be a major draw to the fans attending Super Bowls and will lure them again in January 1986.

With a history dating back to the early 1700s when the area became colonized by the French, and later the Spanish and Africans, the area brims with charm. Its rich cultural tapestry has survived a Civil War, Reconstruction and numerous battles. The city also served as the focal point for history's largest real estate deal—the Louisiana Purchase—which opened the way for a new Republic to win the West and expand its sphere of influence.

In many respects New Orleans is today as it was in the 1800s—steamboats still traverse the river, trolley cars still clamber over tree-lined streets, the Garden District and French Quarter remain as preserved relics from the past, and voodoo sorcery still can be found in dark recesses of the city.

To the visitor, New Orleans is a maze of streets whose names imply location, but aren't to be trusted; West End, for example, is East of East End. The city is filled with unusual sights, smells and sounds—cemeteries where the tombs are entirely above ground, bars that never close, a strange dialect called Cajun that sounds like a foreign tongue, steaming coffee with the distinctive aroma of chicory, pungent herbs—a plethora of pleasing stimuli for all the senses.

Of all the areas, the French Quarter is perhaps the most stimulating—a section of early New Orleans inhabited by the French, razed by fire and rebuilt by the Spaniards, and today one of America's most beloved tourism attractions.

The flavor of this district is

From shanties and cotton fields to smoke-filled rooms and the concert stage, jazz evolved from few joys and frequent blues to become America's most enduring musical art form.

NEW ORLEANS:
Mistress of Mystery

established in part by its architecture, with buildings flush to the sidewalk, inner courtyards and decorative ironwork that is graceful, light and airy. Of its architecture Mark Twain wrote "The houses are massed in blocks; are austerely plain and dignified; uniform of pattern, with here and there a departure from it with pleasing effect.... This charming decoration cannot be successfully imitated, neither is it to be found elsewhere in America."

There is old-world charm blended with the rowdy and raucous atmosphere of Bourbon Street. It was here that America's truest art form was born—JAZZ. This spirited music evolved as a means of expression for Negroes and is a fusion of their homeland folk music and the traditional European music they encountered when they came to New Orleans from Africa as slaves. It remained an obscure music form until WW I, when "swing" swept the country, and it has grown in world-wide popularity ever since. The city is rife with jazz clubs and performances by such "greats" as Pete Fountain, Al Hirt, and the venerable Preservation Hall Jazz Band.

A locally popular form of music gaining in international appeal is *bon temps zydeco*—Cajun music for the good times! Aficionados extoll the up-tempo delights of this music made for free-spirited dancing.

The cooking and restaurants are as notable as in San Francisco, but distinctive due to the link with other cultures and a 200-year refinement to what is now one of America's few native cuisines.

New Orleans is a gastronomical paradise, with recipes geared to ingredients indigenous to the area, especially succulent seafood and mouth-watering produce. Local specialties are derived from an incredibly mixed bag of culinary influences, and generally are referred to as "Creole" cuisine (referring to an association with native Louisianians born of Euro-

Historical homes and museums lend local ambience.

And never forget, everything revolves around Carnival.

Today's visitors encounter traditions of another era.

Iron lace adorns street-side buildings, reminiscent of a Spanish past.

Weddings, funerals, good times—any excuse for music and merriment

"Never forget what you really are, this beautiful old enchantress, this siren at the bend of the river, this New Orleans."

Jim Metcalf's Journal

Pleasures to the palate abound in all manner of charming locales.

Jackson Square—a focal point of local history

Cafe du Monde, where aromatic coffee and beignets are a tantalizing tradition

Chalmette brings alive one battlefield of a war-torn history.

Paddlewheelers represent the romance of New Orleans.

pean heritage). Gumbo, jambalaya, fried okra, bourbon-soaked lobster, Pompano en Papillote, Oysters Rockefeller, and red beans and rice are native to the area.

Pages of literature have been enhanced by the influences experienced by dozens of authors living in or visiting New Orleans. Cable, Twain, O. Henry, Whitman, Williams, Hellman, Faulkner, and Stein stand out on the long list of writers whose works reflect the influence of life in New Orleans.

At the site of Super Bowl XX, visitors to New Orleans will find a never-ending array of museums, restaurants, things to do, side trips, entertainment, and lodging equalled by few cities in America. Here the past survives in harmony with the present, to the delight of all who visit!

art by Terry Mollenauer

SUPER *STATS*

Introducing . . .

GRID GRAPH™

Football is a game of give-and-take, a territorial battle in which yards are gained and lost in the pursuit of points. Since its field dimensions are consistent from stadium to stadium, and its form of play is highly structured, a game of football can be plotted in diagram form. Coaches have long used various charts to measure player performance and play flow. Now, through a unique, sophisticated creation called GridGraph™, the editors and publishers of *Super Bowl by the Bay* make this same information available to the fan.

The following GridGraphs are designed to capture the color and action of Super Bowls I through XVIII, to show in vivid detail how they were played, and how they were won and lost. Competing teams in each game are represented by a series of lines in the predominant colors worn that day. Each *net* possession (encompassing running and passing plays, penalties, and recovered fumbles) is shown by a straight line (—). Net punts are illustrated by broken lines (– –) Net return yardage from kickoffs, punts, interceptions, blocked kicks, and recovered fumbles is signified by a wavy line (〜). The point from which a score is made is shown by (▲) for touchdown and (●) for field goal. Special occurrences such as missed field goals, lost fumbles, points of interception, blocked kicks, recovered on-side kicks, and safeties are marked on each diagram according to accompanying legends where they apply.

We hope that these GridGraphs will help fans see the game of football in a new light. Together with essential game information, scoring summaries, team and individual statistics, and Super Trivia questions to tax your football knowledge, they provide the most comprehensive account of Super Bowl history ever published.

First World Championship Game AFL vs NFL

Vince Lombardi 12-2

Hank Stram 11-2-1

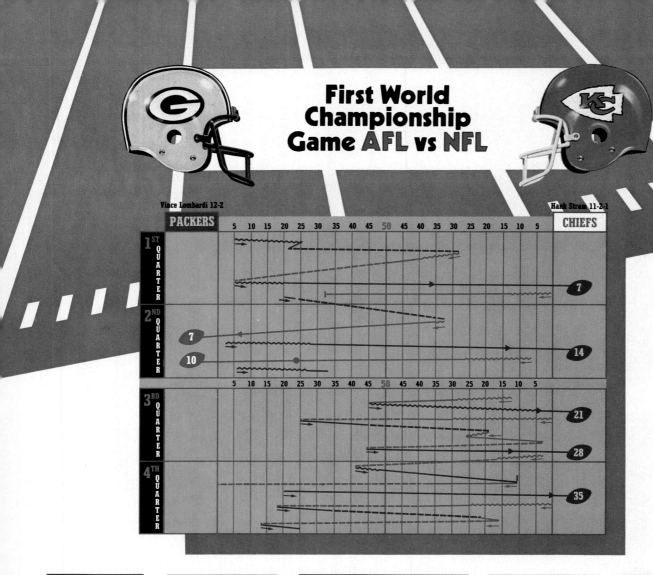

PACKERS

CHIEFS

TEAM STATISTICS

First Downs	21
Total Yards	358
Yards Rushing	130
Yards Passing	228
Penalties	4-40

January 15, 1967
Los Angeles Memorial
Coliseum
Los Angeles, California
1:00 p.m. PST
72 degrees, sunny
Attendance 61,946
Gross Receipts
$2,768,211.64
Winners' Shares $15,000
Losers' Shares $7,500

INDIVIDUAL STATISTICS

Rushing
J. Taylor	(1 TD) 16-53
Pitts	(2 TDs) 11-45
Anderson	4-30
Grabowski	2-2

Passing
Starr	16-23-250
	2 TD, 1 int.
Bratkowski	0-1-0

Receiving
McGee	(2 TDs) 7-138
Dale	4-59
Pitts	2-32
Fleming	2-22
J. Taylor	1-(-1)

Punting
| Chandler | 3-130 |
| Anderson | 1-43 |

Punt Returns
| Anderson | 3-25 |
| Wood | 1-(-2) |

Kickoff Returns
| Adderley | 2-40 |
| Anderson | 1-25 |

Interceptions
| Wood | 1-50 |

Fumbles Recovered
None

SCORING SUMMARY

Kansas City	0	10	0	0 - 10
Green Bay	7	7	14	7 - 35

GB - McGee 37 pass from Starr
(Chandler kick)
KC - McClinton 7 pass from
Dawson
(Mercer kick)
GB - Taylor 14 run
(Chandler kick)
KC - FG Mercer 31
GB - Pitts 5 run
(Chandler kick)
GB - McGee 13 pass from Starr
(Chandler kick)
GB - Pitts 1 run
(Chandler kick)

SUPER TRIVIA

1. Who is the only player to start
one Super Bowl on offense and
another on defense?

2. Name the six members of the
Green Bay Packers' starting
lineup in Super Bowl I who
eventually were enshrined in the
Pro Football Hall of Fame.

INDIVIDUAL STATISTICS

Rushing
Dawson	3-24
Garrett	6-17
McClinton	6-16
Beathard	1-14
Coan	3-1

Passing
Dawson	16-27-211
	1 TD, 1 int.
Beathard	1-5-17

Receiving
Burford	4-67
O. Taylor	4-57
Garrett	3-28
McClinton	(1 TD) 2-34
Arbanas	2-30
Carolan	1-7
Coan	1-5

Punting
| Wilson | 7-317 |

Punt Returns
| Garrett | 2-17 |
| E. Thomas | 1-2 |

Kickoff Returns
| Coan | 4-87 |
| Garrett | 2-43 |

Interceptions
| Mitchell | 1-0 |

Fumbles Recovered
None

TEAM STATISTICS

First Downs	17
Total Yards	239
Yards Rushing	72
Yards Passing	167
Penalties	4-26

PACKERS
Possession Punt Return

CHIEFS
Possession Punt Return

▲ = TOUCHDOWN
● = FIELD GOAL
I = INTERCEPTION
⌐ = MISSED FIELD GOAL

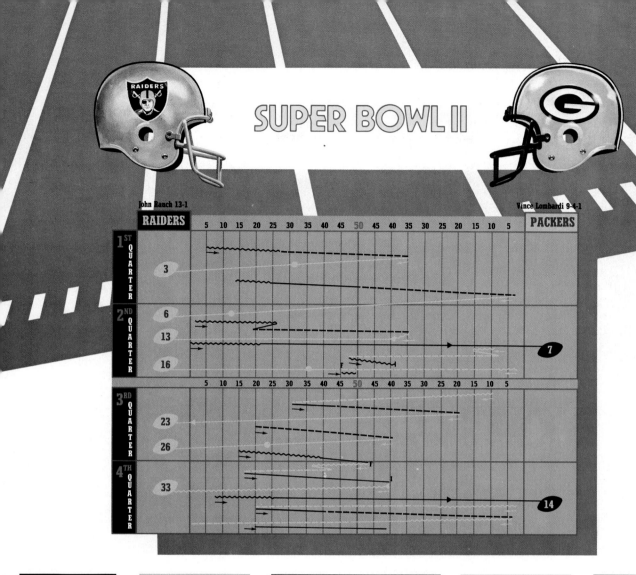

SUPER BOWL II

John Rauch 13-1

| RAIDERS | 5 10 15 20 25 30 35 40 45 **50** 45 40 35 30 25 20 15 10 5 | PACKERS |

Vince Lombardi 9-4-1

1ST QUARTER — 3

2ND QUARTER — 6, 13, 16 — 7

3RD QUARTER — 23, 26

4TH QUARTER — 33 — 14

TEAM STATISTICS

First Downs	16
Total Yards	293
Yards Rushing	107
Yards Passing	186
Penalties	4-31

January 14, 1968
Orange Bowl
Miami, Florida
3:00 p.m. EST
68 degrees, cloudy
Attendance 75,546
Gross Receipts
$3,349,106.89
Winners' Shares $15,000
Losers' Shares $7,500

INDIVIDUAL STATISTICS

Rushing
Dixon		12-54
Todd		2-37
Banaszak		6-16

Passing
Lamonica		15-34-208
		2 TD, 1 int.

Receiving
Miller	(2 TD)	5-84
Banaszak		4-69
Cannon		2-25
Biletnikoff		2-10
Wells		1-17
Dixon		1-3

Punting
Eisheid	6-264

Punt Returns
Bird	2-12

Kickoff Returns
Todd	3-63
Grayson	2-61
Hawkins	1-3
Kocourek	1-0

Interceptions
None

Fumbles Recovered
None

SCORING SUMMARY

Green Bay	3	13	10	7 -	33
Oakland	0	7	0	7 -	14

GB - FG Chandler 39
GB - FG Chandler 20
GB - Dowler 62 pass from Starr
(Chandler kick)
OK - Miller 23 pass from Lamonica
(Blanda kick)
GB - FG Chandler 43
GB - Anderson 2 run
(Chandler kick)
GB - FG Chandler 31
GB - Adderley 60 intercep. return
(Chandler kick)
OK - Miller 23 pass from Lamonica
(Blanda kick)

SUPER TRIVIA

3. Two assistant coaches from the Super Bowl II teams later became head coaches for their respective teams. Name them.

4. Who is the only man to play in a Super Bowl and, later, take a team to a Super Bowl as a head coach?

INDIVIDUAL STATISTICS

Rushing
Wilson		17-62
Anderson	(1 TD)	14-48
Williams		8-36
Starr		1-14
Mercein		1-0

Passing
Starr		13-24-202
		1 TD
Bratkowski		0-0-0

Receiving
Dale		4-43
Fleming		4-35
Dowler	(1 TD)	2-71
Anderson		2-18
McGee		1-35

Punting
Anderson	6-234

Punt Returns
Wood	5-35

Kickoff Returns
Adderley	1-24
Williams	1-18
Crutcher	1-7

Interceptions
Adderley	(1 TD)	1-60

Fumbles Recovered
Caffey	1-0
Robinson	1-16

TEAM STATISTICS

First Downs	19
Total Yards	322
Yards Rushing	160
Yards Passing	162
Penalties	1-12

RAIDERS
Possession   Punt   Return

PACKERS
Possession   Punt   Return

▲ = TOUCHDOWN
● = FIELD GOAL
I = INTERCEPTION
F = FUMBLE
⊣ = MISSED FIELD GOAL

SUPER BOWL III

Don Shula 13-1

Weeb Ewbank 11-3

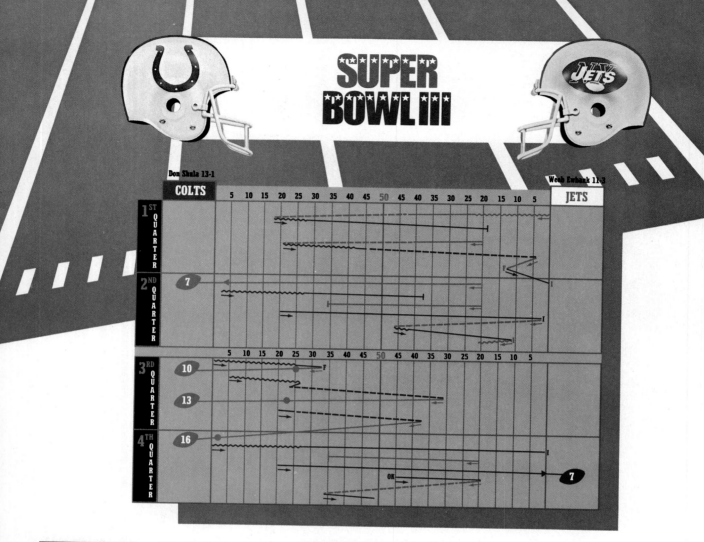

TEAM STATISTICS

First Downs	18
Total Yards	324
Yards Rushing	143
Yards Passing	181
Penalties	3-23

January 12, 1969
Orange Bowl
Miami, Florida
3:00 p.m. EST
73 degrees, overcast
Attendance 75,389
Gross Receipts
$3,374,985.64
Winners' Shares $15,000
Losers' Shares $7,500

INDIVIDUAL STATISTICS

Rushing
Matte	11-116
Hill	(1 TD) 9-29
Unitas	1-0
Morrall	2-(-2)

Passing
Unitas	11-24-110
	1 int.
Morrall	6-17-71
	3 int.

Receiving
Richardson	6-58
Orr	3-42
Mackey	3-35
Matte	2-30
Hill	2-1
Mitchell	1-15

Punting
| Lee | 3-133 |

Punt Returns
| Brown | 4-34 |

Kickoff Returns
| Pearson | 2-59 |
| Brown | 2-46 |

Interceptions
None

Fumbles Recovered
| Porter | 1-0 |

SCORING SUMMARY

New York Jets	0	7	6	3 - 16
Baltimore	0	0	0	7 - 7

NYJ - Snell 4 run
(Turner kick)
NYJ - FG Turner 32
NYJ - FG Turner 30
NYJ - FG Turner 9
BA - Hill 1 run
(Michaels kick)

SUPER TRIVIA

5. What New York sports figure was known as "Broadway Joe" several years before Joe Namath?

6. What university did Colts quarterback Johnny Unitas attend?

INDIVIDUAL STATISTICS

Rushing
Snell	(1 TD) 30-121
Boozer	10-19
Mathis	3-2

Passing
| Namath | 17-28-206 |
| Parilli | 0-1-0 |

Receiving
Sauer	8-133
Snell	4-40
Mathis	3-20
Lammons	2-13

Punting
| Johnson | 4-155 |

Punt Returns
| Baird | 1-0 |

Kickoff Returns
| Christy | 1-25 |

Interceptions
Beverly	2-0
Hudson	1-9
Sample	1-0

Fumbles Recovered
| Baker | 1-0 |

TEAM STATISTICS

First Downs	21
Total Yards	337
Yards Rushing	142
Yards Passing	195
Penalties	5-28

COLTS

Possession Punt Return

JETS

Possession Punt Return

▲ = TOUCHDOWN
● = FIELD GOAL
I = INTERCEPTION
F = FUMBLE
OK = ON-SIDE KICK
⊣ = MISSED FIELD GOAL

SUPER BOWL IV

Hank Stram 11-3

CHIEFS

| 5 | 10 | 15 | 20 | 25 | 30 | 35 | 40 | 45 | 50 | 45 | 40 | 35 | 30 | 25 | 20 | 15 | 10 | 5 | **VIKINGS** |

Bud Grant 12-2

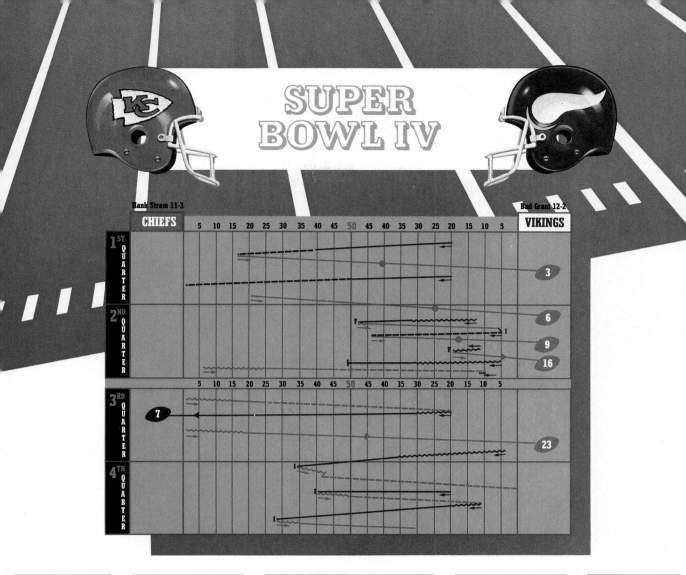

1ST QUARTER

2ND QUARTER

3RD QUARTER

4TH QUARTER

TEAM STATISTICS

First Downs	18
Total Yards	273
Yards Rushing	151
Yards Passing	122
Penalties	4-47

January 11, 1970
Tulane Stadium
New Orleans, Louisiana
2:30 p.m. CST
61 degrees, overcast
Attendance 80,562
Gross Receipts
$3,817,872.69
Winners' Shares $15,000
Losers' Shares $7,500

INDIVIDUAL STATISTICS

Rushing
Garrett	(1 TD)	11-39
Pitts		3-37
Hayes		8-31
McVea		12-26
Dawson		3-11
Holmes		5-7

Passing
Dawson	12-17-142
	1 TD, 1 int.

Receiving
Taylor	(1 TD)	6-81
Pitts		3-33
Garrett		2-25
Hayes		1-3

Punting
Wilson	4-194

Punt Returns
Garrett	1-0

Kickoff Returns
Hayes	2-36

Interceptions
Lanier	1-9
Robinson	1-9
Thomas	1-6

Fumbles Recovered
Robinson	1-2
Prudhomme	1-0

SCORING SUMMARY

Minnesota	0	0	7	0 -	7
Kansas City	3	13	7	0 -	23

KC - FG Stenerud 48
KC - FG Stenerud 32
KC - FG Stenerud 25
KC - Garrett 5 run
    (Stenerud kick)
MN- Osborn 4 run
    (Cox kick)
KC - Taylor 46 pass from Dawson
    (Stenerud kick)

SUPER TRIVIA

7. What kicker holds the field goal distance record in both Super Bowl and Pro Bowl competition?

8. Name the four members of the Vikings' legendary Purple People Eaters defensive line in Super Bowl IV.

INDIVIDUAL STATISTICS

Rushing
Brown		6-26
Reed		4-17
Osborn	(1 TD)	7-15
Kapp		2-9

Passing
Kapp	16-25-183
	2 int.
Cuozzo	1-3-16
	1 int.

Receiving
Henderson	7-111
Brown	3-11
Beasley	2-41
Reed	2-16
Osborn	2-11
Washington	1-9

Punting
Lee	3-111

Punt Returns
West	2-18

Kickoff Returns
West	3-46
Jones	1-33

Interceptions
None

Fumbles Recovered
None

TEAM STATISTICS

First Downs	13
Total Yards	239
Yards Rushing	67
Yards Passing	172
Penalties	6-67

CHIEFS

Possession	Punt	Return
───	---	∿∿

VIKINGS

Possession	Punt	Return
───	---	∿∿

SUPER BOWL V

Tom Landry 10-4

COWBOYS

Don McCafferty 11-2-1

COLTS

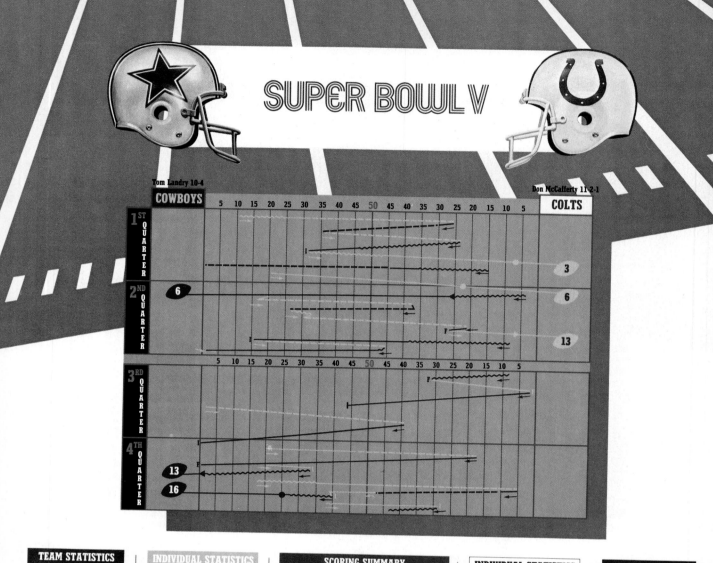

TEAM STATISTICS	
First Downs	10
Total Yards	215
Yards Rushing	102
Yards Passing	113
Penalties	10-133

January 17, 1971
Orange Bowl
Miami, Florida
2:00 p.m. EST
70 degrees, partly cloudy
Attendance 79,204
Gross Receipts
$3,992,280.01
Winners' Shares $15,000
Losers' Shares $7,500

INDIVIDUAL STATISTICS

Rushing
Garrison	12-65
Thomas	18-35
Morton	1-2

Passing
Morton	12-26-127
	1 TD, 3 int.

Receiving
Reeves	5-46
Thomas (1 TD)	4-21
Garrison	2-19
Hayes	1-41

Punting
Widby	9-377

Punt Returns
Hayes	3-9

Kickoff Returns
Harris	1-18
Hill	1-14
Kiner	1-2

Interceptions
Howley	2-22
Renfro	1-0

Fumbles Recovered
Harris	1-0
Pugh	1-0
Flowers	1-0

SCORING SUMMARY

Baltimore	0	6	0	10 -	16
Dallas	3	10	0	0 -	13

DA - FG Clark 14
DA - FG Clark 30
BA - Mackey 75 pass from Unitas
(kick blocked)
DA - Thomas 7 pass from Morton
(Clark kick)
BA - Nowatzke 2 run
(O'Brien kick)
BA - FG O'Brien 32

SUPER TRIVIA

9. Who was Dallas
quarterback Craig Morton's
backup in Super Bowl V?

10. What was Super Bowl V
hero Jim O'Brien's team
nickname?

INDIVIDUAL STATISTICS

Rushing
Nowatzke (1 TD)	10-33
Bulaich	18-28
Unitas	1-4
Havrilak	1-3
Morrall	1-1

Passing
Morrall	7-15-147
	1 int.
Unitas	3-9-88
	1 TD, 2 int.
Havrilak	1-1-25

Receiving
Jefferson	3-52
Mackey (1 TD)	2-80
Hinton	2-51
Havrilak	2-27
Nowatzke	1-45
Bulaich	1-5

Punting
Lee	4-166

Punt Returns
Logan	1-8
Gardin	4-4

Kickoff Returns
Duncan	4-90

Interceptions
Volk	1-30
Logan	1-14
Curtis	1-13

Fumbles Recovered
Duncan	1-0

TEAM STATISTICS	
First Downs	14
Total Yards	329
Yards Rushing	69
Yards Passing	260
Penalties	4-31

COWBOYS
Possession Punt Return

COLTS
Possession Punt Return

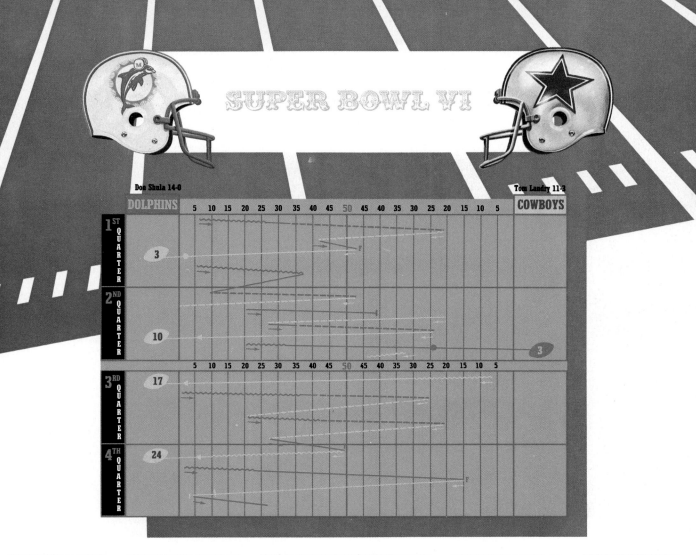

Don Shula 14-0

Tom Landry 11-3

SUPER BOWL VI

DOLPHINS | 5 10 15 20 25 30 35 40 45 50 45 40 35 30 25 20 15 10 5 | COWBOYS

1ST QUARTER — 3
2ND QUARTER — 10 — 3
3RD QUARTER — 17
4TH QUARTER — 24

TEAM STATISTICS

First Downs	10
Total Yards	185
Yards Rushing	80
Yards Passing	105
Penalties	0-0

January 16, 1972
Tulane Stadium
New Orleans, Louisiana
1:30 p.m. CST
39 degrees, sunny
Attendance 81,023
Gross Receipts
$4,041,527.89
Winners' Shares $15,000
Losers' Shares $7,500

INDIVIDUAL STATISTICS

Rushing
Csonka	9-40
Kiick	10-40
Griese	1-0

Passing
Griese	12-23-134
	1 int.

Receiving
Warfield	4-39
Kiick	3-21
Csonka	2-18
Fleming	1-27
Twilley	1-20
Mandich	1-9

Punting
Seiple	5-200

Punt Returns
Scott	1-21

Kickoff Returns
Morris	4-90
Ginn	1-32

Interceptions
None

Fumbles Recovered
Fernandez	1-0

SCORING SUMMARY

Dallas	3 7 7 7 - 24	
Miami	0 3 0 0 - 3	

DA - FG Clark 9
DA - Alworth 7 pass from Staubach
(Clark kick)
MI - FG Yepremian 31
DA - D. Thomas 3 run
(Clark kick)
DA - Ditka 7 pass from Staubach
(Clark kick)

SUPER TRIVIA

11. Who holds the record for most Super Bowl games as head coach?

12. Which Dallas offensive starter in Super Bowl VI now is the head coach of the team Dallas acquired him from?

INDIVIDUAL STATISTICS

Rushing
D. Thomas	(1 TD)	19-95
Garrison		14-74
Hill		7-25
Staubach		5-18
Ditka		1-17
Hayes		1-16
Reeves		1-7

Passing
Staubach	12-19-119
	2 TD

Receiving
D. Thomas		3-17
Alworth	(1 TD)	2-28
Ditka	(1 TD)	2-28
Hayes		2-23
Garrison		2-11
Hill		1-12

Punting
Widby	5-186

Punt Returns
Hayes	1-(-1)

Kickoff Returns
I. Thomas	1-23
Waters	1-11

Interceptions
Howley	1-41

Fumbles Recovered
Howley	1-0
Cole	1-0

TEAM STATISTICS

First Downs	23
Total Yards	352
Yards Rushing	252
Yards Passing	100
Penalties	3-15

DOLPHINS
Possession Punt Return

COWBOYS
Possession Punt Return

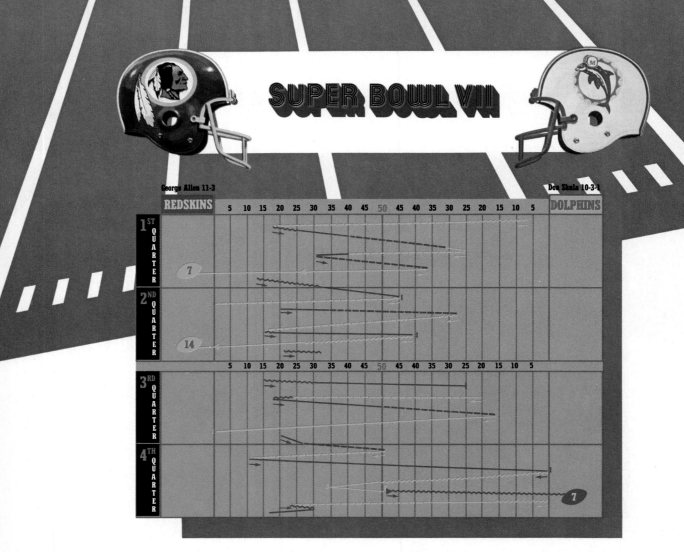

George Allen 11-3

Don Shula 10-3-1

REDSKINS | 5 10 15 20 25 30 35 40 45 50 45 40 35 30 25 20 15 10 5 | **DOLPHINS**

1ST QUARTER — 7
2ND QUARTER — 14
3RD QUARTER
4TH QUARTER — 7

TEAM STATISTICS

First Downs	16
Total Yards	228
Yards Rushing	141
Yards Passing	87
Penalties	3-25

January 14, 1973
Los Angeles Memorial
Coliseum
Los Angeles, California
12:30 p.m. PST
84 degrees, sunny
Attendance 90,182
Gross Receipts
$4,180,086.53
Winners' Shares $15,000
Losers' Shares $7,500

INDIVIDUAL STATISTICS

Rushing
Brown	22-72
Harraway	10-37
Kilmer	2-18
C. Taylor	1-8
Smith	1-6

Passing
Kilmer	14-28-104
	3 int.

Receiving
Jefferson	5-50
Brown	5-26
C. Taylor	2-20
Smith	1-11
Harraway	1-(-3)

Punting
Bragg	5-156

Punt Returns
Haymond	4-9

Kickoff Returns
Haymond	2-30
Mul-Key	1-15

Interceptions
Owens	1-0

Fumbles Recovered
Bass	(1 TD) 1-49

SCORING SUMMARY

Miami	7 7 0 0 - 14
Washington	0 0 0 7 - 7

MI - Twilley 28 pass from Griese
(Yepremian kick)

MI - Kiick 1 run
(Yepremian kick)

WA- Bass 49 fumble recovery
return
(Knight kick)

SUPER TRIVIA

13. Who was Redskins quarterback
Billy Kilmer's backup in Super Bowl
VII?

14. The Dolphins' undefeated
season was an NFL first. However,
one other team did go through an
NFL season without a loss. Name
that team.

INDIVIDUAL STATISTICS

Rushing
Csonka	15-112
Kiick	(1 TD) 12-38
Morris	10-34

Passing
Griese	8-11-88
	1 TD, 1 int.

Receiving
Warfield	3-36
Kiick	2-6
Twilley	(1 TD) 1-28
Mandich	1-19
Csonka	1-(-1)

Punting
Seiple	7-301

Punt Returns
Scott	2-4

Kickoff Returns
Morris	2-33

Interceptions
Scott	2-63
Buoniconti	1-32

Fumbles Recovered
None

TEAM STATISTICS

First Downs	12
Total Yards	253
Yards Rushing	184
Yards Passing	69
Penalties	3-35

REDSKINS
Possession Punt Return

DOLPHINS
Possession Punt Return

▲ = TOUCHDOWN
● = FIELD GOAL
I = INTERCEPTION
F = FUMBLE
B = BLOCKED PUNT
⊣ = MISSED FIELD GOAL

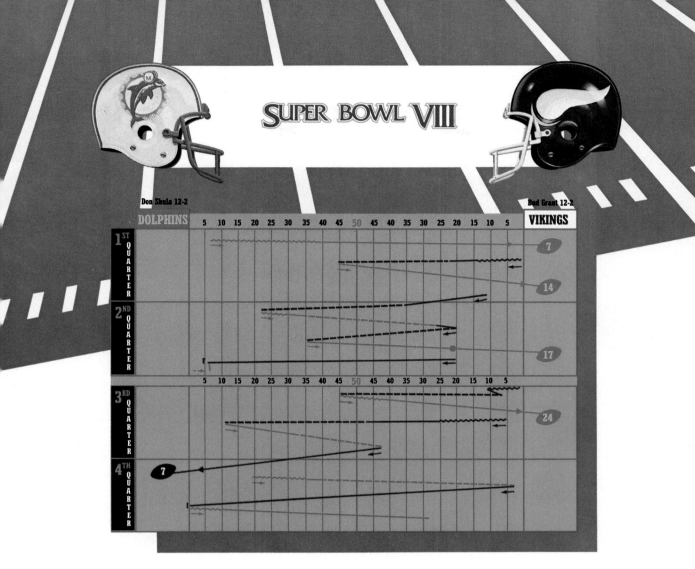

SUPER BOWL VIII

Don Shula 12-2

DOLPHINS

VIKINGS

Bud Grant 12-2

1ST QUARTER					7	
					14	
2ND QUARTER					17	
3RD QUARTER					24	
4TH QUARTER	7					

TEAM STATISTICS	
First Downs	21
Total Yards	259
Yards Rushing	196
Yards Passing	63
Penalties	1-4

January 13, 1974
Rice Stadium
Houston, Texas
2:30 p.m. CDT
50 degrees, overcast
Attendance 71,882
Gross Receipts
$3,953,641.22
Winners' Shares $15,000
Losers' Shares $7,500

INDIVIDUAL STATISTICS

Rushing
Csonka	(2 TD)	33-145
Morris		11-34
Kiick	(1 TD)	7-10
Griese		2-7

Passing
Griese	6-7-73

Receiving
Warfield	2-33
Mandich	2-21
Briscoe	2-19

Punting
Seiple	3-119

Punt Returns
Scott	3-20

Kickoff Returns
Scott	2-47

Interceptions
Johnson	1-10

Fumbles Recovered
Scott	1-0

SCORING SUMMARY

Minnesota	0	0	0	7 -	7	
Miami	14	3	7	0 -	24	

MI - Csonka 5 run
(Yepremian kick)
MI - Kiick 1 run
(Yepremian kick)
MI - FG Yepremian 28
MI - Csonka 2 run
(Yepremian kick)
MN- Tarkenton 4 run
(Cox kick)

SUPER TRIVIA

15. What did Miami do in Super Bowl VIII that no other team had ever done before or since?

16. Which Vikings Super Bowl VIII player once scored a safety against his team by running the wrong way with a recovered fumble?

INDIVIDUAL STATISTICS

Rushing
Reed		11-32
Foreman		7-18
Tarkenton	(1 TD)	4-17
Marinaro		1-3
B. Brown		1-2

Passing
Tarkenton	18-28-182
	1 int.

Receiving
Foreman	5-27
Gilliam	4-44
Voigt	3-46
Marinaro	2-39
B. Brown	1-9
Kingsriter	1-9
Lash	1-9
Reed	1-(-1)

Punting
Eischeid	5-211

Punt Returns
None

Kickoff Returns
Gilliam	2-41
West	2-28

Interceptions
None

Fumbles Recovered
None

TEAM STATISTICS	
First Downs	14
Total Yards	238
Yards Rushing	72
Yards Passing	166
Penalties	7-65

DOLPHINS

Possession Punt Return

VIKINGS

Possession Punt Return

▲ = TOUCHDOWN
● = FIELD GOAL
I = INTERCEPTION
F = FUMBLE

SUPER BOWL IX

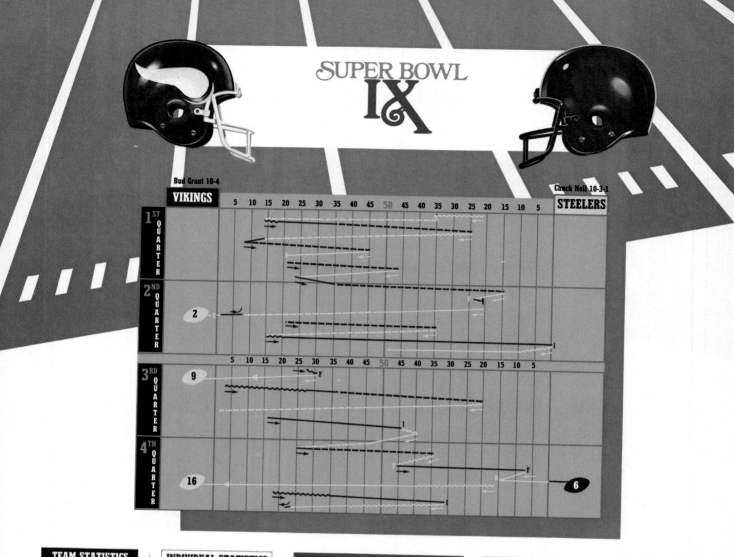

Bud Grant 10-4

VIKINGS

Chuck Noll 10-3-1

STEELERS

1ST QUARTER
2ND QUARTER
3RD QUARTER
4TH QUARTER

2

9

16

6

TEAM STATISTICS	
First Downs	9
Total Yards	119
Yards Rushing	17
Yards Passing	102
Penalties	4-18

January 12, 1975
Tulane Stadium
New Orleans, Louisiana
2:00 p.m. CST
46 degrees, cloudy
Attendance 80,997
Gross Receipts
$5,259,766.90
Winners' Shares $15,000
Losers' Shares $7,500

INDIVIDUAL STATISTICS

Rushing
Foreman	12-18
Tarkenton	1-0
Osborn	8-(-1)

Passing
Tarkenton	11-26-102
	3 int.

Receiving
Foreman	5-50
Voigt	2-31
Osborn	2-7
Gilliam	1-16
Reed	1-(-2)

Punting
Eischeid	6-223

Punt Returns
McCullum	3-11
N. Wright	1-1

Kickoff Returns
McCullum	1-26
McClanahan	1-22
B. Brown	1-2

Interceptions
None

Fumbles Recovered
Poltl	1-0
Krause	1-0

SCORING SUMMARY

Pittsburgh	0	2	7	7	- 16
Minnesota	0	0	0	6	- 6

PI - Safety, White downed
Tarkenton in end zone
PI - Harris 12 run
(Gerela kick)
MN- T. Brown recovered blocked
punt in end zone
(Kick failed)
PI - L. Brown 4 pass from
Bradshaw
(Gerela kick)

SUPER TRIVIA

17. With their victory in Super
Bowl IX, the Steelers won their
first NFL championship ever.
How many years had it taken
them to accomplish this?

18. How many records did the
Vikings set against the Steelers
in Game IX?

INDIVIDUAL STATISTICS

Rushing
Harris	(1 TD)	34-138
Bleier		17-65
Bradshaw		5-33
Swann		1-(-7)

Passing
Bradshaw	9-14-96
	1 TD

Receiving
Brown	(1 TD)	3-49
Stallworth		3-24
Bleier		2-11
Lewis		1-12

Punting
Walden	7-243

Punt Returns
Swann	3-34
Edwards	2-2

Kickoff Returns
Harrison	2-17
Pearson	1-15

Interceptions
Wagner	1-26
Blount	1-10
Greene	1-10

Fumbles Recovered
Kellum	1-0
Greene	1-0

TEAM STATISTICS	
First Downs	17
Total Yards	333
Yards Rushing	249
Yards Passing	84
Penalties	8-122

VIKINGS
Possession Punt Return

STEELERS
Possession Punt Return

▲ = TOUCHDOWN
I = INTERCEPTION
F = FUMBLE LOST
⊣ = MISSED FIELD GOAL
S = SAFETY
B = BLOCKED PUNT

SUPER BOWL X

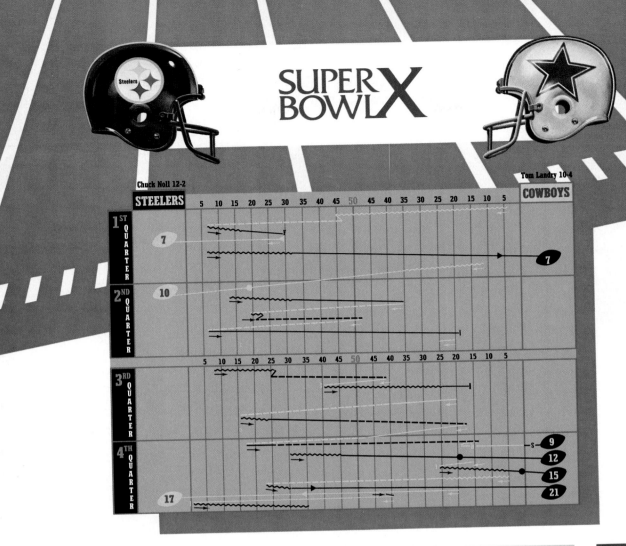

Chuck Noll 12-2

STEELERS

Tom Landry 10-4

COWBOYS

1ST QUARTER
2ND QUARTER
3RD QUARTER
4TH QUARTER

TEAM STATISTICS

First Downs	13
Total Yards	339
Yards Rushing	149
Yards Passing	190
Penalties	0-0

January 18, 1976
Orange Bowl
Miami, Florida
2:00 p.m. EST
57 degrees, clear
Attendance 80,187
Gross Receipts
$5,242,641.25
Winners' Shares $15,000
Losers' Shares $7,500

INDIVIDUAL STATISTICS

Rushing
Harris		27-82
Bleier		15-51
Bradshaw		4-16

Passing
Bradshaw		9-19-209
		2 TD

Receiving
Swann	(1 TD)	4-161
Stallworth		2-8
Harris		1-26
Grossman	(1 TD)	1-7
L. Brown		1-7

Punting
Walden	4-159

Punt Returns
D. Brown	3-14
Edwards	2-17

Kickoff Returns
Blount	3-64
Collier	1-25

Interceptions
Edwards	1-35
Thomas	1-35
Wagner	1-19

Fumbles Recovered
None

SCORING SUMMARY

Dallas	7	3	0	7 -	17
Pittsburgh	7	0	0	14 -	21

DA - D. Pearson 29 pass from Staubach (Fritsch kick)
PI - Grossman 7 pass from Bradshaw (Gerela kick)
DA - FG Fritsch 36
PI - Safety, Harrison blocked Hoopes' punt thru end zone
PI - FG Gerela 36
PI - FG Gerela 18
PI - Swann 64 pass from Bradshaw (Kick failed)
DA - P. Howard 34 pass from Staubach (Fritsch kick)

SUPER TRIVIA

19. Dallas' clutch receiver Preston Pearson played in a previous Super Bowl for another team. Name the team.

20. What record did the Pittsburgh Steel Curtain defense tie in Super Bowl X that it set in Super Bowl IX?

INDIVIDUAL STATISTICS

Rushing
Newhouse		16-56
Staubach		5-22
Dennison		5-16
P. Pearson		5-14

Passing
Staubach		15-24-204
		2 TD, 3 int.

Receiving
P. Pearson		5-53
Young		3-31
D. Pearson	(1 TD)	2-59
Newhouse		2-12
P. Howard	(1 TD)	1-34
Fugett		1-9
Dennison		1-6

Punting
Hoopes	7-245

Punt Returns
Richards	1-5

Kickoff Returns
T. Henderson	lateral 48
P. Pearson	4-48

Interceptions
None

Fumbles Recovered
None

TEAM STATISTICS

First Downs	14
Total Yards	270
Yards Rushing	108
Yards Passing	162
Penalties	2-20

COWBOYS
Possession Punt Return

STEELERS
Possession Punt Return

▲ = TOUCHDOWN
● = FIELD GOAL
I = INTERCEPTION
F = FUMBLE
OK = ON-SIDE KICK RECOVERED

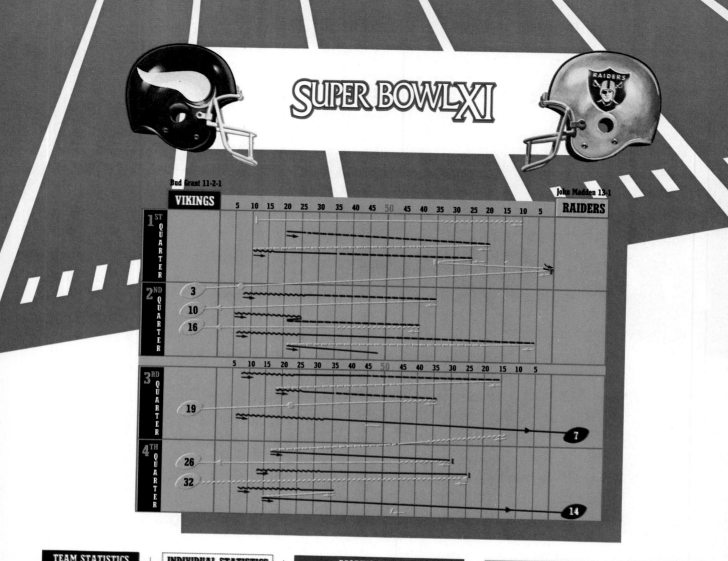

SUPER BOWL XI

Bud Grant 11-2-1

John Madden 13-1

VIKINGS	5 10 15 20 25 30 35 40 45 50 45 40 35 30 25 20 15 10 5	RAIDERS

1ST QUARTER

2ND QUARTER — 3, 10, 16

3RD QUARTER — 19, 7

4TH QUARTER — 26, 32, 14

January 9, 1977
Rose Bowl
Pasadena, California
12:30 p.m. PST
58 degrees, sunny
Attendance 103,438
Gross Receipts
$5,768,772.73
Winners' Shares $15,000
Losers' Shares $7,500

TEAM STATISTICS

First Downs	20
Total Yards	353
Yards Rushing	71
Yards Passing	282
Penalties	2-25

INDIVIDUAL STATISTICS

Rushing
Foreman	17-44
Johnson	2-9
S. White	1-7
Lee	1-4
Miller	2-4
McClanahan	3-3

Passing
Tarkenton	17-35-205
	1 TD, 2 int.
Lee	7-9-81
	1 TD

Receiving
S. White	(1 TD)	5-77
Foreman		5-62
Voigt	(1 TD)	4-49
Miller		4-19
Rashad		3-53
Johnson		3-26

Punting
| Clabo | 7-265 |

Punt Returns
| Willis | 3-14 |

Kickoff Returns
| S. White | 4-79 |
| Willis | 3-57 |

Interceptions
None

Fumbles Recovered
None

SCORING SUMMARY

Oakland	0	16	3	13 - 32
Minnesota	0	0	7	7 - 14

OK - FG Mann 24
OK - Casper 1 pass from Stabler
(Mann kick)
OK - Banaszak 1 run
(Kick failed)
OK - FG Mann 40
MN- S. White 8 pass from
Tarkenton
(Cox kick)
OK - Banaszak 2 run
(Mann kick)
OK - Brown 75 interception return
(Kick failed)
MN- Voigt 13 pass from Lee
(Cox kick)

SUPER TRIVIA

21. What famous pro athlete was Vikings wide receiver Ahmad Rashad's high school backfield mate?

22. Although he was an outstanding punter and placekicker at Southern Mississippi, the Raiders' Ray Guy also excelled at what other position?

INDIVIDUAL STATISTICS

Rushing
Davis		16-137
van Eeghen		18-73
Garrett		4-19
Banaszak	(2 TD)	10-19
Ginn		2-9
Rae		2-9

Passing
| Stabler | 12-19-180 |
| | 1 TD |

Receiving
Biletnikoff		4-79
Casper	(1 TD)	4-70
Branch		3-20
Garrett		1-11

Punting
| Guy | 4-162 |

Punt Returns
| Colzie | 4-43 |

Kickoff Returns
| Garrett | 2-47 |
| Siani | 1-0 |

Interceptions
| Brown | (1 TD) | 1-75 |
| Hall | | 1-16 |

Fumbles Recovered
| Hall | 1-0 |

TEAM STATISTICS

First Downs	21
Total Yards	429
Yards Rushing	266
Yards Passing	163
Penalties	4-30

VIKINGS
Possession Punt Return

RAIDERS
Possession Punt Return

▲ = TOUCHDOWN
● = FIELD GOAL
I = INTERCEPTION
F = FUMBLE
B = BLOCKED PUNT
⊣= MISSED FIELD GOAL

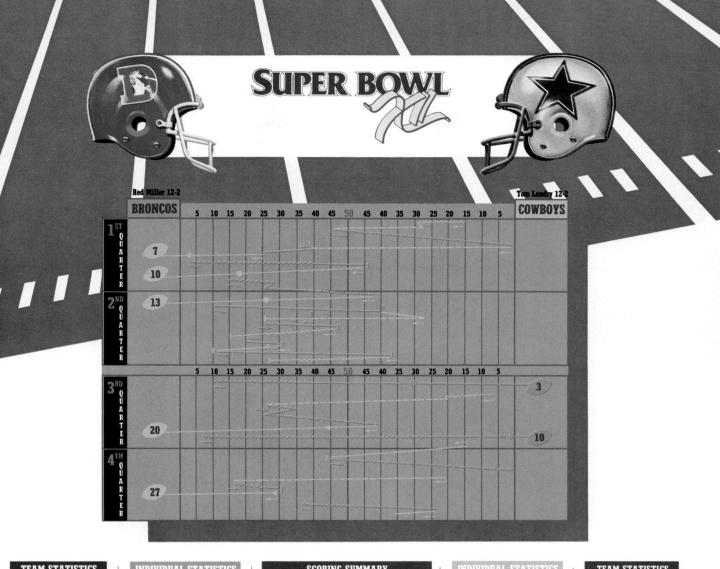

SUPER BOWL XII

Red Miller 12-2

Tom Landry 12-2

BRONCOS	5 10 15 20 25 30 35 40 45 50 45 40 35 30 25 20 15 10 5	COWBOYS

1ST QUARTER
7
10

2ND QUARTER
13

3RD QUARTER
20
3
10

4TH QUARTER
27

INDIVIDUAL STATISTICS

Rushing
Lytle	(1 TD)	10-35
Armstrong		7-27
Weese		3-26
Jensen		1-16
Keyworth		5-9
Perrin		3-8

Passing
Morton	4-15-39
	4 int.
Weese	4-10-22

Receiving
Dolbin	2-24
Odoms	2-9
Moses	1-21
Upchurch	1-9
Jensen	1-5
Perrin	1-(-7)

Punting
Dilts	4-153

Punt Returns
Upchurch	3-22
Schultz	1-0

Kickoff Returns
Upchurch	3-94
Schultz	2-62
Jensen	1-17

Interceptions
None

Fumbles Recovered
T. Jackson	1-0
Carter	1-0

SCORING SUMMARY

Dallas	10	3	7	7	-	27
Denver	0	0	10	0	-	10

DA - Dorsett 3 run
(Herrera kick)
DA - FG Herrera 35
DA - FG Herrera 43
DN - FG Turner 47
DA - Johnson 45 pass from Staubach
(Herrera kick)
DN - Lytle 1 run
(Turner kick)
DA - Richards 29 pass from
Newhouse
(Herrera kick)

SUPER TRIVIA

23. Where did Broncos defensive end Lyle Alzado attend college?

24. How tall is Cowboys defensive end Ed (Too Tall) Jones?

INDIVIDUAL STATISTICS

Rushing
Dorsett	(1 TD)	15-66
Newhouse		14-55
D. White		1-13
P. Pearson		3-11
Staubach		3-6
Laidlaw		1-1
Johnson		1-(-9)

Passing
Staubach	17-25-183
	1 TD
Newhouse	1-1-29
	1 TD
D. White	1-2-5

Receiving
P. Pearson		5-37
DuPree		4-66
Newhouse		3-(-1)
Johnson	(1 TD)	2-53
Richards	(1 TD)	2-38
Dorsett		2-11
D. Pearson		1-13

Punting
D. White	5-208

Punt Returns
Hill	1-1

Kickoff Returns
Johnson	2-29
Brinson	1-22

Interceptions
Washington	1-27
Kyle	1-19
Barnes	1-0
Hughes	1-0

Fumbles Recovered
Hughes	2-21
Kyle	1-0
Huther	1-0

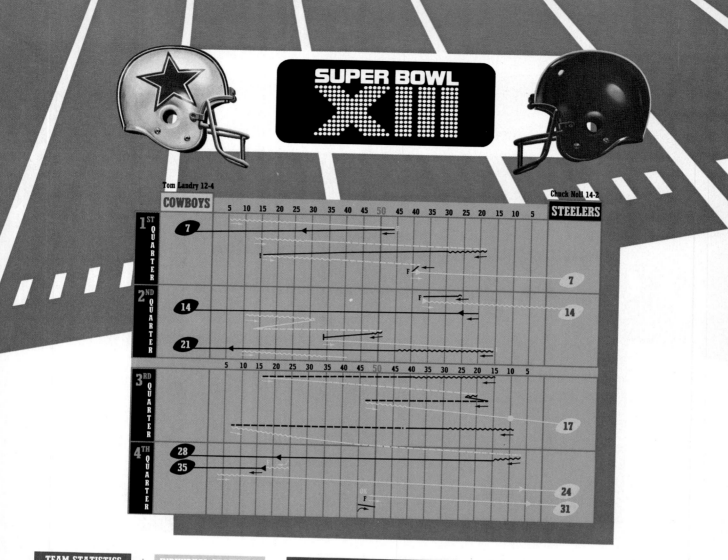

Tom Landry 12-4

COWBOYS

STEELERS

Chuck Noll 14-2

1ST QUARTER		
2ND QUARTER		
3RD QUARTER		
4TH QUARTER		

TEAM STATISTICS

First Downs	21
Total Yards	330
Yards Rushing	154
Yards Passing	176
Penalties	9-89

January 21, 1979
Orange Bowl
Miami, Florida
4:15 p.m. EST
71 degrees, cloudy
Attendance 79,484
Gross Receipts
$8,833,185.26
Winners' Shares $18,000
Losers' Shares $9,000

INDIVIDUAL STATISTICS

Rushing
Dorsett		16-96
Staubach		4-37
Laidlaw		3-12
P. Pearson		1-6
Newhouse		8-3

Passing
| Staubach | | 17-30-228 |
| | | 3 TD, 1 int. |

Receiving
Dorsett		5-44
D. Pearson		4-73
Hill	(1 TD)	2-49
Johnson	(1 TD)	2-30
DuPree	(1 TD)	2-17
P. Pearson		2-15

Punting
| D. White | | 5-198 |

Punt Returns
| Johnson | | 2-33 |

Kickoff Returns
Johnson		3-63
Brinson		2-41
R. White		1-0

Interceptions
| Lewis | | 1-21 |

Fumbles Recovered
| Hegman | (1 TD) | 1-37 |
| Martin, Jones | | 1-0 |

SCORING SUMMARY

| Pittsburgh | 7 | 14 | 0 | 14 - 35 |
| Dallas | 7 | 7 | 3 | 14 - 31 |

PI - Stallworth 28 pass from Bradshaw
    (Gerela kick)
DA - Hill 39 pass from Staubach
    (Septien kick)
DA - Hegman 37 fumble recovery return
    (Septien kick)
PI - Stallworth 75 pass from Bradshaw
    (Gerela kick)
PI - Bleier 7 pass from Bradshaw
    (Gerela kick)
DA - FG Septien 27
PI - Harris 22 run
    (Gerela kick)
PI - Swann 18 pass from Bradshaw
    (Gerela kick)
DA - DuPree 7 pass from Staubach
    (Septien kick)
DA - Johnson 4 pass from Staubach
    (Septien kick)

SUPER TRIVIA

25. What player wore two Super Bowl rings before he ever played in a regular season game?

26. Cowboys quarterback Roger Staubach and Steelers running back Rocky Bleier had an experience in common. What was it?

INDIVIDUAL STATISTICS

Rushing
Harris	(1 TD)	20-68
Bleier		2-3
Bradshaw		2-(-5)

Passing
| Bradshaw | | 17-30-318 |
| | | 4 TD, 1 int. |

Receiving
Swann	(1 TD)	7-124
Stallworth	(2 TD)	3-115
Grossman		3-29
Bell		2-21
Harris		1-22
Bleier	(1 TD)	1-7

Punting
| Colquitt | | 3-129 |

Punt Returns
| Bell | | 4-27 |

Kickoff Returns
| L. Anderson | | 3-45 |

Interceptions
| Blount | | 1-13 |

Fumbles Recovered
| Winston | | 1-0 |
| Banaszak | | 1-0 |

TEAM STATISTICS

First Downs	19
Total Yards	357
Yards Rushing	66
Yards Passing	291
Penalties	5-35

STEELERS
Possession Punt Return
--- ---

COWBOYS
Possession Punt Return

▲ = TOUCHDOWN
● = FIELD GOAL
I = INTERCEPTION
F = FUMBLE
S = SAFETY
⊣ = MISSED FIELD GOAL

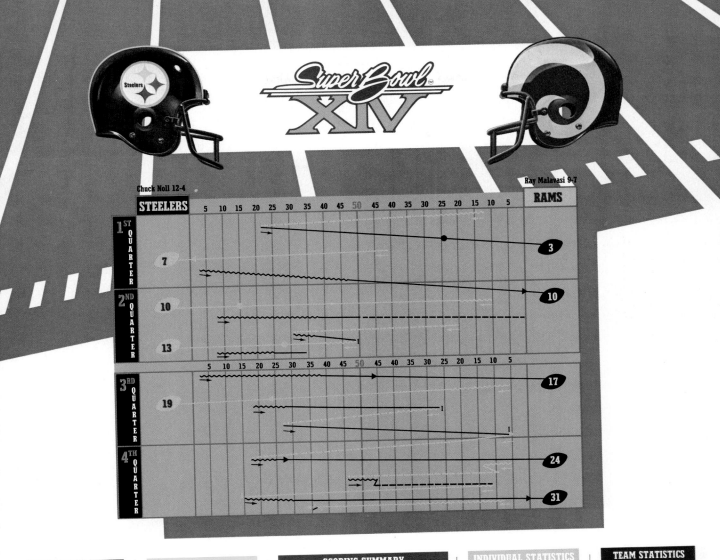

Chuck Noll 12-4

Ray Malavasi 9-7

STEELERS

RAMS

TEAM STATISTICS

First Downs	19
Total Yards	393
Yards Rushing	84
Yards Passing	309
Penalties	6-65

January 20, 1980
Rose Bowl
Pasadena, California
3:15 p.m. PST
67 degrees, sunny
Attendance 103,985
Gross Receipts
$9,489,274.00
Winners' Shares $18,000
Losers' Shares $9,000

INDIVIDUAL STATISTICS

Rushing
Harris	(2 TD) 20-46
Bleier	10-25
Bradshaw	3-9
Thornton	4-4

Passing
| Bradshaw | 14-21-309 |
| | 2 TD, 3 int. |

Receiving
Swann	(1 TD) 5-79
Stallworth	(1 TD) 3-121
Harris	3-66
Cunningham	2-21
Thornton	1-22

Punting
| Colquitt | 2-85 |

Punt Returns
| Bell | 2-17 |
| Smith | 2-14 |

Kickoff Returns
| L. Anderson | 5-162 |

Interceptions
| Lambert | 1-16 |

Fumbles Recovered
None

SCORING SUMMARY

Los Angeles	7	6	6	0 - 19
Pittsburgh	3	7	7	14 - 31

PI - FG Bahr 41
LA - Bryant 1 run
(Corral kick)
PI - Harris 1 run
(Bahr kick)
LA - FG Corral 31
LA - FG Corral 45
PI - Swann 47 pass from Bradshaw
(Bahr kick)
LA - R. Smith 24 pass from
McCutcheon
(Kick failed)
PI - Stallworth 73 pass from
Bradshaw
(Bahr kick)
PI - Harris 1 run
(Bahr kick)

SUPER TRIVIA

27. Who was head coach Chuck
Noll's first Steelers draft choice in
1969?
28. What dubious distinction did
the Rams bring into Super Bowl
XIV?

INDIVIDUAL STATISTICS

Rushing
Tyler	17-60
Bryant	(1 TD) 6-30
McCutcheon	5-10
Ferragamo	1-7

Passing
Ferragamo	15-25-212
	1 int.
McCutcheon	1-1-24
	1 TD

Receiving
Waddy	3-75
Bryant	3-21
Tyler	3-20
Dennard	2-32
Nelson	2-20
D. Hill	1-28
Smith	(1 TD) 1-24
McCutcheon	1-16

Punting
| Clark | 5-220 |

Punt Returns
| Brown | 1-4 |

Kickoff Returns
E. Hill	3-47
Jodat	2-32
Andrews	1-0

Interceptions
Elmendorf	1-10
Brown	1-6
Perry	1-(-1)
Thomas	0-6

Fumbles Recovered
None

TEAM STATISTICS

First Downs	16
Total Yards	301
Yards Rushing	107
Yards Passing	194
Penalties	2-26

STEELERS
Possession Punt Return

RAMS
Possession Punt Return

▲ = TOUCHDOWN
● = FIELD GOAL
I = INTERCEPTION

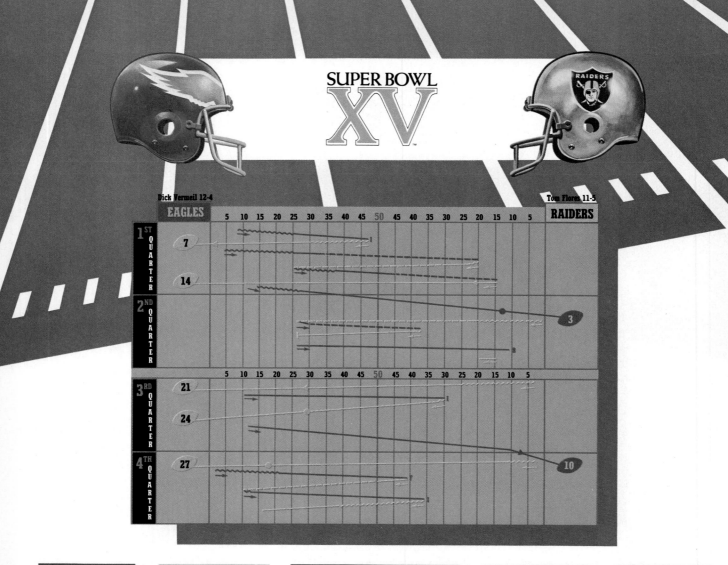

SUPER BOWL XV

Dick Vermeil 12-4

EAGLES

Tom Flores 11-5

RAIDERS

| | 5 10 15 20 25 30 35 40 45 50 45 40 35 30 25 20 15 10 5 | |

1ST QUARTER — 7, 14
2ND QUARTER — 3
3RD QUARTER — 21, 24
4TH QUARTER — 27, 10

TEAM STATISTICS

First Downs	19
Total Yards	360
Yards Rushing	69
Yards Passing	291
Penalties	6-57

January 25, 1981
Louisiana Superdome
New Orleans, Louisiana
5:15 p.m. CST
72 degrees, indoors
Attendance 76,135
Gross Receipts
$10,328,664.57
Winners' Shares $18,000
Losers' Shares $9,000

INDIVIDUAL STATISTICS

Rushing
Montgomery	16-44
Harris	7-14
Giammona	1-7
Harrington	1-4
Jaworski	1-0

Passing
| Jaworski | 18-38-291 |
| | 1 TD, 3 int. |

Receiving
Montgomery	6-91
Carmichael	5-83
Smith	2-59
Krepfle (1 TD)	2-16
Spagnola	1-22
Parker	1-19
Harris	1-1

Punting
| Runager | 3-110 |

Punt Returns
| Sciarra | 2-18 |
| Henry | 1-2 |

Kickoff Returns
| Campfield | 5-87 |
| Harrington | 1-0 |

Interceptions
None

Fumbles Recovered
None

SCORING SUMMARY

| Oakland | 14 | 0 | 10 | 3 - 27 |
| Philadelphia | 0 | 3 | 0 | 7 - 10 |

OK - Branch 2 pass from Plunkett
   (Bahr kick)
OK - King 80 pass from Plunkett
   (Bahr kick)
PH - FG Franklin 30
OK - Branch 29 pass from Plunkett
OK - FG Bahr 46
PH - Krepfle 8 pass from Jaworski
   (Franklin kick)
OK - FG Bahr 35

SUPER TRIVIA

29. Name the quarterback who started the 1980-regular season for the Super Bowl XV champion Oakland Raiders?

30. Prior to taking over at Philadelphia, Dick Vermeil coached at a college in the same city Eagles quarterback Ron Jaworski had played pro football. What city was it?

INDIVIDUAL STATISTICS

Rushing
van Eeghen	19-80
King	6-18
Jensen	3-12
Plunkett	3-9
Whittington	3-(-2)

Passing
| Plunkett | 13-21-261 |
| | 3 TD |

Receiving
Branch (2 TD)	5-67
Chandler	4-77
King (1 TD)	2-93
Chester	2-24

Punting
| Guy | 3-126 |

Punt Returns
| Matthews | 2-1 |

Kickoff Returns
| Matthews | 2-29 |
| Moody | 1-19 |

Interceptions
| Martin | 3-44 |

Fumbles Recovered
| Jones | 1-0 |

TEAM STATISTICS

First Downs	17
Total Yards	377
Yards Rushing	117
Yards Passing	260
Penalties	5-37

EAGLES
Possession   Punt   Return

RAIDERS
Possession   Punt   Return

▲ = TOUCHDOWN
● = FIELD GOAL
I = INTERCEPTION
F = FUMBLE
B = BLOCKED PUNT

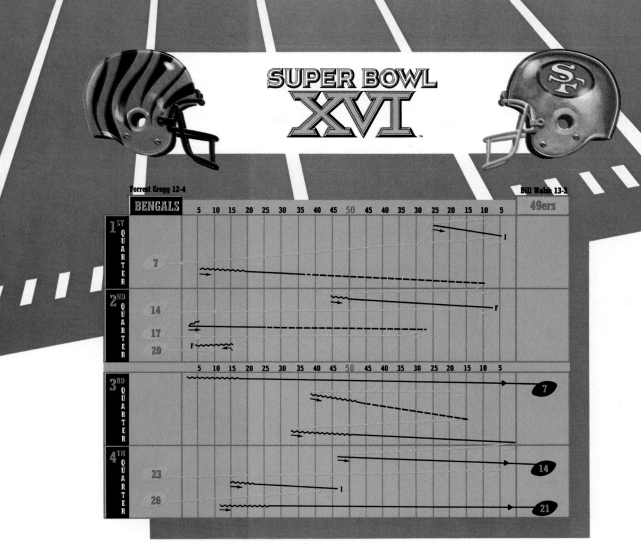

Forrest Gregg 12-4

Bill Walsh 13-3

SUPER BOWL XVI

BENGALS | 5 10 15 20 25 30 35 40 45 50 45 40 35 30 25 20 15 10 5 | **49ers**

1ST QUARTER
2ND QUARTER
3RD QUARTER
4TH QUARTER

TEAM STATISTICS	
First Downs	24
Total Yards	356
Yards Rushing	72
Yards Passing	284
Penalties	8-57

January 24, 1982
Pontiac Silverdome
Pontiac, Michigan
4:00 p.m. EST
70 degrees, indoors
Attendance 81,270
Gross Receipts
$10,641,034.83
Winners' Shares $18,000
Losers' Shares $9,000

INDIVIDUAL STATISTICS

Rushing
Johnson 14-36
Alexander 5-17
Anderson (1 TD) 4-15
A. Griffin 1-4

Passing
Anderson 25-34-300
2 TD, 2 int.

Receiving
Ross (2 TD) 11-104
Collinsworth 5-107
Curtis 3-42
Kreider 2-36
Johnson 2-8
Alexander 2-3

Punting
McInally 3-131

Punt Returns
Fuller 4-35

Kickoff Returns
Verser 5-52
A. Griffin 1-0
Frazier 1-0

Interceptions
None

Fumbles Recovered
Simmons 1-0

SCORING SUMMARY

San Francisco   7 13 0   6 - 26
Cincinnati   0   0 7 14 - 21

SF - Montana 1 run
       (Wersching kick)
SF - Cooper 11 pass from Montana
       (Wersching kick)
SF - FG Wersching 22
SF - FG Wersching 26
CI - Anderson 5 run
       (Breech kick)
CI - Ross 4 pass from Anderson
       (Breech kick)
SF - FG Wersching 40
SF - FG Wersching 23
CI - Ross 3 pass from Anderson
       (Breech kick)

SUPER TRIVIA

31. Who was the first rookie defensive back in Super Bowl history to make an interception?
32. Which member of the 1982 Cincinnati Bengals has a law degree?

INDIVIDUAL STATISTICS

Rushing
Patton 17-55
Cooper 9-34
Montana (1 TD) 6-18
Ring 5-17
Davis 2-5
Clark 1-(-2)

Passing
Montana 14-22-157
1 TD

Receiving
Solomon 4-52
Clark 4-45
Cooper (1 TD) 2-15
Wilson 1-22
Young 1-14
Patton 1-6
Ring 1-3

Punting
Miller 4-185

Punt Returns
Hicks 1-6

Kickoff Returns
Hicks 1-23
Lawrence 1-17
Clark 1-0

Interceptions
Hicks 1-27
Wright 1-25

Fumbles Recovered
Thomas 1-0
McColl 1-0

TEAM STATISTICS	
First Downs	20
Total Yards	275
Yards Rushing	127
Yards Passing	148
Penalties	8-65

BENGALS
Possession Punt Return

49ers
Possession Punt Return

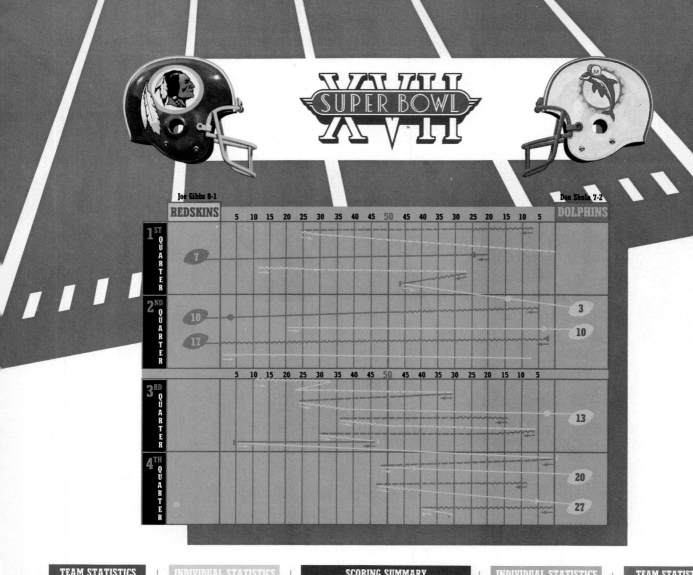

Joe Gibbs 8-1

REDSKINS | 5 10 15 20 25 30 35 40 45 50 45 40 35 30 25 20 15 10 5 | **DOLPHINS**

Don Shula 7-2

1ST QUARTER — 7

2ND QUARTER — 10, 17 — 3, 10

3RD QUARTER — 13

4TH QUARTER — 20, 27

TEAM STATISTICS

First Downs	24
Total Yards	400
Yards Rushing	276
Yards Passing	124
Penalties	5-36

January 30, 1983
Rose Bowl
Pasadena, California
3:00 p.m. PST
61 degrees, clear
Attendance 103,667
Gross Receipts
$19,997,330.86
Winners' Shares $36,000
Losers' Shares $18,000

INDIVIDUAL STATISTICS

Rushing
Riggins	(1 TD)	38-166
Garrett		1-44
Harmon		9-40
Theismann		3-20
Walker		1-6

Passing
Theismann	15-23-143
	2 TD, 2 int.

Receiving
Brown	(1 TD)	6-60
Warren		5-28
Garrett	(1 TD)	2-13
Walker		1-27
Riggins		1-15

Punting
Hayes	4-168

Punt Returns
Nelms	6-52

Kickoff Returns
Nelms	2-44
Wonsley	1-13

Interceptions
Murphy	1-0

Fumbles Recovered
Butz	1-0

SCORING SUMMARY

Miami	7	10	0	0	17
Washington	0	10	3	14	27

MI - Cefalo 76 pass from Woodley
(von Schamann kick)
WA - FG Moseley 31
WA - FG von Schamann 20
WA - Garrett 4 pass from Theismann
(Moseley kick)
MI - Walker 98 kickoff return
(von Schamann kick)
WA - FG Moseley 20
WA - Riggins 43 run
(Moseley kick)
WA - Brown 6 pass from Theismann
(Moseley kick)

SUPER TRIVIA

33. What NFL team did John Riggins play for before the Redskins?

34. Which two Miami Super Bowl XVII players were with the Dolphins in Super Bowl VII against the Redskins?

INDIVIDUAL STATISTICS

Rushing
Franklin	16-49
Nathan	7-26
Woodley	4-16
Vigorito	1-4
Harris	1-1

Passing
Woodley	4-14-97
	1 TD, 1 int.
Strock	0-3-0

Receiving
Cefalo	(1 TD)	2-82
Harris		2-15

Punting
Orosz	6-227

Punt Returns
Vigorito	2-22

Kickoff Returns
Walker	(1 TD)	4-190
L. Blackwood		2-32

Interceptions
Duke	1-0
L. Blackwood	1-0

Fumbles Recovered
None

TEAM STATISTICS

First Downs	9
Total Yards	176
Yards Rushing	96
Yards Passing	80
Penalties	4-55

REDSKINS
Possession Punt Return

DOLPHINS
Possession Punt Return

▲ = TOUCHDOWN
● = FIELD GOAL
I = INTERCEPTION
F = FUMBLE

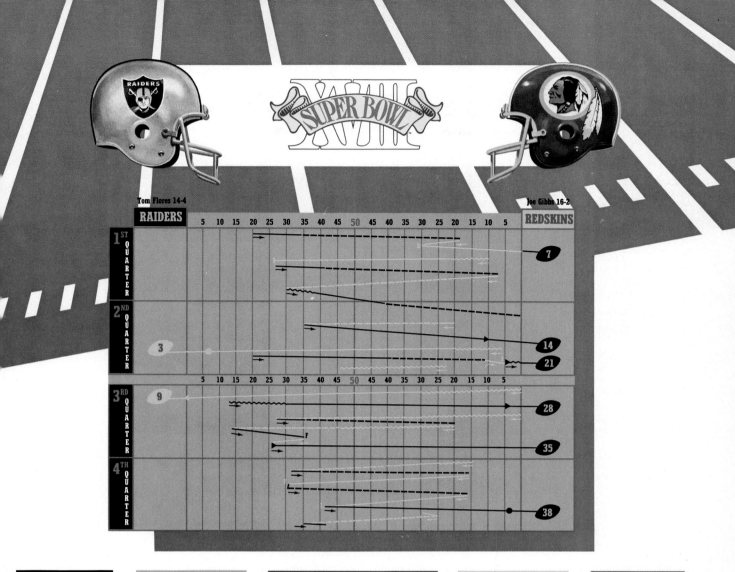

Tom Flores 14-4

RAIDERS | 5 10 15 20 25 30 35 40 45 50 45 40 35 30 25 20 15 10 5 | **REDSKINS**

Joe Gibbs 16-2

1ST QUARTER — 7

2ND QUARTER — 3 — 14 — 21

3RD QUARTER — 9 — 28 — 35

4TH QUARTER — 38

TEAM STATISTICS

First Downs	18
Total Yards	385
Yards Rushing	231
Yards Passing	154
Penalties	7-56

January 22, 1984
Tampa Stadium
Tampa, Florida
4:45 p.m. CST
68 degrees, partly cloudy
Attendance 72,920
Gross Receipts
$13,280,500.00
Winners' Shares $36,000
Losers' Shares $18,000

INDIVIDUAL STATISTICS

Rushing
Allen	(2 TD)	20-191
Pruitt		5-17
King		3-12
Willis		1-7
Hawkins		3-6
Plunkett		1-(-2)

Passing
Plunkett		16-25-172
		1 TD

Receiving
Branch	(1 TD)	6-94
Christensen		4-32
Hawkins		2-20
King		2-8
Allen		2-18

Punting
Guy	7-299

Punt Returns
Pruitt	1-8
Watts	1-0

Kickoff Returns
Pruitt	1-17

Interceptions
Squirek	(1 TD)	1-5
Haynes		1-0

Fumbles Recovered
R. Martin	1-0

SCORING SUMMARY

Washington	0 3 6 0 - 9
Los Angeles Raiders	7 14 14 3 - 38

LA - Jensen blocked kick recovered
    in end zone
        (Bahr kick)
LA - Branch 12 pass from Plunkett
        (Bahr kick)
WA- FG Moseley 24
LA - Squirek 5 interception return
        (Bahr kick)
WA- Riggins 1 run
        (Kick blocked)
LA - Allen 5 run
        (Bahr kick)
LA - Allen 74 run
        (Bahr kick)
LA - FG Bahr 21

SUPER TRIVIA

35. Raiders head coach Tom
Flores gained what special
distinction with the Super Bowl
XVIII victory?

36. What record did the
Washington offense set in the
regular season prior to Super
Bowl XVIII?

INDIVIDUAL STATISTICS

Rushing
Riggins	(1 TD)	26-64
Theismann		3-18
J. Washington		3-8

Passing
Theismann		16-35-243
		2 int.

Receiving
Didier	5-65
Brown	3-93
J. Washington	3-20
Giaquinto	2-21
Monk	1-26
Garrett	1-17
Riggins	1-1

Punting
J. Hayes	7-259

Punt Returns
Green	1-34
Giaquinto	1-1

Kickoff Returns
Garrett	5-100
Grant	1-32
Kimball	1-0

Interceptions
None

Fumbles Recovered
G. Williams	1-0
A. Washington	1-0

TEAM STATISTICS

First Downs	19
Total Yards	283
Yards Rushing	90
Yards Passing	193
Penalties	4-62

RAIDERS

Possession	Punt	Return
———	---	~~~

REDSKINS

| Possession | Punt | Return |

▲ = TOUCHDOWN
● = FIELD GOAL
I = INTERCEPTION
F = FUMBLE
B = BLOCKED PUNT

SUPER TRIVIA ANSWERS

1. E.J. Holub of the Kansas City Chiefs played linebacker in Super Bowl I and center in Super Bowl IV.

2. Herb Adderley, Willie Davis, Forrest Gregg, Ray Nitschke, Bart Starr, and Jim Taylor.

3. Phil Bengtson, Green Bay's defensive coach at Super Bowl II, was head coach of the Packers from 1968 to 1970. John Madden, the Raiders' Super Bowl II linebackers coach, was the team's head coach from 1969 to 1978.

4. Forrest Gregg (the Packers' current head coach) played in Super Bowls I and II with Green Bay and VI with Dallas. He was Cincinnati's head coach in Super Bowl XVI.

5. Joe Pepitone, who played first base for the New York Yankees (1962-69), was the original Broadway Joe. Namath was given the nickname in 1965.

6. Louisville

7. Jan Stenerud kicked record 48-yard field goals in Super Bowl IV and the 1972 Pro Bowl.

8. Carl Eller (LE), Gary Larsen (LT), Alan Page (RT), Jim Marshall (RE)

9. Roger Staubach

10. O'Brien's teammates called him "Lassie" because of his long hair.

11. Don Shula and Tom Landry, the opposing coaches in Super Bowl VI, have coached five games each. Shula coached the Colts in Super Bowl III and the Dolphins in Games VI, VII, VIII, and XVII. Landry coached the Cowboys in Super Bowls V, VI, X, XII, and XIII.

12. Mike Ditka, who played tight end, now is Chicago's head coach.

13. Sam Wyche, the current Cincinnati head coach. Sonny Jurgensen injured his foot during the regular season, leaving Wyche as the only other active quarterback on Washington's roster for the game.

14. Green Bay in 1929 had a 12-0-1 record.

15. They played in three consecutive Super Bowls.

16. Defensive end Jim Marshall in 1964

17. Forty two years

18. Five: fewest first downs, game (9); fewest yards gained, game (117); fewest yards gained, rushing, game (17); lowest average gain, rushing (0.81); and most consecutive games lost (2).

19. Pittsburgh, Super Bowl IX

20. Most safeties, game (1)

21. Chicago Cubs third baseman Ron Cey. They attended Mt. Tahoma High School in Tacoma, Washington, in the late 1960s.

22. Guy was a safety and had 18 career interceptions.

23. Yankton, in South Dakota. Alzado was the first player ever drafted from the school.

24. Six feet, nine inches

25. Quarterback Cliff Stoudt was on the Super Bowl XIII and XIV champion Pittsburgh Steelers, but did not play in a regular season game until 1980, his third year.

26. Both served in the military in Vietnam.

27. Defensive tackle Joe Greene. Although Greene was an All-America at North Texas State, the reaction in Pittsburgh was less than enthusiastic. Local sportswriters asked, "Joe who?" After four Super Bowls and 10 Pro Bowls, Greene answered the question well.

28. They had the poorest regular season record of any Super Bowl participant, 9-7.

29. Dan Pastorini started the season, but broke his leg in the fifth game. He was replaced by Jim Plunkett.

30. Los Angeles. Vermeil coached at UCLA; Jaworski played for the Rams from 1974 to 1976.

31. Eric Wright, cornerback, San Francisco 49ers, Super Bowl XVI

32. Ken Anderson received his law degree in 1981 from Chase Law School at Northern Kentucky University.

33. The New York Jets

34. Guard Bob Kuechenberg and fensive end Vern Den Herder

35. He became the only man ever to win Super Bowl rings as a player (Kansas City, Game IV), assistant coach (Raiders, Game XI) and head coach.

36. Most points scored, season (541)

CREDITS

Photography

Super Bowl by the Bay is proud to present the photographic work of Gerald French, Photo File, created expressly for this book. The Editor is grateful for the creative efforts of photographer Rick Cummings and for photos provided by Tom Meyers.

Except where noted at specific photographs, chapters of this book are the work of the following photographers: Dave Bush, Superfanitis Attacks Tampa; Gerald French, San Francisco, Peninsula, Carmel/Monterey, South Bay, Yosemite, Lake Tahoe and Wine Country; Rick Cummings, East Bay, North Bay; and Tom Meyers, Sacramento.

The following individuals and organizations deserve special thanks for providing information and/or photography:

Alpine Meadows, American Conservatory Theatre, Bank of America, Concord Pavilion, Cow Palace, Dalmo Victor Operations Bell Aerospace/Textron, DuDell and Associates, Gilroy Garlic Festival, Hanford Associates, Larsen Helicopters, Lawrence Livermore Laboratory, Lick Observatory, Louisiana Office of Touism, MGM Grand Hotel-Reno, Marine World/Africa USA, Marriott's Great America, Paul Masson Vineyards, Montalvo Center for the Arts, Monterey Bay Aquarium, North Tahoe-Truckee Snowfest Committee, Oceanic Society, Pan American World Airways, Inc., Pebble Beach Company, Terry Pimsleur and Company, Port of Oakland, the Rosicrucian Order, Saks Fifth Avenue, San Francisco Giants Baseball Club, San Fransico Opera, San Jose Convention/Visitors Bureau, Santa Cruz Beach Boardwalk, Seeq Technology, Inc. Sheraton-Palace Hotel, Dick Skuse Public Relations, Southern Pacific Railroad, Stanford Alumni Association, Stanford Athletic Department, Tahoe North Visitors & Convention Bureau, Tampa Chamber of Commerce, Tom Watson's Harness Shop, Westin St. Francis, Winchester Mystery House, Yosemite Park and Curry Company.

GridGraph™

Created by

Richard Keller, Jack Little

Type for this book was set in Stymie Bold Condensed, Garamond Light, and Garamond Light Italic on a Varityper Comp/Edit 6400. It was printed on 70 lb. Multiweb by W.A. Krueger Co., New Berlin, Wisconsin. Color separations were prepared by American Color Corporation, Focus 4 Inc. and W.A. Krueger Co.

Editor's Kudos

Appreciation is extended to those restaurants and facilities who offered hospitality and patience during our photo sessions, as well as those people we commandeered to serve as "models." Of these, certain facilities deserve special recognition for their extraordinary assistance:

The Barnyard, Blue Fox, Buena Vista Winery, Carey-Nob Hill Limo, Central Fish Company, Centrella Hotel, Fandango, Gingerbread House, Il Fornaio, Kabuki Hot Spring, Leslie Salt, the Mandarin, Marine World/Africa USA, Masa's, Orsborn Group, Quail Lodge and Seoul Garden.

Bohn & Bland Publishers, Inc., extend special thanks to:

Valerie Anderson
Lyle and Catherine Barter
Sandi Blakeley
Corrine Bland
Frank and Nora Bland
Geoff Bland
Karen Bland
Jackie Brewster
Jack Castin
Jim Cathcart
John Chow
Chuicjabd Pat Church
Hazel Church
Will Dashell
George DeLong
Ben Ferguson
Norman and Juliann Fredicks
Greg Hamilton
Robert and Glenda Hesseltine
Lisa Kaiser
Patty Kloch
Tony and Mabel Litvin
William and Lucille Mellish
Neil Perlman
Tony Sherchuck
Walter Shjeflo
Don Smith
Kevin Smith
Leanna Snyder
David Soares
Raquel Soria
John Steen
Michael Stephen
Rick Stubblefield
Chart Watchers
Lots Witfall
David Williams
David Yu
Joe Zaccone

bohn&bland Publishers, Inc.